BEHAVIOR:
THE CONTROL OF
PERCEPTION

ABOUT THE AUTHOR

William T. Powers received his B.S. in physics and did his graduate work in psychology at Northwestern University. He has consulted for The Center for the Teaching Profession and was formerly Chief Systems Engineer of the Department of Astronomy at Northwestern. He has published articles in psychology, astronomy and electronics, and has invented and designed a number of electronic instruments.

First published 1973 by
Aldine Publishing Company
529 South Wabash Avenue
Chicago, Illinois 60605

ISBN 0–202–25113–6
Library of Congress Catalog Number 73–75697

Printed in the United States of America

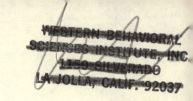

BEHAVIOR: THE CONTROL OF PERCEPTION

William T. Powers

Chicago
ALDINE PUBLISHING COMPANY

This book is dedicated
to
Donald T. Campbell and Hugh G. Petrie
for their vision and generosity
and to
Treval C. Powers
from whom I still have much to learn
and most particularly to
my wife, Mary
who has had to share me with this book
for fifteen years

Contents

Preface

This book represents, I hope, a step on the path back to a concept of man as autonomous, and away from the concept of man as automaton. Yet in allowing my humanistic bias to hold sway, I do not think I have denied science. Indeed, to most readers the first part of this book will seem a direct denial of my hope, for it gives a deliberately and specifically mechanistic picture of how the central nervous system behaves.

Only after the mechanistic model is thoroughly understood will the reader see that it leads beyond ordinary mechanism and that it is capable of describing the interface between what we can represent as mechanism and what we cannot yet represent at all, but only experience.

The traditional arguments between mechanists and humanists are represented by the dispute over purposiveness in behavior. The mechanists have argued that since organisms are made of matter, they are subject to the same determinism as any physical system, living or not, and in particular are bound by the cause-effect laws governing the behavior of matter. Hence we have *behaviorism,* which treats input as cause and output as effect and all that lies between as an automatic machine having properties but no purposes. The humanists have denied this picture on intuitive and subjective grounds, claiming that no machine can experience its inputs as well as respond to them, or conceptualize its own existence, or see the need for building a machine.

This book presents an approach which may bring together these apparently irreconcilable points of view. The conclusion we are led to by the thinking in this book is that there *is* mechanism in behavior—but it is not the mechanism the behaviorists have in mind, for it is capable of having inner purposes in the full humanistic sense. On the other hand we are led also to seek not just a model of behavioral mechanisms, but a deep awareness that we are constructing a model; and we are encouraged to apply the model to ourselves. This process puts experience before theory but paradoxically shows that much which seems uniquely human is after all only acquired mechanism. The human remainder, the factor distinguishing man from animal or machine, is visible in the model only as a ghost, through its transcendant effects on the model itself.

Is that the Soul of which I speak? The Atman? The Awareness? Of course it is. It is myself, yourself. But I have not been forced by this theory to conclude that this factor, this self, has to be treated either with tact or with reverence. It is a perfectly natural part of the totality we call a human being. It has functions in this otherwise mechanistically representable structure, and is not just along for the ride. Animals may have it, too. If it does not seem subject to the laws of physics, I take that as evidence that physics is still in an early stage of development. Whatever its nature, and I am sure it has a nature, it is adequately understandable through its effects on experience—and, incidentally, on learning. Adequately, that is, for any purpose I can now conceive.

Scientists who view progress as a series of narrow escapes from metaphysical traps may find this book tough going in places, especially those places where I cheerfully give in to the temptation to anthropomorphize. It is precisely that kind of scientist who has the most to gain by understanding this book. If I anthropomorphize, be assured that I have done so with reasonable care and for a purpose. It is necessary, in order to understand the organization of human behavior, to recognize that one is constrained by any property he would impose on his experimental subjects if they too are human. What is necessary is not to avoid attributing human properties to human beings, but to avoid attributing such properties arbitrarily. There is at least one method, which is fully described later in the book, for testing the appropriateness of anthropomorphisms.

It is a long way through this book, both in words and in new concepts. To save the reader a long wait for what will never appear, I should state now that the theory nowhere predicts how a particular person will react to a particular event. I have not been concerned with the kind of theory which predicts that event A will probably lead to behavior B. To me such theories are not theories at all, but summaries of observations. They in no way answer the questions I have been interested in, such as the question of what kind of organization is required to permit a person to reproduce in present time an experience contained in his present-time memories of the past. Not a particular experience—*any* experience.

In that same vein, I have not been concerned with relating behavior to antecedent events. Rather, the central problem has been to find a plausible model which can behave at all. This has required a long effort to penetrate beneath surface descriptions to see what is being taken for granted. For example, it will be shown later that the brain does *not* command the muscles to act. That concept implies properties which the neuromuscular system simply does not have. It ignores the fact that we move about balanced on jointed sticks supported only by flabby rubber bands of variable tension. There is just no way the brain can select a muscle tension that will produce one and only one behavioral effect, even if that tension is accurately produced.

The result of this approach is a model nearly devoid of specific behavioral content. I once felt that it was my duty to supply the model with content as well as form, but I am wiser now, and much more impressed with my ignorance. What *is* up to me is in this book. What I do best is in this book. Others who know more about behavior and many other subjects are the ones to put the content in. Where I have tried to make the form more comprehensible by suggesting content I have stepped over the bounds of my knowledge and have probably made mistakes. I trust that they can be corrected without obscuring what is most important about this model—and that is this: Behavior is the process by which organisms control their input sensory data. For human beings, behavior is the control of perception. That is what is important about the model—that, and all that is implied by it.

BEHAVIOR:
THE CONTROL OF
PERCEPTION

1

The Dilemmas of Behaviorism

Since this book represents a break with traditional psychologies, it is appropriate to begin with a close look at behaviorism, the branch of psychology begun in America by John Broadus Watson near the start of this century. While many psychologists overtly reject the mechanistic formalisms of behaviorism, they adhere almost universally to its basic concepts and methods in one way or another. A humanistic psychologist, for example, may reject the idea that painful stimuli act on a passive nervous system to cause an organ to secrete adrenalin, but he may be perfectly willing to say that stress acts on a person to make him anxious. Even when stimulus and response do not show up in such disguises, it is widely agreed that a valid experiment requires that one establish fixed experimental conditions, manipulate a single variable, or several, and observe the consequent effects on behavior. Running throughout psychology (and almost identical to what is termed "scientific method" in psychology) is a particular concept of cause and effect. The cause, the immediate physical cause of what an organism does, lies outside that organism; the best the organism can do is to modulate the connection from the stimulus that is the cause to the behavior that is the effect. Those psychologists who find this point of view at variance with their own appreciation of human behavior simply do not compete at that level of discourse; they tend to withdraw from "scientific" psychology and to turn to humanistic and clinical pursuits.

1

Both within and without behaviorism there is one fundamental concept that underlies studies of behavior: a model of the nervous system and of its relationship to the external world, accepted in medicine, neurology, psychiatry, psychology in general, and even in modern cybernetics. It is a simple and compelling model. The basis for this model is the well-established fact that nervous systems are joined to receptors and effectors—sense organs and muscles. With or without direct contact, the environment can apparently act on the nervous system in such a way as to cause the muscles to tense, moving the organism. There are input devices by means of which the environment affects the nervous system, and there are output devices by means of which the nervous system affects the environment. All evidence points to the fact that *within* the nervous system the general course of events following stimulation is from the input devices, through the nervous system, and back outward to the output devices. This is borne out not only by the tracing of neural impulses inside the nervous system, but by observing the time sequence of events. Stimulus always precedes response, even if only by a small fraction of a second.

It is tempting to think of the brain as something that acts to modify the streams of sensory impulses, as if the brain were a sort of complex filter lying between the sensory receptors and the muscles. D. O. Hebb (1964), in an elementary textbook of psychology that is still in use, writes,

> . . . a fundamental question: How do sensory events guide behavior, and how close is their control? The influence they exert is by means of the nervous system, which is essentially a transmitter of excitations from *receptors* (sensory cells) to *effectors* (muscles and glands). . . . When transmission is relatively direct, we are dealing with *reflective* or *sense-dominated* behavior. When certain complications are involved, we are dealing with behavior that is under the control of both sensory events and mediating processes (ideas, thinking). Behaviorally, our question is: How do we distinguish between the two forms of response to the environment?

A great deal of effort in behavioral research today is devoted to exploring behavior in terms just like these. Even in many modern computer-oriented studies bristling with engineering terminology, the basic experimental design involves application of a stimulus and measuring its consequences somewhere downstream inside the brain or in overt behavior. Conceiving of the brain as a coherent detector (Trehub 1971), or as a transfer function, or as a transition-probability matrix (Broadbent 1971), makes no essential difference in the basic concept. Adding memory to the model merely puts a delay in the process of transmission. The basic model of how sensory events act on the brain to produce or change behavior remains, in all but technological details, the same as it was when first presented by Descartes 300 years ago:

> In order to understand how the brain can be excited by external objects which affect the organs of sense, so that all the members can be moved in a thousand different ways, imagine that the delicate threads which arise from inside of the brain and form the marrow of the nerves, are so disposed in all those parts which serve as the organs of any sense that they can easily be set in motion by the objects of the senses, and that whenever they are so set in motion, even ever so little, they pull upon the parts of the brain whence they originate, and so open certain pores on the internal surface of the brain. Through these pores the animal spirits in the ventricles pass into the nerves and then into the muscles which carry out movements like those to which we are incited when our senses are affected in that way (*L'Homme,* 1662).

Behind John Watson's thinking in the early 1900s was the brilliant example of physics which Watson took as his model of scientific research. He wished to do away with the vague metaphors and empty entity-filled language that abounded in psychology and to substitute an experimental approach modeled after that of physics in which only that which was publicly observable would be admitted as evidence. He felt that ultimately all behavior would be explainable, at least in principle, given full knowledge of environmental effects on an organism. By studying the effects of controlled objective stimuli on the objectively observed actions of animals or people, he planned to derive laws of behavior, generalizations from many individual observations, which could then be used to predict the behavior that would follow from any stimulus. With enthusiastic optimism, he wrote, "Regardless of how complicated the stimulus-response relations may be, the behaviorist does not admit for a moment that any human reactions cannot be so described" (1913).

To the present moment, substantial numbers of scientists still agree in principle with Watson, even though after sixty years of progress they can see more difficulties than he saw. In principle, one should be able to trace physical cause and effect from the stimulus object right up to the sensory receptors of the organism, and from the tensions in the muscles to their ultimate effects in the physical world, leaving only the gap occupied by the organism to be analyzed empirically. Knowing the history of all effects on the organism and all previous responses, how could this fail to result in perfect prediction of future responses to future stimuli?

This idea is a direct offshoot of a basic physical principle—that the present state of a physical system, if fully known, completely predicts the next state of the system. Thus, one does not need to know the history of the system save for the purpose of determining general laws. Guthrie (1942) put it this way: "What [the boy] is doing at any time is our best indicator of what he will be doing the next moment." (p. 19) Now as in Watson's time, those who consider themselves strictly scientific students of behavior believe that underlying all behavior are the physical (and chemical) laws governing the matter of which organisms are constructed. Since these laws apply whether a molecule is part of an organism or part of a rock, the basic determinism of physics *must* apply to behavior in the final analysis and therefore so must any laws which deal with that same behavior in ways less specific than the molecular. Quantum mechanics may have raised some basic doubts about these articles of faith, but not serious or specific enough doubts to have changed the course of behavioral research—yet.

There is little wonder that a humanistic psychologist might feel cowed by such awesome arguments. Behind them one feels the weight of centuries; one senses the implacable pressure of a logical development of iron-clad concepts toward inevitable ends. No humanist that I know has ever successfully challenged a behaviorist in this arena. All counter-arguments are given from the safe side of the fence and rely on appeal to mysteries and metaphysics, to intuition and insight. What else can be done when one finds his hands weaponless?

As monolithic as this conceptual structure seems, it is vulnerable. The orderly march of cause and effect from stimulus object to sensory receptor, and from muscle tension to the eventual behavioral result, does not exist. It was *imagined,* I suppose, because to imagine anything else (it seemed) would have meant the denial of physical reality. The basic orderliness was assumed because it *had* to be assumed. Without it, stimulus-response ideas, and indeed any ideas of an orderly empirical investigation of responses to the environment, would have been left with no conceptual base, no justification.

In fact, it is not true that a stimulus which results in a regular behavioral result always acts on the nervous system in the same way. Nor is it true that a stimulus which *does* act on the nervous system in a consistent way always produces the same behavioral result. Nor is it true that a given set of muscle tensions always produces the same observable behavior. And, finally, it is not true that when a given observable behavior repeats, the muscle tensions that cause it are the same every time. Where order had been assumed, there is instead apparent chaos.

The fact that the achievement of Watson's goal was not going to be straightforward must have been realized quite early—I suspect in something like five minutes after the start of the first behavioral experiment of this kind. But the realization of *what* was wrong grew only slowly and incompletely. The perversity of experimental subjects could not escape notice—for instance, the rat which turned left 99 times in a row to get food in the only place food had ever appeared, turning right on the 100th trial; or the human subject who had performed perfectly for three days, forgetting his instructions; or the student with an IQ of 190 flunking out of school. Psychologists learned very early the uses of statistics.

At first behaviorists explained away these irregularities by pointing out that one could not possibly control all of the stimuli to which an organism was subject before and during an experiment. Of course one had to expect random variations in behavior if there were random stimuli flying about. But despite patient measures to eliminate random stimuli, and to eliminate differences in inherited characteristics and upbringing, the irregularities remained, and they remained large. By the time I took elementary psychology in 1948 (the year in which Wiener [1948] published his *Cybernetics*), the theorists of behaviorism had temporarily solved the problem by attributing the unpredictability of behavior to a universal property of living organisms: *variability*. Somehow that failed to hit the mark.

There have been many attempts by behaviorists to cope with the mysterious way in which behavior relates regularly to stimulus-events through the medium of apparently random processes. While the theorists were struggling, the rest of experimental psychology was learning t-tests and chi-square tests and regression calculations and all the other complex paraphernalia of statistics, because the variability often got so bad that only by the use of extensive statistical tests could one find out whether anything at all had happened in an experiment. "Significance" in experimental results had come to mean something other than "importance." It now means a little triumph over nature's noise level.

The true definition of the conceptual difficulty with behaviorism and all branches of psychology adhering to the same model was eventually stated by a leading behaviorist, the late Egon Brunswik, when he formulated his "empirical law of distal achievements through vicarious mediation." This was an empirical law, not an explanation of how this phenomenon could possibly occur in a universe subject to physical laws. I have never been sure of what "vicarious mediation" means, and I have never known anyone who was, but Brunswik (1952) nevertheless succeeded in laying out the problem clearly in one simple diagram, his (adapted) "Lens Model" (fig. 1.1).

On the left in figure 1.1 is a "distal focus"—here, a stimulus object remote from the organism, which on different occasions can affect the sense organs of that organism in different ways. The varying amounts and kinds of effect are symbolized by the rays diverging from the distal focus and reaching the organism by different paths, each path representing the effect in a given instance of behavior and the bundle representing the whole set of variations from instance to instance.

On the right is another distal focus, now representing some particular consequence of an organism's behavior, such as the depres-

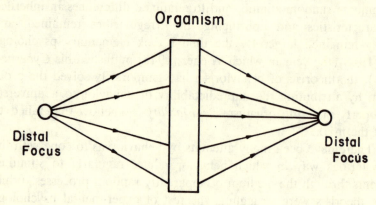

FIGURE 1.1.   *The lens model.*

sion of a lever by a rat that has been trained to feed itself in this way. The bundle of rays reaching this distal focus by different paths represents the collection of different detailed muscular acts by which the *same* behavioral result is achieved, again over many instances of this behavior. If the distal focus on the left represents a signal light telling the rat that pressing the lever will result in food, then this diagram would be intended to represent the fact that the organism does the same thing (depresses the lever) each time the same stimulus (the signal light) occurs, but that the signal light has different effects on the retinas of the rat's eyes on each trial, and that the rat gets the lever to go down using different muscle tensions, and perhaps even different means (such as sitting on the lever) to accomplish the final contact closure on each trial.

The "lens," of course, is the organism, which behaves as if it is focusing the divergent effects from the stimulus object into behavioral effects which converge to a common final "achievement."

The quotation marks around "achievement" are Brunswik's and point to the real problem that lies behind the attempt to formulate an empirical law of vicarious mediation. If an organism is seen to be altering its behavior in an environment that is full of disturbances in such a way as to keep producing the same final result, one might be tempted to think that the organism intends to produce that final result and is simply varying its outputs as necessary so as to keep that final result happening over and over. It seems as if there is purpose in behavior. A large portion of the theoretical effort in psychology has been devoted to explaining away all of the cases in which it seemed that purpose was involved, for behaviorism is founded on the premise that not purpose but environmental stimulation is the cause of behavior.

Purpose, of course, is invisible and, as many behaviorists have pointed out, one cannot even see the goal toward which a purpose is guiding behavior until behavior does finally reach the goal state. Guthrie (1952), until nearly the end of his career as a major behaviorist, was certain that purpose was only an illusion:

> The goal is often spoken of as a cause. The absurdity of this is evident in those cases in which the goal does not yet exist until activity has produced it. Goals do not determine activity; but stimuli may incite activity that is directed toward a goal previously attained by the activity because the stimuli remain associated with the movements that ended in the goal attainment. (p. 52)

Many others have agreed with Guthrie. As late as 1968, and at a cybernetics conference at that, the following statement was made: "I have always regarded a drop of water sliding down a slightly inclined plane as showing all the manifestations of purposeful behavior. It is going downhill because it 'wants to get somewhere' and it does so by an erratic and quite unpredictable path" (Gerard 1968, p. 26). Brunswik (1952) cites a similar idea with approval:

> The theorist of classical behaviorism, Albert P. Weiss, provided the crucial model to deal with doubtful cases of this kind in his "raindrop analogy" of purposive behavior. He pointed at the convergence of originally diverse occurrences toward a common characteristic end stage in behavior and compared it with the way raindrops originally scattered over a wide area are eventually carried to a common point in the sea (p. 17).

Such models of purposive behavior have the common property of depending on an unseen force that guides behavior to a common end—that is the function of gravity in the water-drop analogy. In older times the unseen force that led human behavior to a pre-destined end was thought to be God even by scientists. In neither case is there any admission that something *inside the organism* might be responsible for purposive behavior, despite the fact that organisms normally move only when and as their brains direct their muscles to make them move.

Clearly, the goal of all these discussions was to do away with the illusion of purposiveness and to substitute a picture in which control remained in the natural forces of an organism's environment. This determination to shake off the impression of purposiveness in behavior was doomed to frustration, however, because all behavior is purposive all of the time, and the purposes are selected by the brain, not by the environment: the illusion is no illusion, but it will take a while yet to prove that.

REFERENCES

Broadbent, D. *Decision and Stress*. New York: Academic Press, 1971.
Brunswik, E. *The Conceptual Framework of Psychology*. Chicago: University of Chicago Press, 1952.
Campbell, D. "Pattern Matching as an Essential in Distal Knowing."

Chapter 2 in *The Psychology of Egon Brunswik,* edited by K. Hammond. New York: Holt, Rinehart, & Winston, 1966.

Gerard, R. "The Neurophysiology of Purposive Behavior." In *Purposive Systems,* edited by H. von Foerster et al. New York: Spartan Books, 1968.

Guthrie, E. "Conditioning: A Theory of Learning in Terms of Stimulus, Response, and Association." Chapter I in *The Psychology of Learning,* edited by McConnell et al., National Society for the Study of Education. Chicago: University of Chicago Press, 1952 ed.

Hebb, D. O. *A Textbook of Psychology.* Philadelphia; Saunders, 1964 ed.

Trehub, A. "The Brain as a Parallel Coherent Detector." *Science* 174 (1971): 722.

Watson, J. "Psychology as the Behaviorist Views It," *Psychological Review* 20 (1913): 158–77.

Wiener, N. *Cybernetics.* New York: John Wiley, 1948.

Leading Questions: Chapter 1

1. A man exercising raises a dumbbell slowly at arm's length. In what direction do his muscle forces act on the dumbbell? (Upward) Now he begins slowly to lower the dumbbell. In what direction do his muscle forces *now* act on the dumbbell?

2. A woman is pulling a reluctant little boy by the hand toward a schoolroom door. In what direction do the boy's walking movements carry his body? (Forward) In what direction would the leg-muscle forces tend to move the boy's body? Do movements depend only on muscle forces?

3. A man stands before a large screen tracking a moving spot of light by keeping his finger on it. The effective *stimulus* is the distance of the spot from the finger. The *response* to a given stimulus is expressible as the position and velocity of the finger relative to the spot. Is the stimulus measure independent of the response measure? Is any independent measure possible? Is there any response that does not entail a change in the stimulus?

4. Behaviorists say that in apparent goal-seeking behavior, the goal is reached because stimuli at each stage of the process evoke the next response leading toward the goal. If a man is operating remote guidance controls to steer a toy car through a maze toward a goal, what will his response be if the car spontaneously moves along the correct path at all times? What would happen if the man *did* produce any steering movements?

2

Models and Generalizations

The conceptual collapse of behaviorism came about only in part because nature failed to fit the premises. Another kind of conceptual error has caused difficulties in behavioral research, paradoxically through *failure* to adopt the methods of physics. There is in psychological research (and many of the other "soft" sciences) what I consider to be a misunderstanding of the way in which physics has constructed theories, especially its classical theories.

It is often taught in elementary science that theorizing is a process of generalization from specific observations. The term *generalization,* however, is *too* general, for it can be used to refer to three quite different strategies. It can mean a process of extrapolation, through which one extends a series of observations a short way into the future; it can mean abstraction, the classification of specific observations into categories; or it can mean model building, which I intend here to mean the interpretation of specific observations as consequences of underlying causes. Psychology has been built almost exclusively on the first two senses of generalization, whereas the greatest successes of physics have come from use of the third.

I propose to use the third method, the method of model building, in this book, which means that the behavioral theory to be found here will be different in nature from customary theories in psychology. The purpose of this chapter is to make clear the difference between my approach and that of most other theorists in psychology and similar disciplines.

10

Extrapolation

When one is confronted with an unknown phenomenon, the first and only available procedure is to observe. After some period of observation, regularities become apparent, and the first type of generalization becomes possible. If this new phenomenon were the motions of Mars across the star background, one could begin by observing successive positions of the planet relative to the stars, thus generating a table of positions. It would quickly become clear that each day the position changed by the same amount, and on a map the points would lie on a very slightly curved line. A reasonable course would be to extend the curve some way into the future, thus predicting where the planet will be found several days or weeks ahead.

This simplest form of generalization relies on only one postulate: The future is a smooth extension of the past. Over short enough periods of time, such generalizations are valid and useful. They can be used not only to deal with ongoing events but also with more complex cause-effect situations. If many different rats always respond to the sight of a food pellet by eating it, one can generalize by predicting that the *next* time a food pellet is presented to a rat, the rat will eat it. A large portion of psychology is organized around this sort of approach. Industrial psychologists observing productivity alter working conditions in a plant, and, after observing the effects over a period of time, recommend that certain conditions be established on the assumption that if those conditions increased productivity in the past, they will continue to do so in the future. Aptitude tests are given to job applicants, and the results are judged by how others with similar scores have performed on various jobs on the theory that a person with a given score will perform in the same way that others in the past with the same score have performed. This is bread-and-butter psychology—and medicine, and sociology, and anthropology, and a host of other -ologies. It can hardly be called "science," save for the fact that all science has to start like this.

Simple extrapolation usually fails after a while. The planet Mars does not actually appear at equally-spaced intervals in the sky each night. Over a period of months it will even stop and then reverse its path for a while, describing a loop among the stars. A rat may grow old or be satiated and fail to take the food. As in the famous Western Electric Hawthorne Works experiment, in which a group of workers performed well when under study (the "Hawthorne effect"), the workers may go back to their old habits as soon as the researchers turn off the limelight. A man may be hired because of an aptitude for numbers, and thoroughly confuse the bookkeeping.

Extrapolation fails because conditions change, because observations may be made at a time when the true state of affairs cannot be seen, and most often, especially in psychology, because the phenomena themselves are subject to unpredictable variations. Conditions can be allowed for, and the true state of affairs will eventually be observed, but nothing can be done to prevent the variations, the noise that renders the basic observations highly uncertain.

There are two ways to deal with random variations: average them out or trace them to their causes. The causes of most behavioral variations are not known, hence psychologists turn to statistics to render their extrapolations less variable. One no longer says, "Rats will eat food," but, "94 out of 100 rats will eat food." The industrial concern expects the aptitude tests to be useful in the long run, but not necessarily for an individual worker. Increasing the length of time that rats go without food is expected to increase the speed of maze-running toward a food reward, but only by some amount averaged over many experiments with many rats. (It is unfortunate but true that measures and predictions obtainable only through averaging the performance of many persons are applied to individuals, so that a person's life may be seriously affected by his performance on a test that is valid *only* for predicting behavior en masse. The practice of evaluating individuals by means of tests that have only statistical validity is a perversion of science, but is not important in the conceptual scheme, so I must reluctantly put aside the rest of *that* lecture.)

The use of statistics has become a mainstay of psychology, to the point where it is a substitute for thought, creativity, and evaluation. If A correlates with B, the experiment is a success, regardless of its significance in any but the statistical sense. In the world of statistical extrapolation, a "model" is a statistical treatment. This kind of science has nothing to do with this book.

Abstraction

Statistical treatments, however, may reveal a stable cause-effect relationship which could not be seen as clearly without the averaging. At this point it is common to search for an *abstract generalization* that can be used in place of individual observations and that may show relationships to other abstract generalizations less variable than the relationship to be seen in the raw data.

An elementary example of an abstract generalization would be to report experiments with rats and food pellets by saying, "Rodents accept nourishment." A rat is a rodent, but so is a rabbit; food pellets are nourishment, but so is a carrot. By substituting more general terms for the specifics actually involved in an experiment, one offers a generalization that includes cases (at least in dictionary terms) other than the one observed. If the generalization proves valid on test, that is, if one finds that both rabbits and rats will eat both food pellets and carrots, the generalization is lent credibility and one may be encouraged to test it with other rodents and other examples of nourishment.

A more relevant example of this kind of generalization is the observation that *intermittent reinforcement is more effective than continuous reinforcement in motivating learning*. The terms *intermittent* and *continuous* refer to a whole class of temporal patterns: rewarding the animal for every successful trial or, according to some schedule, occasionally omitting the reward. *Reinforcement* is the term for any object or event capable of causing learning. *Learning* covers a host of phenomena from learning a hand-eye coordination to learning a girl's telephone number.

Since this is a generalization, it is commonly supposed to represent a law of behavior, for while it may fail to apply in individual cases, it remains approximately true for many kinds of reinforcing rewards and many types of learning. (Abstract generalizations are not *expected* to hold true all of the time.) Sometimes such generalizations are *very* accurate (the path of a body about the sun is an ellipse); others are less reliable (an unresolved Oedipal conflict may cause sexual aberrations); some are always true, but so vague that they are trivial (self-respect depends on right living).

The problem with abstract generalizations is that they are superficial, in the literal sense. They deal only with the surface appearances of a phenomenon. Most often, their true basis is nothing more solid than verbal custom or common sense. *Intelligence,* for example, is said by the more cautious psychologists to be a person's score on a particular intelligence test, but the items on these tests were not selected at random—they were intended, and still are, to reveal how smart people are. *Positive reinforcement* is said to be any stimulus that increases the probability of a given response to a given stimulus, but behind this idea is the common-sense notion of a *reward;* we still have no idea of what is rewarding about a reward, or what we mean by "rewarding," except in terms of the very learning effects we wish to account for.

Abstract generalizations begin with observations of the visible symptoms of an inner organization and progress outward from the organism and upward into verbal abstraction, going farther and farther from the source of the symptoms and having less and less to say about any one instance of behavior. They represent, in my opinion, at best a temporary measure for improving predictions when en masse predictions are needed, and at worst a mechanism for creating the illusion of understanding.

Model Building

In physics both extrapolation and abstract generalization are used and misused, but the power of physical theories did not finally develop until physical *models* became central. A model in the sense I intend is a description of subsystems within the system being studied, each having its own properties and all—interacting together according to their individual properties—being responsible for observed appearances.

The kinetic theory of heat grew out of such model building. The observations, the appearances, were generalized first: Substances have *heat capacity,* which is a measure of the *temperature rise* resulting from adding a specific number of *calories* of heat per unit *mass.* This generalization remains useful. The explanatory model developed to account for these surface appearances, however, is more powerful and precise.

The "subsystems" in this model are molecules, and the individual properties of the molecules that are used in the model are the masses, velocities, sizes, and shapes of the molecules. The molecules interact according to universal principles of conservation of energy and momentum, thus producing the phenomena we see on the surface. The surface appearance is seen to be a statistical average measure that depends on the molecules, speed, their mass, and their collision rate with each other and (for gases) with the molecules in the walls of the container.

It can be argued that psychologists *have* tried building models of this kind, but I do not think this is true to any significant degree.

Rather, I think they have *tried* but did not understand how a model of this type is constructed and so have ended by creating abstract generalizations that sounded like models but were not models. (There are, of course, significant exceptions, some of which I will mention later.)

Several examples come to mind. Freud's id, ego, and superego might possibly qualify as models except for one fact: They were defined in terms of the symptoms they produced, which means that their individual properties were not *underlying* properties but simply subdivisions of observed symptoms. Another would be Clark Hull's theory (1940) of habit strength. A "habit" in this "mathematico-deductive" theory was spoken of as existing inside an organism, but its strength was measured by seeing for how long a time a behavior pattern would persist after the rewards used to establish it were terminated. The entities in this theory were not inner properties of an organism interacting with each other, but simply ways of classifying observable behavior patterns. The term *strength* may sound as if it refers to a property of some inner organization that accounts for the persistence that is seen, but habit strength is in fact defined in terms of the *consequences* of some property which remains un-named and unknown.

Pseudomodels like Hull's and Freud's and many others represent earnest attempts to penetrate beneath the surface appearances of behavior. They could not have succeeded in any significant way because they were based on unspoken subjective criteria. I suppose it was hoped that if the *right* entities could be seen in behavior, they would turn out to have some correlation with the actual inner operation of nervous systems, but the brain itself remained an enigma, a hopelessly complex structure beyond analysis. There was little to guide the guesswork. The problem is that there are too many overlapping ways to categorize the regularities of behavior, and they can't *all* correspond to the brain's inner organization. To find some reason to choose one way of looking at behavior over another, one needs information from outside the conceptual scheme. Self-consistency alone is not enough to provide a basis for choice, since many different schemes are self-consistent.

Before the kinetic theory of heat could be developed, a hint from the inside of matter had to be found. The main concept preceding the kinetic theory was that of *caloric,* the "capacity for heat" of a substance. This term has a family resemblance to "habit strength" and "reinforcing value" (of a stimulus) in that it sounds as if it refers to an inner property, but it is in fact defined wholly in terms of observed events.

The first hint came from Rumford's and then Davy's experiments with frictional heating, which showed that matter apparently contained an *unlimited* amount of "caloric" (comparable, say, to the unlimited strength of certain habits such as calling oneself by a certain name, or the unlimited—negative—reinforcement value of a bullet). This development occurred just at the time when the molecular theory of matter was gaining experimental support, and the evidence for the molecular theory (crowned by the discovery of *Brownian movements* of tiny particles suspended in liquids) was the hint from inside matter needed to provide a true *model* for the nature of heat. Once heat was identified as the observable consequence of *motion inside matter,* all the mysterious observations fell into place.

They fell into place, however, not by becoming mutually consistent, but because they could now be seen as consequences of a common underlying phenomenon. "Caloric" was revealed as a misleading construct and became obsolete, leaving for posterity only the name of a unit of heat, the *calorie.*

During the past 25 years, there have been many attempts to construct models of the brain phenomena underlying behavior. My model represents another attempt. Among the earliest of these attempts was the model of McCulloch and Pitts (1943). The approach taken by McCulloch and his co-workers was to begin with basic facts about the nervous system, and from them develop a "logical calculus" of nerve activity that might develop into a description of the phenomena underlying behavior. In this period during and just after World War II, there was a tremendous creative effort that resulted in the appearance of information theory, computer theory, servomechanism theory, and especially cybernetics, the brainchild of Norbert Wiener (1948).

Developments in this new line of theorizing have followed two main branches, one specifically following up McCulloch's nerve-net analysis and the other using the new terminology and techniques but following the old externalized approach that lies behind "caloric" and "habit strength." I say that without criticism. It is very difficult not only to find those crucial hints from inside but even to realize when they are needed. Even when one deliberately looks inside, as McCulloch did, there are no guideposts to provide assurance that one is looking without prejudice at what he finds or from the point of view that will finally bring order out of chaos.

Neither complexity nor explanatory power distinguishes the "internal" from the "external" theory. D. O. Hebb's "cell-assembly" theory (1949) is almost totally lacking in explanatory power, but it is a true attempt to describe an organization inside the brain that does not itself demonstrate observable behavior but by its properties accounts for observed behavior. The TOTE (Test-Operate-Test-Exit) unit of Miller, Galanter, and Pribram's model (1960) has considerable explanatory power (in that it contains an organizational principle that applies to a great range of behavior), but it is not a model of the brain; rather, it is a model of the behavior that is caused by the brain.

Most of modern cybernetics, including related computer-simulation studies of thought processes, is in the class of externalized theories rather than models in the sense intended here. The thought-simulation programs of Newell and Simon (1963); the theorem proving programs of Gelernter (1963), and many other such attempts to duplicate human thought rest on descriptions of *what* the brain does, not concepts of the functions in the brain that make it capable of doing these things. One cannot help feeling, of course, that all these lines of research are slowly converging toward a new picture of human nature—after all, the molecular theory of matter was first suspected (as long ago as Lucretius) because of indirect evidence and not initially on the basis of observing underlying phenomena.

Still, I think there is a certain amount of confusion extant about the difference between a model for *causes* of behavior and a model for *consequences* of organization (I claim no exemption for myself). One often sees block diagrams of behavioral organization, but a close inspection usually shows that the blocks are not subsystems inside the behaving system, but subdivisions of its externally observable behavior. As long as one is only dividing observed behavior into units that seem to hang together in some way, he has the problem that many different ways of subdividing the same whole will result in a self-consistent description. What is needed to build a compelling model of internal causes of behavior is some hint from nature, some suggestion that will point the theorist in the right direction and tell him how to look at what little of the insides of the nervous system is known.

This book presents a model of the brain's internal organization which as far as I can tell now is of the same type as the molecular theory of matter, in that the entities that are supposed to reside in the brain have *individual* properties as molecules have individual masses and velocities. Observed behavior is deduced not from past examples of behavior, but from the way in which these internal entities interact with each other and the external world. Of course these entities have been carefully chosen to behave properly when put together, but they have also been selected to fit anatomical hints about the nervous system (as far as I understand them), physical models of the organism and its environment, subjective experience, and elementary mathematical logic. Many models might be consistent with one or two of these classes of knowledge, but not many will satisfy *all* these criteria.

REFERENCES

Gelernter, H., et al. "Empirical Explorations of the Geometry-Theorem Proving Machine." In *Computers and Thought,* edited by E. Feigenbaum and J. Feldman. New York: McGraw-Hill, 1963.

Hebb, D. O. *Organization of Behavior.* New York: John Wiley, 1949.

Hull, C., et al. *Mathematico-Deductive Theory of Rote Learning.* New Haven: Yale University Press, 1940.

McCulloch, W., and Pitts, W. "A Logical Calculus of the Ideas Immanent in Nervous Activity." *Bulletin of Mathematical Biophysics* 5 (1943): 115.

Miller, G., Galanter, E., and Pribram, K. *Plans and the Structure of Behavior;* New York: Holt, Rinehart & Winston, 1960.

Newell, A., and Simon, H. "GPS, A Program that Simulates Human Thought." In *Computers and Thought,* edited by E. Feigenbaum, and J. Feldman. New York: McGraw-Hill, 1963.

Wiener, N. *Cybernetics.* New York: John Wiley, 1948.

LEADING QUESTIONS: CHAPTER 2

1. A statistical generalization: Hiawatha shoots four arrows. A target with its bullseye is located ten feet to the right of a pine tree. The arrows pass six feet, eight feet, twelve feet, and fourteen feet to the right of the pine tree, level with the bullseye. Where does Hiawatha's average shot go?

2. An extrapolation: Xeno's tortoise is ten feet from a stone wall. At noon exactly, it heads toward the stone wall at a speed of one foot per minute. Where will the tortoise be at one minute past noon? nine minutes past noon? eleven minutes past noon?

Premises

One man, John Von Neumann, was largely responsible for the two major classes of modern automatic computers, analogue computers and digital computers. His first "differential analyzer" was a mechanical contraption that solved simultaneous differential equations with pulleys, cables, levers, and balls rolling on disks. His first "stored program digital computer" was by today's standards also crude. Nevertheless, both inventions have profoundly affected modern engineering and science—and modern theorists.

The Digital-Computer Premise

An unfortunate coincidence caused almost every theorist following Von Neumann to select the *digital* computer as the basic model of nervous-system activity. The coincidence was the fact that nerves behave in an all-or-none fashion: They generate an impulse or they do not, depending on whether the stimulation is above or below a threshold level. The comparison with the binary on-off elements of a digital computer was obvious, and was immediately taken up as the basis for a huge amount of theoretical effort.

McCulloch's (1972) nerve-net analysis was based on this concept; so was Wiener's "stationary time series" analysis in *Cybernetics* (1948). Many others have continued in this tradition, and the mathematical theorems have multiplied and prospered. The

19

main difficulty with such analyses is that they quite regularly require assumptions about the nervous system that are contrary to known fact.

In a typical analysis, activity in a nerve network is described in terms of *time states*. A given nerve cell which receives impulses from several fibers coming from other nerve cells has a *threshold of firing:* If an impulse arrives at the cell in each incoming fiber, there will be a summing (over some short interval) of excitatory effects; the threshold will be exceeded; and the cell will be triggered to produce an impulse. If too few incoming impulses arrive together, the nerve cell receiving them will *not* fire.

A time state refers to a whole set of nerve cells which are receiving multiple impulses at a given moment. Some of the cells will fire and some will not, creating a pattern of *on* cells and *off* cells which is called the state of the neural network at that moment of time (Arbib 1964).

Given the initial time state of *on* and *off* cells, one can then proceed to the next time state, when the impulses generated by the cell firings have reached a new set of cells. Once again, some of these cells will receive enough multiple impulses from different incoming fibers to fire them, and some will not. Thus one can proceed time state by time state to describe the activity of the network of nerves.

The assumption contrary to fact is simply that these time states are synchronized. In real nervous systems summation effects do occur in each nerve cell that is stimulated by incoming impulses, but the summing occurs at random times owing to variations of conduction speed in various paths. The cells which change state at a given moment may be anywhere within the whole network. Thus there is a basic difference between nerve networks and the computing flip-flops in a digital computer: There is no clock in the nervous system to cause changes of state to occur in neat sequence. Electrical rhythms in the brain that have been observed are far too slow to do the necessary clocking; they are results, not causes, just as the interference caused in radio reception by an operating computer is a result, not a cause, of the program that is running.

Comparison of nerve activity to digital computing elements is not only factually suspect; it is of no practical help in experimental work. The *only* correlations that have been found between nervous-system activity and behavior have been discovered through measurement of what I have come to term *neural currents*: the rate at which impulses pass a given point, averaged over just enough time to *erase* the discrete nature of nerve impulses.

For these reasons I am not going to accept the digital-computer premise for a theory of nerve activity.

The Analogue-Computer Premise

In effect, I am choosing to use Von Neumann's other invention as a conceptual model for nervous system operation: the analogue computer. More basically, the choice is for a *continuous* representation over a *discrete* representation, although the concept of quantitative analogues is also of great usefulness. The meaning of this can be illustrated by a comparison of nerve impulses with the discrete charges that carry electric current.

We know now that electric current is not a flow of continuous substance, but the drift of tiny individually charged particles (electrons) through the atomic matrix of a conductor. That was not the initial picture, however, nor is it the concept that is used in modern electronic and electrical engineering (except at levels of current so low that effects of individual charges can be seen). For purely practical reasons, engineers treat electric current as a smoothly variable continuous quantity and ignore what they know to be too detailed a representation of reality for their purposes.

The level of detail one accepts as basic must be consistent with the level of detail in the phenomena to be described in these basic terms. One can always, for other purposes, analyze further. If we wish to describe the activity of the nervous system that correlates with the phenomena of direct experience, and constitutes the inner component of such behaviors as walking, talking, and execution of action patterns in general, then it would be inappropriate to begin with an individual neural impulse. No one neural impulse has any discernible relationship to observations (objective or subjective) of *behavior*. Even if we knew where all neural impulses were at any given instant, the listing of their locations would convey only meaningless detail, like a half-tone photograph viewed under a microscope. If we want understanding of relationships, we must keep the level of detail consistent and comprehensible, inside and outside of the organism.

Neural Currents

As the basic measure of nervous-system activity, therefore, I choose to use *neural current,* defined as *the number of impulses passing through a cross section of all parallel redundant fibers in a given bundle per unit time.* The appropriateness of this measure depends on the *maximum* neural current normally expected to occur in a given bundle of fibers. If the maximum in a bundle of 50 fibers is 200 impulses per second in each fiber, the maximum neural current will be 10,000 impulses per second, and statistical variations will not be important at any level of neural current in proportion to the whole normal range of operation (they will be roughly 1 percent of the maximum, or less).

The use of neural current is appropriate, for example, in considering the stimulation of a whole muscle, especially in terms of the forces thereby developed on the tendons and thus on the bones. The impulses going to the muscle arrive via hundreds of individual pathways, each terminating on one tiny contractile fiber, but the net force developed depends on all these parallel events, not on any one of them. The individual random twitches are averaged out.

The only quantity inside the nervous system that correlates with the net force exerted by, say, the biceps muscle is the neural current obtained by counting all the impulses reaching that muscle per unit time. That is essentially the same as counting the impulses passing a cross section of all the parallel motor-nerve fibers running from the spinal cord to the biceps muscle. I am doing nothing more here than formalizing a measure that is commonly used in neurology and physiology, even if not instrumented with just this definition in mind.

The single-impulse model of neural activity treats the convergence of separate trains of impulses on a single nerve cell by instant-to-instant evaluation of the summation of excitatory effects. The neural-current model handles the same situation in terms of continuous average summation effects. Unlike the time-state analysis, the neural-current analysis handles this summation effect easily whether several small (low repetition rate) signals are converging, or one large (high repetition rate) signal is present. Binary computing elements do not distinguish the rate at which input events occur (in normal operation), and so a digital-computer model cannot handle the common situation in which one high-frequency current can cause a nerve cell to fire, while two low-frequency currents cannot.

Neural impulses may either increase the tendency of a nerve cell to fire (excitatory effects) or may decrease that tendency (inhibitory effects). The difference seems to reside in the type of nerve cell in which the impulse originates: "Renshaw cells" are apparently specialized to emit an inhibitory substance at the end of the outgoing impulse-conducting fiber (Wooldridge 1963). Therefore in the summation of neural currents, some currents contribute positively to the net excitation of the receiving nerve cell, while others contribute negatively.

Some connections seem to involve such low thresholds that only a few impulses arriving at once—even just one—can fire the following nerve cell. In a case where two impulses are required, and at relatively low neural currents, the chance of two independently originated impulses arriving nearly enough at the same instant is the *product* of the probabilities of arrival of an impulse in each incoming path per unit time. Thus the neural current generated by the receiving cell is proportional not to the sum of incoming neural currents, but to their product.

Neural Analogue Computers

The nervous system, no matter what kind of computer to which we liken it, does not operate according to the forms we find convenient to express mathematically. At best, mathematical descriptions can only provide a form that is reasonably close to reality. The "summation" of neural currents is only roughly linear—$2 + 2$ may equal about 4, but $4 + 4$ may equal a little less than 7; $7 + 7$ may equal 8, and $\frac{1}{2} + \frac{1}{2}$ may equal 0. This nonlinearity means that everything we would like to call "summation" also contains a little of what we would see as "multiplication," and vice versa.

Nevertheless, many other nonlinear systems have been successfully understood on the basis of linear approximations, and if we do not demand great precision, such approximations can be suggestive of interesting arrangements in the nervous system. At least this degree of approximation (if not more) is required to make the digital approach plausible, so the neural-current analysis rests on no shakier premises than the digital analysis.

In the next few pages, the basic elements of a model of neural function will be developed, not as a complete treatment of the continuous-variable approach, but as a sort of existence theorem to justify the general shift from discrete to continuous representation of behavioral variables. (Some reference will be made, later in the book, to specific computing functions to be described here.)

All of this may sound highly abstract at this point, but if we follow the model through—order by order, level by level (and if the model represents, as I think it does, a near approximation of how and why humans behave as they do)—we will eventually by its logic come to conclude that the brain's model of reality, as far as consciousness is concerned, *is* reality—there is nothing else to perceive. That is, the behavior of the model given in this book is the behavior of reality; when one acts to affect reality, he is acting so as to affect his model, and he has no inkling, save for physics, of what he is really doing to the external world in the process of making his brain's model behave in various ways. He cannot of course sense the neural networks that cause the implicit properties of one model to be represented explicitly at a higher level as a different kind of model; he perceives only the consequences of these transformations. What we do, finally, is simply add to our brain's many existing models a new model, one which represents transformations we cannot perceive. (This process of making a model of the brain's model is not infinitely regressive, however, any more than it is infinitely regressive to define, say, a well-formed function, in logic, as a relationship between two well-formed functions.)

Moreover, if ultimately we accept as a fact the idea that *all* objects of perception are neural signals, we can see that there is no reason for shutting off present-time perception in order to observe subjectively derived perceptions: such perceptions will appear precisely as real and objective as configurations, sensations, and motion. We do not have to use our imagination in order to perceive such things; we need only look around. What is difficult, of course, is getting used to the idea that what we see indicates the existence of a perceptual transformation and only secondarily and hypothetically something actually occurring in an external reality. We need to learn to look not at the meanings and implications of the events, but at the events themselves, and ask what else is "obviously" going on.

It may be difficult initially to grasp the idea that all neural signals are alike. A face, for example, is certainly not like an automobile, but in the model presented in this book both will be represented, albeit in different places in the brain, by the presence of a single neural signal. Once we happen to be noticing "on-ness," for example, we can continue: the saucer is *on* the table, the table is *on* the floor. The system that detects the relationship "on" (in this model the sixth-order system) responds in each case to "on-ness," even though the configurations involved are quite different. (A different system responds if we pay attention to "in-ness" instead of "on-ness"; the spoon is *in* the cup, the cup is *in* the room.

A world perceived in terms no higher than sixth order, however, would consist only of objects and events in relationship; that is, relationships would be observed or caused to exist, first one and then another set of them, but once a particular relationship had appeared in experience, that would be the end of it. And even at the sixth order it will be evident that the model has passed beyond systems whose operation can be spelled out in much detail, but still there seems to be a need to guess at higher levels of organization, and the next, the seventh level of this book's model, is concerned with something of which individual relationships (and lower-order perceptions) are only components.

The seventh level of human organization is concerned with *programs,* a term used in exactly the sense of computer programs, a string of relationships, events, movements, configurations, sensations, and intensities. But there is more to a program than a particular relationship among events, and the difference is that a program contains choice points. In fact *only* the choice points are critical at the seventh level, because what happens between them is fully describable in lower-order terms as relationships, sequences, motions, etc. What makes a string of lower-order perceptions into a program is that at each test point the string branches into several paths, and what will happen at each branch point depends on the outcome of the test.

A program, then, is a *network of contingencies,* not a list. There can be main programs and subroutines; branch points may be two-way or multiple-way, and can loop back to earlier points in the program or skip parts of programs. This is the kind of organization the brain needs in order to carry out what we call *thinking*. Sixth-order systems can recognize when events satisfy logical or other relationships (the door is open or shut), but the program level is required in order to carry out manipulations of these relationships (if the door is open, walk through it; if not, open it and *then* walk through.)

It is often said that computers do not think because they do not select their own programs; they do the bidding of a human operator. If a programmed computer is not fully human, however, then neither would a person be whose highest level of organization was the seventh order of systems in this book's model. Another level is required in order to permit behavior to include *choice of program* by a means other than another program, and one way to find higher-order controlled quantities is to ask *why* lower-order quantities are controlled. In the present case, this amounts to asking why a collection of programs is executed over and over. For example, why does a bookkeeper balance the books?

The answers to such questions would probably be a statement of some general principle; for example, because things ought to come out even, or because a man has to make a living, or because a person has to maintain a certain status.

Another term that seems applicable at this level is *role*. When a man says, "I am a bookkeeper," the phrase denotes a set of complex skills at the program level—the ability to carry out behaviors in a network of choice points. The phrase also implies a definite set of principles. Bookkeepers are supposed to be trustworthy, painstaking, thorough, orderly, and accurate in their work. In the same way, being a father implies responsibility and being a playboy implies hedonism—but these characteristics can be seen over a range of values from absent to maximally present. If a father says he behaves responsibly, he may mean that he does so with respect to a setting of the reference signal ("I am responsible") which is lower than that of other fathers—and reference levels for principles can always be seen as values. In speaking loosely of values, we tend to forget that a term like *honesty* describes something variable, since it is tacitly if unrealistically assumed that one always seeks to maximize qualities generally accepted as good. In behavioral organization, then, a value is merely that state of a controlled quantity one has accepted as good.

We will get to these matters—and more—in succeeding chapters. For now, we begin by laying some conceptual foundations for later discussions, with a simple model of neural conduction. Trains of neural impulses are generated either by a sensory receptor or a nerve cell excited by other neural impulses. These are neural currents which propagate rapidly enough that they may be considered to exist simultaneously over the whole length of a nerve fiber. The impulses travel in the direction from the cell body to synaptic knobs terminating the fiber just a few microns away from the next cell body in the chain. They do not "jump the gap" to the next cell; rather, they act to speed up or slow down the spontaneous repetitive firings of the next cell body. That is a correct picture when the rates of firing are near the middle of the normal range of operation. With *no* input impulses arriving, a cell body will seldom fire spontaneously.

A *large* input neural current results in repetitive release of many tiny quanta of excitatory or inhibitory substance per unit time, having a large effect on the rate at which the following cell body recovers from each firing and fires again, and hence having a large effect on the neural current generated by that receiving cell body. Thus input neural currents have quantitative effects on output neural currents, although there is no one-to-one correspondence required between incoming and outgoing impulses.

In the following discussion we will consider a basic array of analogue computing functions based on this linear-approximation approach.

Addition of positive neural currents is diagrammed in figure 3.1. *Open* circles indicate *excitation*. If I is used (as in electricity) to designate current, then $I_3 = (I_1 + I_2)$. The plus signs emphasize the *excitatory* effects.

Subtraction of neural currents can be indicated by using a blacked-out circle and a minus sign (or either alone) to indicate

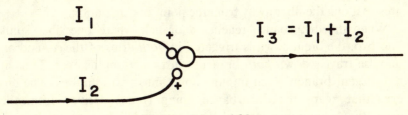

FIGURE 3.1. *Adder.*

inhibition (see fig. 3.2). This is the general case of algebraic summation; $I_3 = I_1 + (-I_2)$, or $I_3 = I_1 - I_2$. If the negative current is equal to or greater than the positive current, the output current I_3 is *zero*. This is the first main difference between neural and electrical currents. All currents are in units of impulses per second, or frequency of firing. A frequency of firing, in impulses per second, cannot go negative—the nervous system cannot "owe" impulses, and we can count only the number that occurs in a unit of time, which must be zero or greater.

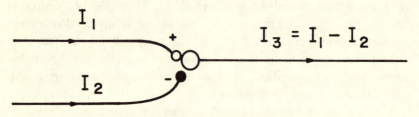

FIGURE 3.2.   *Subtractor.*

The second main difference is in the meaning of positive and negative signs. In electricity all current carriers have the same effects, and sign indicates direction of current flow. In neural current analysis all currents resulting from firing of a neuron flow in one direction only (away from the cell body) and sign indicates *only* excitatory or inhibitory effect.

The third important difference can be seen when a neural current reaches a branch in a nerve fiber. To see what happens we must return to the single-impulse level of analysis. A nerve impulse is an electrochemical breakdown phenomenon. A drastic but highly localized change in the walls of the nerve-fiber tube permits the flow of ions in and out of the fiber, and this sudden flow triggers a similar event in the adjacent section that has not just undergone this change. Thus a wave of chemical activity progresses along the fiber away from the point of origination.

When the disturbance reaches a branch where one fiber splits into two, the breakdown is triggered in *both* arms of the Y, and an impulse travels down *both* branches just as strong as ever. Thus at a divergent branch, each impulse splits into two impulses. The energy that keeps the disturbance going is not derived from the event that originally triggered the impulse, but is continually sup-

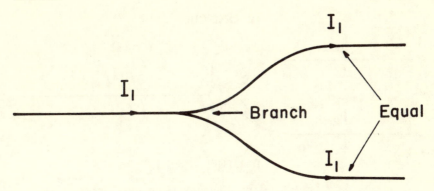

FIGURE 3.3. *Nonconservation of neural current.*

plied to the fiber, along its whole length, from the surrounding fluids. *No conservation law is needed.*

This means that when a fiber splits, the current is not weakened at all, but is duplicated. This is shown diagrammatically in figure 3.3. From this *non*conservation law can be derived the concept of the weighting of currents. In the simplest case we have an *amplifier* (see fig. 3.4). The *n*-way branch duplicates the original current *n* times; these *n* copies are then summed at a neural junction, and the current leaving the following cell is *n* times the magnitude of the incoming current (roughly). Even though the duplicated impulses arrive at the junction at nearly the same time, they can initiate many impulses if the net excitatory effect greatly exceeds the firing threshold. The neural current is thus amplified by a factor of *n*.

Several different neural currents may reach a receiving cell body after *each* has split into several branches, a very common arrangement throughout the nervous system (see fig. 3.5). In this case the effect of each input current on the output current I_3 depends on the number of branches that form. The relative contribution, or *weight,* of each input current thus depends on the num-

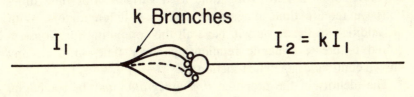

FIGURE 3.4. *Amplifier.*

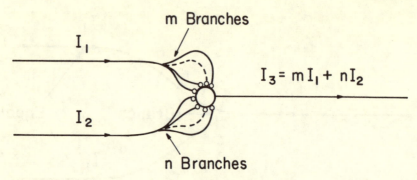

FIGURE 3.5. *Weighted summation.*

ber of branches: $I_3 = mI_1 + nI_2$. This is a *weighted summation,* which can include negative contributions, a computing function that can have considerable significance. (Note that overall proportionality factors are being left out for simplicity.)

As mentioned, if simultaneous arrival of impulses in two (or more) paths is required to initiate *one* output impulse, especially when recovery time is *very fast* after a firing, the output frequency varies as the *product* of the input frequencies (see fig. 3.6). If one input is inhibitory, we obtain approximate *division* of the excitatory current by the inhibitory current.

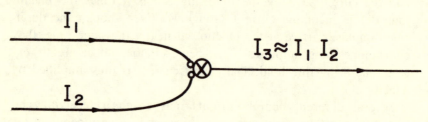

FIGURE 3.6. *Multiplier.*

So far we have all the computing functions required to develop any relationship among neural currents that can be expressed in *algebraic* terms not involving time as a variable. For time functions we require time integrations and time differentiators. With the addition of these, we will have all the computing functions required to create dynamic relationships over time—in fact, any known continuous analytic function.

The identity of the proposed *time integrator* may be something of a surprise. It has long been assigned an entirely different role.

Time integration is accomplished by so-called "reverberating circuits," that is, closed chains of neural connections.

Imagine a single impulse entering from the left in figure 3.7, and a receiving cell body with a threshold of less than one impulse—it will fire for *each* incoming impulse in any input path. The second cell is similar. Recalling that impulses *duplicate* at branches in a fiber, it is clear that after the initial impulse from the left, cell 1 and cell 2 will fire alternately, forever, as if a single impulse were racing around and around the closed loop.

Every time cell 2 fires, a duplicate impulse will travel off to the right, and the neural output current I_4 will be equal to the rate at which cell 2 fires. If the transit time around the loop is $\frac{1}{10}$ second, the neural current I_4 will have a magnitude of 10 impulses per second.

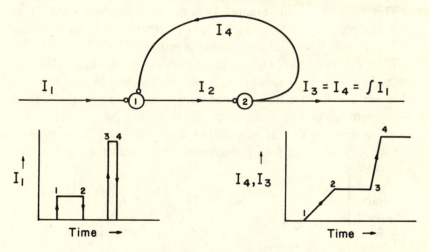

FIGURE 3.7. *Time-integrator.*

Assuming that the output current is 10, let a second impulse arrive from the left. Immediately the output jumps to 20, since now *two* impulses make the round trip every $\frac{1}{10}$ second. If a succession of five more impulses enter from the left, the output current will increase by 50 more, to 70 (impulses per second).

The *rate* at which impulses leave this circuit on the right is equal to 10 times the *total number* of impulses that have entered from the left, regardless of how long they took to arrive. Of course the closed circuit must be long enough to allow the necessary number of impulses to be circulating at once.

This means that I_4 is proportional to the time integral of I_1, or to the time integral of the net excitatory signal if several sources contribute inputs of both signs. As with other analogue integrators, neural integrators are probably not perfect—an impulse will *not* circulate forever, but has some finite lifetime in the loop. Also, if a circulating impulse arrives back at cell 1 just as a new input impulse arrives, only one impulse can survive. The cell can generate only one impulse at a time. As the number of circulating impulses approaches the capacity of the loop, the input cell will more and more often be firing just as a new input impulse arrives, and accumulation must eventually level off due to such "coincidence losses." The metabolic energy supply that actually drives the impulses can be exhausted, which also limits the lifetime of an impulse.

This integrator will respond to negative (inhibitory) inputs as well as excitatory ones, since a train of inhibitory input impulses will eventually destroy all circulating impulses.

Time differentiation can be accomplished in two quite different ways. One involves *habituation,* a fatiguelike drop in rate of firing of a nerve cell after abrupt appearance of a steady input signal. Many sensory endings, especially the annulospiral sensors in the muscles, respond in this way. When a steady stimulus is applied, the sensory nerve at first generates a large neural current which

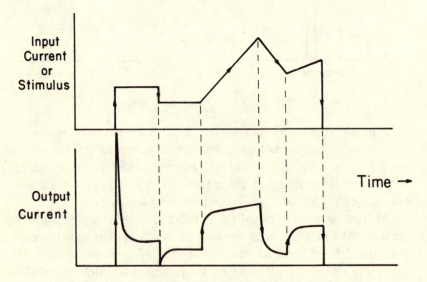

FIGURE 3.8.   *Differentiator: Input-output relationships.*

immediately declines to a much smaller value. If the stimulation is then lessened slightly, the neural current will drop sharply, then rise again somewhat (see fig. 3.8). This kind of response can be represented as a combination of first derivative response and proportional response, though in some cases the proportional part is all but missing.

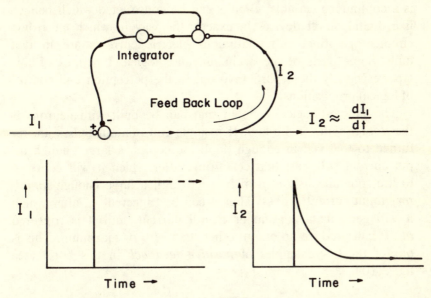

FIGURE 3.9. *Differentiator: Using integrator in feedback loop.*

A second way of achieving time differentiation is to connect a neural integrator in a negative feedback loop (see fig. 3.9). The integrator's output inhibits an input amplifier, but the amount of inhibition starts at zero and increases at a rate depending on the output current I_2, so that the output current shows the same response to changes that the habituating sensory ending shows. As drawn in figure 3.9, of course, this differentiator could be used only once and would not respond properly to a *decrease* in input current. The added design required to make a complete differentiator is left as an exercise for the reader, being fairly obvious.

These components—algebraic summer, amplifier, integrator, and differentiator—together with the multiplying function mentioned earlier are the standard set of building blocks for analogue computing. All of these arrangements can be found in the nervous system, but of course the input-output relationships will not be linear as in the idealized model. Nevertheless, these kinds of computing blocks can be interconnected in an endless variety of ways to create any imaginable relationship between an input current and one or more output currents.

There is one last class of computing functions that has to be considered—*logical* functions. Despite the fact that neural current is a continuous variable, circuits can be constructed which behave like digital on-off devices in exactly the way in which electronic circuits operating with continuous electric currents are in fact built. Some parts of the brain may use logical functions of this type, especially those parts involved in the perception and control of logical propositions.

The simplest logical element that can be built with neurons is the *storage* unit, or flip-flop. If a single cell's output pulses are returned to that cell in enough duplicate copies, a large enough input current will start that cell firing, after which it will continue to fire spontaneously at a high speed until a large enough *inhibitory* input current arrives. Thus it can be triggered *on,* after which it will generate a continuous neural current until it is triggered *off.* It can produce no output other than zero or maximum. This is one of the few examples of *positive feedback* in this book (see fig. 3.10).

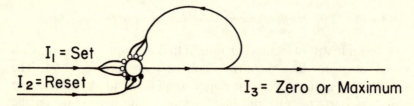

I₁ = Set

I₂ = Reset

I₃ = Zero or Maximum

FIGURE 3.10.   *Set-Reset Flip-Flop.*

Given the definition of *one* and *zero* as maximum and zero neural current respectively, and identifying inhibition as the *not* operator, it is possible to go on from here to design logic circuits functionally identical to those used in digital computers. Since neural currents instead of single impulses are used to represent one and zero, there is no clocking problem to contend with: The logic can be "asynchronous." Those who are not already familiar with logic circuitry can find unlimited detail in the literature (for example, Richards 1971). This is a point of interest only, however, since I will not use logic design circuits in the model proposed in this book, or for that matter try to set up *any* specific computing designs. A proper investigation of the nervous system will tell us the proper design details by direct measurement of output-input relationships in terms of neural current.

A Premise Concerning Perception

The foregoing discussion of computing functions has been in preparation for a discussion of how we will be dealing with the activities of the nervous system in this book's model. The most important activity to be dealt with is *perception,* which we know consciously as *what is* and *what happens* around us, to us, and inside of us. I am not going to subdivide perception in the way the dictionary suggests, separating sensations and concepts from perception. When I refer to perception, I mean in general the entire set of events, following stimulation, that occurs in the *input* part of the brain, all the way from sensory receptors to the highest centers in the cerebral cortex.

More specifically, *perception* is to be distinguished from *conscious perception.* A perception is occurring if the neural current corresponding to that perception has a magnitude greater than zero. The perception is *conscious* if there is reason to believe that awareness is involved also. Thus we can speak of perception as a brain phenomenon, and leave the subject of consciousness for later discussion. Clearly there are often sensory responses going on in nerves with no consciousness of the presence of these signals; for example, consider the pressure sensation from the seat you are in. Presence of perceptual neural currents is a necessary prerequisite of conscious perception, but is not sufficient to assure consciousness of that perception. Thus many perceptions may be involved in behavior even though the subject is not always paying attention to them.

A "perception" means a neural current in a single fiber or bundle of redundant fibers which has a magnitude that is related to the magnitudes of some set of primary sensory-nerve stimulations. I suspect, although I cannot prove, that every distinct object of awareness *is* one such neural current. The neurologist Jerzy Konorski (1967) has arrived at essentially the same conclusion for different, and perhaps better, reasons than mine.

A neural current that is a perception I will call a *perceptual signal*. The first perceptual signals to arise in the nervous system are produced by the sensory endings themselves as a direct result of a physical phenomenon just outside the nervous system. A light intensity, a chemical concentration, an influx or outflow of heat, or a mechanical deformation can cause these *first-order* perceptions to arise. If one is aware of these perceptual signals directly, he perceives only *intensity,* for that is all that these single signals can represent—they carry no added information to identify the kind of intensity.

Perceptual signals are continuous functions of something outside the nervous system. Some receptors emphasize rates of change. All of them habituate to some extent so that the zero of the perceptual scale may wander. Nevertheless, an acceptably accurate general statement is that the state of the perceptual signals of first order reflects the state of the immediate environment impinging on the sensory receptors on a continuing basis. It is simply not true that perceptions arise mainly from brief stimuli or changes in stimulation. Look around: *That* is perception. It is always there.

Suppose now that a set of first-order perceptual signals enters a neural computer, a collection of analogue computing devices like those we have just discussed. The outputs of these devices will be neural currents that represent weighted sums, differences, or other functions of the incoming neural currents. Any one of the output currents is a specific function of the many input currents. As those input currents vary in magnitude, so will the output current vary, in accordance with the relationships defined by the intervening computing devices. If an intervening device performed simple summation of two first-order currents, the output or *second-order* current would remain constant if one first-order current increased while the other decreased by the same amount.

In that example, a second-order current depends on physical events impinging on sensory endings, but not in the same way as the first-order currents depend on the same external phenomena. The second-order current varies according to the sum of two physically distinct effects, and not either one alone. It can remain constant while both of the first-order signals on which it depends change, and hence while both physical effects change. This means that a second-order neural current corresponds in magnitude not to any single local physical effect, but to the magnitude of some more general variable—temperature, for example, or pressure, rather than local flow of heat or local mechanical deformation.

It is also true that a second-order perception may correspond to nothing of physical significance. One can see how second-order perceptions might correspond to some physically meaningful attribute of the outer world such as temperature, but that significance depends entirely on the kind of computing functions involved. There is nothing to prevent the nervous system from performing computations leading to second-order perceptual signals that have no external significance. A taste sensation such as the distinctive taste of lemonade results from combining sweet and acid sensory responses, but there is nothing contained in the glass that corresponds to the sum of these sensory responses. The sugar concentration and the acid concentration do not physically add to each other. They are simply in the same general location. Yet the total lemonade taste is just as unitary a perception as is the image of the glass.

We are led by this kind of reasoning to a peculiar concept of perception. The brain may be full of many perceptual signals, but the relationships between those signals and the external reality on which they depend seems utterly arbitrary. At least we have no assurance that any given perception has significance outside of a human brain. It could be that none of them have, not even the first-order perceptions. We may strongly suspect that there is a real universe out there, beginning a millimeter outside of our nervous systems, but *our perceptions are not that universe.* They *depend on it,* but the form of that dependence is determined in the brain, by the neural computers which create perceptual signals layer by layer through transformations of one set of neural currents into another.

What might we learn about that external reality by learning more about ourselves? What assumptions have we made about reality that are really no more than limitations of our brains?

A Premise about Brain Organization

The neural currents (which I will refer to regularly as *signals* from now on) corresponding to perceptions are related to one another by the computing functions that cause one signal to be a function of others. These computing networks can be called *perceptual functions* and can be represented in a block diagram by a

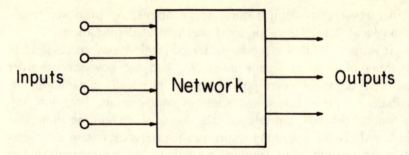

FIGURE 3.11. *Likely organization of neural network.*

box receiving several signals and emitting *one* signal. If an actual neural network emits multiple output signals as in figure 3.11, we will simply consider it to be a collection of functions, one for each output signal, as in figure 3.12.

Karl Pribram has recently suggested the possibility that the brain is like a hologram which is a light-interference pattern on film from *any part* of which can be reconstructed the image recorded on the film. A functional block diagram of the brain's organization, however, can remain valid even if it were later to be discovered that each function is a distributed property of the brain and each perception is a pattern of neural currents pervading the brain. Some features of the brain suggest separation of function and localization of perceptions; that is, if the brain is like

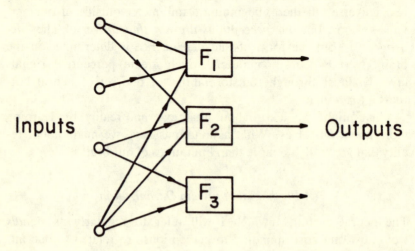

FIGURE 3.12. *Functional representation of neural network (one function per output).*

a hologram, perhaps it is more like a collection of localized holograms. Perhaps, also, the brain is *not* like a hologram.

In the model described here, which is the brain model that is part of the theory to be developed in this book, the basic elements of organization are *neural signals* and *neural functions,* where *functions* is to be taken in the sense of the form of a many-to-one relationship between signals.

Summary

In the remainder of this book we will adhere to the basic premises given in this chapter, even though no formal use may be made of some of them. We will assume that neither single neurones nor single impulses are significant elements of behavior, taking instead computing functions (neural networks) as the least element of organization, and continuously variable neural currents (in units of impulses per second) as the carriers of information to and from computing functions. The principal purpose of laying out these premises in some detail, even more detail than is really essential, has been to show that there *is* a defensible alternative to the strict digital-computer model of the brain that has been so popular for several decades.

The analogue or continuous variable model provides a way to describe perceptions as the outcome of a process whereby an external state of affairs is continually represented inside the brain as one or more continuous neural signals. These signals—perceptual signals—*are* reality as far as the brain experiences reality, yet are functionally dependent on something else, a supposed external reality, which is not the same thing as experienced reality.

It is convenient to think of the brain as a collection of localized functions, and of neural signals as occurring in definite pathways linking functions together. The model, however, will not be invalidated if these elements prove some day to be distributed over large volumes of the brain. The organizational properties of this model do not depend on its geometrical properties.

References

Arbib, M. *Brains, Machines, and Mathematics.* New York: McGraw-Hill, 1964.

Konorski, J. *Integrative Activity of the Brain.* Chicago: Univ. of Chicago Press, 1967.

McCulloch, W. & Pitts, W. "A Logical Calculus of the Ideas Immanent in Nervous Activity." In *Modern Systems Research for the Behavioral Scientist,* edited by Buckley, W. Chicago: Aldine, 1972.

Pribram, K. "Some Dimensions of Remembering; Steps toward a Neuropsychological Model of Memory." In *Perception and Action,* edited by K. H. Pribram. Baltimore: Penguin Books, 1969.

Richards, R. *Digital Design.* New York: Wiley-Interscience, 1971.

Weiner, N. *Cybernetics.* New York: John Wiley, 1948.

Wooldridge, D. E. *The Machinery of the Brain.* New York: McGraw-Hill, 1963.

LEADING QUESTIONS: CHAPTER 3

1. How many brief, abrupt stimuli have you experienced in the last ten minutes? Were you aware during that time of any continuous stimuli?

2. How many brief, abrupt responses have you made in the last ten minutes? Have any of your actions been smoothly varying or continuous?

3. When you steer a car around a curve, do you make a steering movement, wait to see the result, make another movement, wait to see the result, and so forth? Or does it seem that the steering motions and their results vary smoothly and continuously during the same time interval?

4. Does a continuous-variable model rule out perception of brief, abrupt events? execution of brief, abrupt responses? instantaneous responses?

Feedback and Behavior

Now that the general outline has been established for the brain model that is part of this theory, two last steps remain to be taken before the model itself can be developed: (1) an analysis of the role of feedback as objectively observable in behavior, and (2) an introduction to the internal structure and properties of negative feedback control systems; that is, the inner organization of such systems that explains the outward appearance of their interactions with their surroundings.

The Fact of Feedback

What an organism senses affects what it does, *and what it does affects what it senses*. Only the first half of that commonplace observation has been incorporated into most psychological concepts of nervous system organization. The effects of behavior in altering subsequent stimuli, and even in directly causing stimulation, have certainly been noticed, but there has as yet been no *correct* analysis of this in any fully developed psychological theory.

The most common treatment of the effects of an organism's actions on the stimuli affecting it is to carry out the analysis stepwise: First, a stimulus causes a response via the organism, then the response causes a *new* stimulus or modifies the next stimulus, and the cycle begins again. As Hebb (1964) puts it, "Any behavioral response to a single stimulation thus produces a sensory feedback which can act as the initiator of a second response, whose feedback initiates a third response, and so on." (p. 58)

This type of analysis is a natural first approximation to describing a closed loop of causes and effects, but it is incorrect. If one tried to match this description to any one variable in a closed loop—either a particular stimulus or a particular response—he would see that the model does not behave like the real organism. The model behaves in a series of discrete, well-separated responses alternating with discrete stimuli. The real organism behaves in a smoothly continuous manner, with both responses and stimuli continually changing and continually interacting. The model can never stop once the cycle is started. The real behavior goes swiftly to an end condition and ceases.

A step toward a better model can be seen in John Annett's analysis of feedback in human behavior (1969). Here he notes R. B. Miller's distinction between *action* feedback (which occurs during a response) and *learning* feedback (which occurs later). Action feedback occurs as soon as a response begins and can affect the response while it is happening. Learning feedback, which Annett prefers to call by an older terminology, *knowledge of results* (KR), is generally delayed enough to prevent the response from being directly affected by it. Annett correctly recognizes behavior with action feedback as an example of *servomechanism* behavior and illustrates this type of device with a diagram essentially like the one Norbert Wiener used in 1948 as a model for a *kinesthetic feedback control system*. Wiener's diagram was essentially figure 4.1 (one of several similar diagrams).

Kinesthetic feedback is accomplished entirely within the behaving organism. The "feedback takeoff" consists of nerve endings excited directly by muscle contractions or their immediate effects on tissues and tendons. The "subtractor" is in the spinal cord. The "compensator-effector" role is played by the muscle. The effect of an arrangement such as that in figure 4.1, as Wiener himself put it (1948), is to make "the performance relatively independent of the characteristic and changes of characteristic of the effector used."

We will look into such special properties of feedback control systems in the next chapter. For now, the relevant aspect of Wiener's diagram is the fact that it is drawn so that one may consider the *whole* unit in terms of stimulus and response, just as behaviorists have always done. Whether Wiener intended this or not, his illustration of feedback has led many psychologists to overlook a much wider application of this diagram—indeed, a crucial one as we will soon see. As long as this type of immediate and continuous feedback is assumed to be restricted to systems inside the organism, externally observable behavior can continue to be conceived of in stimulus-response terms.

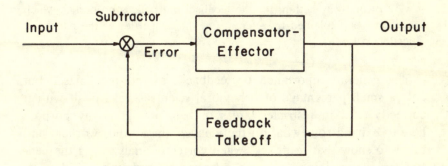

FIGURE 4.1.   *Wiener's feedback model of neuromuscular control system.*

Annett's study of feedback in human behavior is concentrated on external, delayed feedback, or knowledge of results. In a thorough fashion he deals with most major areas of behavior: motor tasks, perceptual properties, judgments, and learning. In every area, feedback is found to be essential in one way or another to successful performance. Knowledge of results at some level is required to enable the subject to carry out a given behavior at all— much less, well. The childhood game of "hot and cold" is a direct example of what Annett means by "KR." Without someone telling "it" whether he is getting closer to or farther from the hidden object, finding the object would be impossible save by chance. In this game, feedback is complex: "Its" spatial relationship to the hidden object causes the other players to say "hot" or "cold," and "its" perception of those words is the basis for his actions that change his relationship to the object. The circle of cause and effect is closed—thus there *is* feedback, by definition.

William Ashby (1952) long ago tried to make clear the reason for which feedback of *any* kind—but especially external—must be taken into account to arrive at a correct picture of behavioral organization:

> It is necessary to point to this existence of feedback in the relation between the free-living organism and its environment because most physiological experiments are deliberately arranged to avoid feedback . . . The importance of feedback lies in the fact that systems which possess it have certain properties . . . which cannot be shown by systems lacking it. Systems with feedback cannot adequately be treated as if they were of one-way action, for the feedback introduces properties which can only be explained by reference to the properties of the particular feedback used.

The general importance of feedback is well recognized, but only a small percentage of behavioral scientists have dealt with it correctly even in restricted areas of behavior. It is my purpose here to expand somewhat on the ideas of these other workers and to try to show that feedback, when correctly analyzed, is the central and determining factor in *all* observed behavior. If that effort succeeds, perhaps feedback will finally take its proper place in psychology. Wiener discovered not just an interesting detail of muscular coordination, but a fundamental principle that will totally change our concept of human and even animal nature.

Feedback as Control

A classical example of a behavioral feedback situation (if anything only twenty-five years old can be called "classical") is the *tracking experiment* in which a subject manipulates a control lever to cause a cursor—say, a moving spot of light—to track a moving target (Taylor and Birmingham 1948). Since the purpose of much of this kind of research concerns the tools of war, the main point of interest is how well the subject tracks the target, and not particularly how the situation looks to the subject.

From the subject's point of view, however, this is clearly a *control* task: He is trying to keep the spot and the moving target in a particular relationship, namely, spot on target. If there is feedback, it involves the position of the spot relative to the target and not in an absolute coordinate system.

That there is feedback is easy to verify. If the spot drifts to the right of the target, the subject moves the control stick to the left and corrects the error; if the spot drifts left, the subject responds to the right. The response to an error is always such as to *reduce* the error. An error affects the subject's control-stick movements and the control-stick movements affect the error—that is the closed cause-effect loop that defines feedback. The fact that any error results in a *reduction* of error means that the feedback is *negative*. If the feedback were positive, any small drift of the spot to either side would cause the subject to move the stick so as to make the spot move *further* in the same direction—clearly, that would hardly result in tracking! Positive feedback plays no significant part in normal behavior.

As this experiment stands, an important fact is still invisible. To make it visible, I shall whisper in the subject's ear, after which we observe that now the spot is *off* the target. In fact, it still moves with the target, but now remains always a few inches to the right. Another whisper, and it stays a few inches to the left. Another—a foot to the left.

I have been telling the subject, of course, to do exactly what was observed. How verbal instructions do this is beside the point here. What is important is that the subject is not simply responding to "error" as we naively saw the situation at first. He is responding to an error, but the error is of a totally different kind. It is the difference between some condition of the situation as the subject sees it, and what we might call a *reference condition,* as he understands it. The initial reference condition was spot on target. After the verbal instructions, the reference condition became successively spot a few inches right of target, a few inches left, and a foot left. A relationship which a moment before constituted an error became the no-error condition, and vice versa.

The reference condition is not directly observable—in fact it is extremely easy to take for granted, and only demands attention when, as in the imaginary example, it suddenly changes to a new state. Once noticed, it is easy to define. It is that state of the environment being observed by the subject that calls for *no response*. At first, there would have been no movements of the control stick if the spot had stayed on the target by itself. Later, there would

have been no movements of the control stick if the spot had spontaneously stayed a distance to the right of the target which the
subject would accept as "a few inches."

One can be forgiven for failing to notice a crucial variable in an
experiment if he has accidentally arranged matters so that the variable never varies during the experiment. Saying, "Make the spot
track the target," fixes the reference condition and renders its existence unnoticeable. Attention is drawn to the errors, for the experimenter has the same reference condition in mind. He does not
find anything remarkable in the fact that *errors are always corrected with respect to a reference condition*. Instead, he is interested in the details of the situation—speed and accuracy of tracking.
The tracking itself as evidence of the subject's internal organization
goes almost unnoticed.

The reference condition determines where the spot of light will
be; the target does *not*. The motions of the target simply tend to
cause a disturbance of the actual state of affairs away from the
reference condition, and the subject moves the stick in any way
that is required to cancel the effects of those disturbances before
any large errors result. The lack of "control" on the part of the
target can be made plain with another whisper: "Hold the spot on
the left margin of the screen." The target moves on, alone.

The reference condition is understood, translated into specifics,
and maintained inside the subject. Whether or not this is done in
response to some other event—a whisper—is irrelevant to the actions which take place relative to that reference condition. The
reference condition is a *perceptual* condition—the perceived state
of affairs, naturally from the subject's point of view and not the
experimenter's, that calls for no effort.

If the present-time state of affairs leads to perception of the *actual* condition of some variable, then operationally the reference
condition is like a perception of the *goal* condition of that variable.
The subject behaves exactly as if he is comparing the perceived
state of affairs with a reference perception of how that perception "should" look. In effect, there are two perceptions (perceptual signals) in the subject's brain, but only one of them corresponds to the present-time environment. The other is fixed, and is
not affected by the movements of the control stick.

If we build no model of the subject's brain, we can only speak
of the reference perception in as-if terms: The reference perception is a hypothetical construct. As observers we see only the spot

and the target, and if we look closely we may find that the reference condition seldom actually occurs except in passing. It can be determined only as the center about which the actual relationship wanders slightly, as if at random.

Nevertheless, that *is* an objective way of defining the reference condition, and a clear definition of the term *control* can be given wholly in such objective terms. The subject can be said to control a variable with respect to a reference condition if every disturbance tending to cause a deviation from the reference condition calls forth a behavior which results in opposition to the disturbance. If very small deviations call forth the maximum possible corrective effort, then control would be called "tight," for no disturbance within the subject's capacity to resist could then cause any large deviation. (Any feedback control system can be overwhelmed by large disturbances, but then it is not operating normally.)

When feedback is found in the relationship between an organism and its environment, it will either be so weak that it can be ignored, or be negative—it will never be strong and positive. (Remember the comment about positive feedback in the tracking situation.) Since behavioral feedback of any significance is always negative, it follows that there will always be a tendency to move toward a zero-error condition calling for no effort, and thus one will always be able to discover the reference condition (if he is clever enough). By the same token, one will always be able to discover what the subject is controlling, for if disturbances are applied which do not in fact disturb the controlled aspect of the environment, the subject's behavior will not oppose the disturbance. Only when one has found the correct definition will the proposed controlled quantity be protected against disturbance by the subject's actions.

The foregoing analysis is probably acceptable as useful in those situations where feedback is clearly present to a significant degree. The question remains as to its generality—how much of the time is this sort of analysis applicable? The answer I propose is— *all of the time*. The main proposition in this book is that all behavior is oriented all of the time around the control of certain quantities with respect to specific reference conditions. The only reason for which any higher organism acts is to counteract the effects of disturbances (constant or varying) on controlled quantities it senses. When the nature of these controlled quantities is known together with the corresponding reference conditions, variability all but disappears from behavior.

Provided that this somewhat sweeping assertion is accepted, we can see immediately why the stimulus-response concept of behaviorism has *had* to fail, and we can also see that the apparent randomness of the connections from specific stimuli to specific responses (chap. 1) is no more than an unfortunate illusion.

The controlled quantity does not directly cause behavior: Only the *difference* (if any) between that quantity and its reference condition calls for a "response." Furthermore, it is not the actual environmental situation that leads to responses, but that situation as perceived by the organism.

Keeping these facts in mind, we may ask, "What is the relationship between the organism's actions and the perceived situation?" The answer is: *That depends on what disturbances are acting.* If there are no effects in the environment tending to drive the controlled quantity away from its reference condition, there will be no change in the organism's pattern of behavior. *Any* disturbance, however, will call for an action which opposes the effects of the disturbance on the controlled quantity. (Note that the action by no means has to interfere with the *cause* of the disturbance.) All that is required is for the action to have effects on the controlled quantity equal and opposite to the effects of the disturbing event. In short, what I have been calling disturbances must really be thought of as potential disturbances—events or forces that would disturb the controlled quantity if the organism did nothing.

For the organism to have control over any sensed condition of the environment, all that is necessary is for it to possess the means to cause that condition as perceived to vary in each of the possible ways it can vary. Given only that, a negative feedback control system can be set up by suitable connections inside the organism. There is no need to sense the causes of any disturbance, because all that disturbance can do is tend to make the controlled condition change in one or more of the possible ways it can change— and the mature organism is already set up to exert forces that can prevent those changes. Sensing the cause of a disturbance and anticipating its effects can sometimes improve control ("feed-forward") but is by no means necessary, and usually is not even possible.

This means that when an event occurs that tends to disturb a controlled quantity, the organism will respond. The response, however, will be related to the cause of the disturbance only indirectly, through a commonly affected quantity—the one under control by the organism. (You will notice I use several terms interchangeably—*quantity, condition, variable,* and so on. No one term is sufficiently general, so by refusing to choose I am hoping to convey generality.)

I would not be surprised if some readers have up to here been translating "controlled quantity" as *stimulus.* We can now see that the stimulus is not, except by chance, the same thing that the organism is controlling. Far more likely to be identified as the stimulus is the event tending to disturb the controlled quantity, which I somewhat inaccurately call "the disturbance." The disturbance *always* calls for a response, even though as the organism moves about and as the environment changes, greatly different responses may occur as the effects of a given disturbance on the controlled quantity change. In fact, the most obvious cause-effect relationship is between disturbance and action. The controlled quantity, if the organism is well-organized for control, does not change appreciably, and that fact renders it somewhat hard to notice. Why should one look for something that does not change when the stimulus is applied, while something else—the organism's actions—shows such a prompt and attention-getting reaction?

The existence of a controlled aspect of the environment provides an explanation for why a given action follows from a given disturbance. It also explains why different disturbances may be followed by the same action and why repetition of the same disturbance may result in different actions. There is no mysterious "focusing" of remote stimuli on remote consequences of responses. Once one has identified what the organism is controlling and the reference condition, the relationship of a whole family of seemingly unrelated responses to a whole family of seemingly unrelated stimuli becomes completely predictable. By the same token there is no longer any reason to investigate such stimulus-response relationships after they have revealed what is controlled.

Purposive Behavior

This interpretation resolves another difficulty in traditional psychology—that of justifying any particular way of defining "the response." In the final analysis the nervous system can *only* cause muscles to tense. The consequences of those tensions are determined not by the nervous system but by physical laws that have nothing to do with the nervous system. By the time the consequences of muscle tension have produced the complex results we see as "actions," there is no longer any regular dependence of results on specific muscle tensions—and a whole array of side effects has been produced, any one of which is to some degree a consequence of muscle tension and thus potentially a response.

When any concept of purpose is disallowed, there is no way of choosing objectively* one consequence of muscle tensions to call the response over another; *all* consequences are equally valid "response measures." If every time you make a threatening move I duck and my hat falls off, the position of my hat is just as good a measure of my response as any other. Then, of course, if my hat falls off for some other reason, it may be concluded that I have responded to a threat, just as one will conclude from the record that a rat has responded in his operant-conditioning cage if there is a momentary short circuit in the apparatus.

The concept of feedback control permits us to state which consequences of muscle tensions are relevant and which are mere side effects of no importance. The *only* relevant effects are those which can cause the controlled quantity to vary.

In a similar way the feedback analysis allows us to say which aspects of a stimulus object or event are relevant to behavior, and which are not. Only those aspects are relevant that are disturbances with respect to a controlled quantity or condition or variable or situation. All other aspects, however striking, are important only to the experimenter.

In this context we can speak of *purpose* freely. *The purpose of any given behavior is to prevent controlled perceptions from changing away from the reference condition.* Purpose implies goal: *The goal of any behavior is defined as the reference condition of the controlled perception.* Both purpose and goal, therefore, can be objectively determined for any behavioral situation in terms of the objective situation corresponding to the hypothetical perceptions. Of course the perceptions are not really "hypothetical," that is, the subject does not think of his perception of the situation that way, nor does the experimenter.

---

*That is, according to clearly stated rules applicable by anyone who understands them.

A Hierarchy of Purposes

Saying that an organism does not control its actions but only its perceptions leads to contradictions as soon as more than one behavior is investigated. The man in the tracking situation cannot choose any hand position he likes because he is trying to keep the spot on the target, and the target position determines what hand position is required to accomplish that purpose. If we were to ask the man to stop tracking, however, and hold the control stick steady against force disturbances, it would become clear immediately that he *can* control his hand position—since he is doing so, relative to this new reference position.

In that case, by the same logic, we could point to the muscle tensions in the man's arm as being the means of control and show that force disturbances control those muscle tensions; that is, the man cannot arbitrarily choose the muscle tensions if he is to control his hand position.

One more step takes us to the end of this road. If the man decides (or agrees) to tense his biceps muscle, he will do so to the exact degree he chooses, and now there is no way to materially disturb the controlled variable without surgical, chemical, or electrical intervention, all of which violate the conditions of normal behavior.

Control of the spot-target relationship, control of hand position, and control of muscle tensions are not simply three different control actions within the man's repertoire. These control actions are hierarchically related, with control of muscle tensions being at the bottom of the hierarchy.

For each task it would be possible to define a reference condition in terms of objective measurements, although some electronic tricks are needed to investigate muscle-tension control in the intact organism. If we assume that the control-system organization remains the same from task to task—that is, that both muscle tension and hand position remain under control in the tracking task—there is only one way to avoid building in conflict among these systems. In order for the man to maintain the reference condition spot on target with the target moving, the reference condition for hand position must change. In order for the hand to be kept in any one position against mechanical disturbances, the reference condition for muscle tension must change. Each level of organization but the lowest corrects its own errors by altering the definition of the reference condition for the level below.

This hierarchy can be extended no further downward, but it can be extended upward without difficulty. We could, for example, ask the subject to make the spot oscillate back and forth from one side of the moving target to the other. Now the reference condition for spot position is varying in order to keep a repetitive change going. Then we could ask that the speed of this oscillation alternate between slow and fast—a few slow cycles, then a few fast cycles, and so on. Now the reference for speed of oscillation is being adjusted back and forth in a simple repetitive sequence—fast, slow, fast, slow. We could then provide a signal light, and ask that this sequence be halted (at slow or fast) while the light is on. That would require altering the reference condition for the sequence in relationship to the light. The highest-level reference condition is now a logical relationship: [(A and B) or (not-A and not-B)] is *true*.

During all of this, the target can continue to move (slowly) back and forth at random. The control stick can be mechanically disturbed, too, without preventing the higher-level purposes from being carried out. Each level of control organization continues to resist disturbances of the variable associated with it, even though the reference condition that defines what constitutes a disturbance may change. There is a hierarchy of control, a hierarchy of controlled perceptions, and a hierarchy of *adjustable* goal-perceptions-purposes. There is, in short, a hierarchy of negative feedback control organizations visible in the subject's behavior.

Time Scales

Every control action, however small the disturbance, is limited in speed of error correction. An absolute limit is set by transmission lags inside and outside the controlling system, and all real control systems are further slowed by the fact that all changes require time. A control system that is too rapid in its response to disturbance will be *unstable*. It will sense its own actions as disturbances and try to correct for them, thus driving itself into spontaneous and usually violent oscillation and thereby ceasing to act as a control system. Efficient control systems must be so designed that they ignore disturbances that come and go too rapidly. In effect, the control system must contain a filter that averages the controlled perception over a time just long enough to permit stable overall control.

This necessary limitation on control speed means that for every control system there will be some speed of variation of disturbances above which the disturbances cannot be counteracted. That is not to say that the system tries and fails to counteract fast disturbances: *It does not even try*. If it were designed to react too fast, it would have to be unstable and would be unable to control anything. The result is that fast enough disturbances cease to be perceived, as the flickering of a movie fades and disappears when the projector is brought up to the proper speed. The objective flicker is still there as large as ever, as a photoelectric cell could prove, but it no longer exists for the human observer, whose retina simply averages out the rapid changes in light intensity.

In a hierarchy of control organizations, the lowest-level systems have the fastest response, but their speed is nevertheless limited. An organization which adjusts the reference condition for the lower system as its means of correcting its own errors, therefore, is subject not only to its own characteristic speed limitations but those of the lower system as well. The result is that the higher in the hierarchy one looks at behavior, the longer becomes the averaging time and the longer a disturbance may act without being corrected.

In effect, fast enough variations in the controlled quantity are nothing but noise with respect to behavior. The subject averages them out and so must the observer if he is to get a true concept of behavioral organization. Failure to realize this will mislead the observer into trying to make sense of noise, an amusing pastime in Las Vegas perhaps, but a waste of laboratory time.

The observer who is not called on to make corrections but only to watch, especially if he observes with automatic instruments or just by watching for key events, can often see disturbances that the subject fails to correct. His attention can fasten on events which he knows to constitute disturbances, but which in fact do not exist for the subject because they come and go too fast.

One basic way of investigating control organizations is to apply moderate disturbances and look for the countering behavior. In the light of speed considerations, it is now obvious that these disturbances must be applied and the results evaluated on the proper

time scale. If the experimenter postulates that a subject is controlling his self-respect, then he may find that the subject will ignore
a downgrading word, a derogatory sentence, or even a discourag-
ing conversation. It may take several interviews before the subject
begins to alter his general interaction with the experimenter in an
attempt to correct this high-level error. The same slowness to respond will be seen when the experimenter decides that he has detected a corrective reaction and stops being nasty. The subject can
no more correct for a sudden disappearance than a sudden onset
of a high-level type of disturbance. An equal number of positive
words, complimentary sentences, and encouraging conversations
will have to occur before the subject ceases his corrective efforts.
Psychologists who believe that intermittent reinforcement is more
effective than continuous reinforcement should give this whole
speed-of-reaction problem serious thought—for a long enough
time.

Summary

This chapter has presented a rather dense array of concepts. Let
us finish by going over the key points.

The fact of feedback is established simply by noting that sensory inputs *affect and are affected by* behavior. This circle of cause
and effect cannot be correctly analyzed as an alternating sequence. Visible behavior does not have that form. Rather, the type
of analysis used in servomechanism theory must be used.

All behavioral feedback is *negative* feedback. Positive feedback
models do not behave properly. Negative feedback can be seen as
feedback *control* when the existence of the *reference condition* is
recognized, for behavior always tends to resist disturbances of the
controlled quantity away from that condition. The reference condition and the controlled quantity can be objectively defined in
terms of reaction to disturbances.

Behavior can be seen as purposive or goal-directed if it is recognized that the purpose of any act is to resist disturbances and
that the reference condition describes the goal of behavior.

There is a hierarchy of feedback control: Higher-level organizations counter disturbances by changing the reference condition for
a lower-level organization. All levels of organization are in action

at once, each controlling one kind of quantity and capable of counteracting corresponding classes of disturbance.

All of these concepts apply to an objective analysis of behavior, and require no model of the behaving system itself. Therefore, it is not necessary to talk of perceptions, however convenient.

REFERENCES

Annett, J. *Feedback and Human Behavior*. Baltimore: Penguin Books, 1969.

Ashby, W. R. *Design for a Brain*. New York: John Wiley, 1952.

Hebb, D. D. *A Textbook of Psychology*. Philadelphia: Saunders, 1964.

Taylor, F. & Birmingham, H. "Studies of Tracking Behavior," *Journal of Experimental Psychology* 38 (1948): 783–95.

LEADING QUESTIONS: CHAPTER 4

1. Without looking at it, clench your right hand into a fist. How do you tell it *is* clenched? How do you detect the fact that your own muscles are acting? Would you class these impressions as perceptions?

2. Is there anything other than a perception that enables you to know that you are clenching your fist? that you are making a muscular effort?

3. Now use that hand to pick up something—this book, for example. Can you still perceive the efforts and other impressions that signify efforts? Does it now seem that they are outputs, the actions that bring about "picking up"? Are you not still aware of them as perceptions?

4. Is there any act you can execute that is not known to you in the form of a perception? Do you know of any act of yours in any other way? Do you know of anything, inside you or outside you, in any other way?

5. Can you think of anything you do that you experience as something other than sensory feedback effects of your outputs?

6. Using the smallest effort you can find, can you make the visual image of these words disappear entirely?

7. Can you shift the visual image of this page so that it occupies the left side of your field of vision?

8. Can you replace the visual image of this page with a visual image of the ceiling?

9. Hold one hand out, palm up and elbow bent, at waist level as if ready to receive something. With the other hand place this book on that hand. How does the arm respond to the disturbance due to the book's weight? Hint: Watch the tendon in the crook of the elbow.

10. What is the purpose of the steering movements you make while driving a car?

11. A man swats at a mosquito and hits himself in the face. Is hitting himself in the face part of his behavior?

12. You close your hand for the purpose of grasping a raw egg. Do you control the amount of sensed pressure you exert on the egg?

13. To what goal might the action of grasping an egg contribute?

14. How many hierarchically ordered purposes can you think of, starting with grasping an egg? Each purpose should in turn become the necessary means for accomplishing a higher-level purpose.

5

The Control-system Unit
of Organization

The concepts of the previous chapter constitute a conceptual model of behavior, similar in form and nature (although not in content) to many other psychological models. In this chapter a model of the behaving system will be developed in order to account for these objectively observable phenomena.

System models are common in engineering but not in behavioral or social science. Outside of engineering the term *system* often appears to mean a network of disembodied relationships that link behaving entities together, whereas an engineer would probably translate the term to mean a diagram of the insides of a behaving entity. The difference is somewhat subtle, so before going on to develop the control-system model, let us first examine a diagram of the conceptual model we have just been through, the model describing the tracking situation (see fig. 5.1).

The first fact to notice is that *the organism does not appear in this diagram*. Every box in figure 5.1 represents something that can be objectively determined by normal scientific procedures. The "muscle-tensions" box would be displayed as a feedback system if we allowed neurological data into the picture, but that would inevitably lead us deep inside the organism where this diagram no longer applies.

There are, without the muscle-tensions system explicit, two feedback loops visible. Between the dashed lines is part of the stick-control loop. At the top is part of the spot-target relationship con-

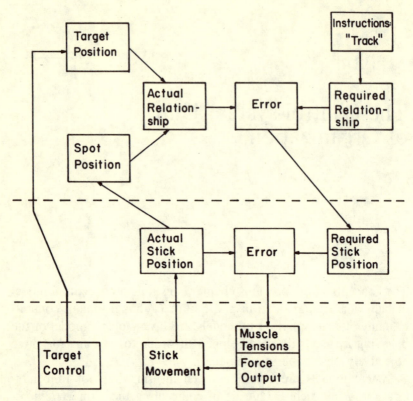

FIGURE 5.1. *A two-level model of feedback relationships in a tracking experiment.*

trol loop. At the bottom is the physical cause-effect chain that closes both loops.

The higher loop is seen most easily by lumping the lower parts of the diagram, below the upper dashed line, together. An error in spot-target relationship (whatever the reference condition) affects the lower systems in such a way as to cause the spot to move. The spot moves, of course, in the direction which reduces the error. Motions of the target cause error. The resulting spot motions prevent the error from becoming large (if the target does not move too fast).

The lower system, for a stationary target, will operate with respect to a fixed reference stick position. Disturbing forces that tend to move the stick result in an error in stick position, and that error causes changes in muscle forces which oppose the disturbing force and prevent the position error from becoming large.

If the effects of the disturbing force are not completely canceled by the muscle forces, the stick will move slightly and the spot will move, creating a relationship error. This will result in a slight readjustment of the reference stick position, just enough so that even *with* the incomplete cancellation of the force disturbance, the spot stays *on* the target (or "a few inches to the right" and so on).

This kind of model of feedback relationships can be used to analyze very complex behaviors with normal scientific procedures, especially if one remembers to use the time scale on which transient errors are averaged out (as appropriate for each level). Many more levels can be added, and many separate control loops may exist at a given level.

The behaving organism appears in figure 5.1 only as a muscle tension. Nevertheless, this diagram would be meaningless without a behaving organism behind it, nor could it exist until a behaving organism put it on paper. The diagram is crammed with unspoken assumptions, subjective phenomena objectivized, and imaginary concepts which might have no physical significance. The fact that such a diagram could serve as the basis for a scientific study of behavior tells far more about behavioral science than about behavior.

The Role of the Brain

A brain is required in order to perceive a relationship—either a self-evident relationship out there in the real environment, or a hypothetical one inside an organism. The only way in which an actual spot position and a reference spot position can lead to realization that an error exists is for a brain to perceive the elements, the relationships, and the error—the subject's brain. What the experimenter perceives has no effect on the subject's muscles. If it appears that the subject's actions stabilize a particular relationship between spot and target, then the cause lies in the subject, not in the spot or in the target. The spot and the target are what they are, and they are where they are. The physical world doesn't care whether any particular arrangement constitutes an "error" or a "relationship." Only the subject and the experimenter care. The only way to account for what we see happening without overlaying the physical world with entities the physicists say do not exist is to turn our attention to the *real* cause of these events, the brain, and to try to guess how it does these things. By admitting subjective phenomena into the model, we shall end by being more objective, that is, more honest about the fact that we know only appearances.

A brain model must contain elements that correspond to every box and every arrow in figure 5.1 except the boxes stacked on the left, which represent the physical-world part of behavior (and the associated connecting arrows which stand for physical laws). Thus, in the brain model we do not speak of the "actual" target-spot relationship, but of a perceptual signal which has that meaning and which is derived from visual sensations by computing processes in the nervous system. The "reference relationship" does not hang in conceptual limbo. It corresponds to a real neural signal which functions as a reference because of its position in the brain and as a relationship because of what it stands for. The "error" does not exist simply because the perceptual signal is different from the reference signal (the perceptual signal is different from *many* other signals). It appears as the result of a neural computing process, as a specific neural signal that results when the perceptual signal is subtracted specifically from the reference signal. We name these signals and this process in terms of physical-world counterparts in order to make the model consistent with physical models. Only in that sense can we identify the relationship signal as "standing for the actual target-spot relationship." To the brain, that signal *is* that relationship which exists nowhere else and in no other form. "Relationship" (of this specific kind) is *how that neural signal is apprehended when one is conscious of it.* What that conscious perception corresponds to in the physical world is a question that can only be answered in terms of the proper brain model.

Let us proceed, then, to develop the approach that will lead to a model of the brain's part in the feedback control process that can be observed in objective terms. This model building is an iterative process; that is, the farther we carry it, the less we will have reason to believe that those "objective" observations ever were objective, and the more we will see the need to extend and improve the model.

The Control-system Unit of Organization

For any given feedback control behavior, a block diagram of the behaving system and its environment can be drawn as in figure 5.2. The controlled quantity which we observe objectively is in the box labeled "remote physical phenomena." These phenomenon are af-

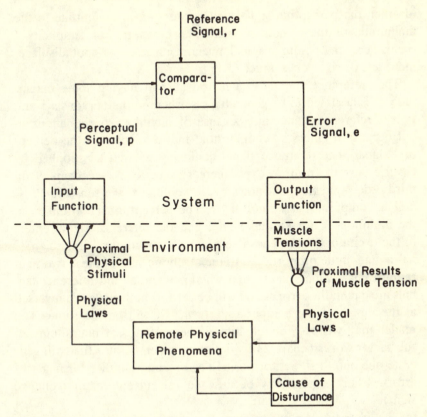

FIGURE 5.2. *General model of a feedback control system and its local environment.*

fected in two ways: as a result of the immediate (proximal) results of muscle tensions, and by other events not directly controlled (if at all) by the nervous system: the "cause of disturbance." The remote physical phenomena in turn affect the minute detailed physical variables ("proximal physical stimuli") which can cause the sensory endings of the nervous system to generate neural currents. In the environment, therefore, we have the entities of physics and the laws relating them.

The neural currents resulting from physical stimulation of nerve endings enter an "input function." This is a neural computing device which generates a neural current—the "perceptual signal"—that varies as a function of sensory-ending stimulations. If this input function has the form of the inverse of the function relating a one-dimensional remote physical phenomenon to the proximal stimuli, then the perceptual signal will correspond in magnitude to the magnitude of the remote physical phenomenon. For simplicity I speak here of one-dimensional phenomena such as spot displacement left or right of a target.

The "reference signal" is a neural current having some magnitude. It is assumed to be generated elsewhere in the nervous system. It is a reference signal not because of anything special about it, but because it enters a "comparator" that also receives the perceptual signal. The reference signal could just as well be supplied by electric current from an experimenter's electrode (see chap. 9 on third-order systems—but not now, it wouldn't make sense yet).

The comparator is a *subtractor*. The perceptual signal enters in the inhibitory sense (minus sign), and the reference signal enters in the excitatory sense (positive sign). The resulting "error signal" has a magnitude proportional to the algebraic sum of these two neural currents—which means that when perceptual and reference signals are equal, the error signal will be zero. If both signs are reversed at the inputs of the comparator, the result will be the same. The reader may wish to remind himself here of how a neural-current subtractor works (chap. 2) by designing a comparator that will generate one output signal for positive errors, and another for negative errors. (This is necessary because neural currents cannot change sign.)

The error signal now enters an "output function," which converts a given magnitude and sign of error into increases and decreases of muscle tensions. The output function need not be complex. The effect of a given neural current on a given muscle can only be to increase or decrease the muscle tension. The effect of a given muscle tension on the one-dimensional remote physical phenomenon can only be to increase or decrease its magnitude, and therefore (through the proximal stimuli and the input function) to increase or decrease the magnitude of the perceptual signal. Thus for each muscle, a proper initial choice of inhibition or excitation will result in a lessening of the error signal (increasing the perceptual signal if it is less than the reference signal, and the opposite). As long as the environment retains the same properties, feedback will remain negative and control will be seen.

The effectiveness of this control system depends on its *sensitivity*. In the present context, that term does not refer to the system's ability to detect inputs near the lower threshold of intensity, but rather to the *loop gain,* another concept entirely. The loop gain can be measured directly only by breaking the feedback loop—for example, by cutting the physical connection from the proximal results of muscle tension to the remote physical phenomena.

With the loop thus broken, we may then substitute for the effects of muscle tension an artificial, known disturbance. A small change in the remote physical phenomena will then occur, followed by a change in proximal physical stimuli, the perceptual signal, the error signal, and finally the muscle tensions and their proximal physical effects. There the chain stops, because the loop has been intentionally broken at that point.

We now compare the magnitude of the artificial, known disturbance that began the chain with the resulting proximal muscle effects that normally would act where we applied the disturbance. The ratio of natural to artificial effects is the loop gain, which we symbolize by A. In the tracking experiment, A could be measured by momentarily (and surreptitiously) disconnecting the link that gives handle position control over spot position, and manually disturbing the link to create a small known deviation of the spot. The subject, trying to correct the error, would move the handle (the "proximal muscle effects") by some amount, probably large. The ratio of handle movement (at the place where we disconnected the link) to artificial link movement would be A, the loop gain or system sensitivity.

The system sensitivity determines how effective any disturbance will be in actually causing a change in the controlled quantity. The amount of effect the disturbance would have if the control system did not resist is reduced by a factor of $\frac{1}{1+A}$, so that if A, the system sensitivity, were only 10 (very low for most behavioral control systems), the effects of the disturbance would be only $\frac{1}{11}$ of the unresisted effect. (See Appendix for details.)

By similar calculations it can be shown that with no disturbance acting, the perceptual signal will have a magnitude of $\frac{A}{1+A}$ times the magnitude of the reference signal; that is, with a system sensitivity of 10, the magnitude of the perceptual signal is $\frac{10}{11}$ of the reference signal. In terms of behavioral observations, the controlled quantity will have a magnitude that is $^{10}\!/_{11}$ of the reference magnitude (determined by applying disturbances). When disturbances are applied, all of their effects on the input of the behavioral system, including effects on the perceptual signal, are reduced to about one-A^{th} of the magnitude of what the result would be if no resistance occurred.

A large increase in system sensitivity does not imply "more response to stimuli"—it implies tighter control. The higher the system sensitivity, the more closely will the perceptual signal track the reference signal, and the less effect disturbances will have; in other words, the more exactly will the system's muscle forces cancel the effects of disturbances on the controlled quantity and the perceptual signal. For a system with a sensitivity of 10, a disturbance of 10 pounds will call forth a countereffort of 9.1 pounds. If A is 100, the countering effort will be 9.9 pounds; if A is 10,000, the effort will be 9.999 pounds. Increased sensitivity means not *more* response but *more precise* response. By the same reasoning, the actual behavior of the system is nearly independent of system sensitivity as long as sensitivity is greater than 5 or 10.

A useful way to think of system sensitivity is as *sensitivity to error*. Error must be considered not in absolute terms but as a fraction of the total range of magnitude of the perceptual signal (or of the objective controlled quantity), for that places error in proper relationship to the system's normal range of operation. Sensitivity to error can then be expressed in terms of the maximum fractional error that is required to produce the maximum possible resistance to disturbance. The maximum resistance is determined either by the strength of the muscles involved or by limits in the effects a muscle can have in the environment to counteract a disturbance. The logical way to measure these output effects is in terms of effects on the controlled quantity.

When sensitivity to error is known, one can see immediately how good a control system exists. If a 1 percent error can produce 100 pounds of corrective force, which we will here stipulate as the most force the system can generate, then two facts are known: First, the system can operate properly only if disturbances are equivalent to less than 100 pounds of force; and second, in this range the difference between actual and reference perceptions will be less than or equal to 1 percent of the largest perceptual signal (or in objective terms, the observed error will be less than 1 percent of the total possible range of the controlled quantity). It is assumed throughout that during any measurements, nothing varies faster than the system can react without instability.

Goal-directed Behavior

With this control-system unit of behavioral organization, we have built a model for one particular organization inside the behaving system which accounts in the simplest possible way for what is observed in one objective experiment. The most important explanatory feature is the reference signal, because that is what accounts for the *reference condition of the controlled quantity*. Without the model and its reference signal, there is no way at all to account for the reference condition. One can only observe its apparent existence.

This reference condition is exactly what is meant by a *goal,* and the fact that it is not connected to any observable physical phenomenon is what has caused behaviorists to reject the notion of goal-directed behavior. In the control-system unit of behavioral organization, we can now trace this hypothetical goal to its physical counterpart, the reference signal. Whatever the perceptual signal corresponds to in the physical world, the reference signal is equivalent to the state in which the perceptual signal will be when the external quantity is *at* the reference condition. Recall that the reference condition was empirically defined as that condition of the controlled quantity calling for *no* response. In the model we see that same condition as the condition of *zero error signal*. Since the error signal drives the system's output, zero error implies zero output effort. Thus with this model, one can accept the concept of a goal without introducing either time travel or metaphysics.

There is a difference, however, between the customary idea of a goal and the understanding that comes from the control-system model. It is customarily to think of a goal as something one sets and then slowly works toward, perhaps never coming close to achieving it. A control system *could* operate that way—the reference signal could possibly be set at a magnitude to which no available output effort could bring the perceptual signal—but in that case the control system would be operating far outside the control range, and could not perform very well, if at all. It would simply produce maximum output all of the time regardless of what the environment did, like a robot toy "walking" with its face against the wall. Goals *can* be defined as unreachable, but to do so negates all the fine organization of the brain.

Furthermore, setting goals that are unreachable can have the effect of simply turning off all efforts. One could, on a ninety-degree summer day, set the furnace thermostat to a comfortable seventy-five degrees—but the furnace cannot cool the house, so it simply remains off until the temperature, for other reasons falls below seventy-five degrees. In the same way, a person can set goals that require doing less than nothing (such as wanting not to be noticed), as a result of which his output will approach that state as closely as possible—nothing—until some event beyond his control (such as his death) achieves the goal *for* him.

In the control-system model, goal-directed behavior means behavior which maintains perceptions at the goal state all of the time. If a high-level system is operating, one must remember to allow for speed limitations. Transient errors can occur, but the process of correcting them cannot occur rapidly, so if there is any change of behavior at all (before the disturbance disappears of its own accord), that change must be slow, and the error correction must be correspondingly slow. However, from the appropriate point of view (that of the controlling system), the errors are never permitted to become large. They are "instantly" counteracted, although from an inappropriate point of view an "instant" may contain many detailed variations.

In the tracking experiment the experimenter is interested in the details of the control movements so he uses instruments that record errors on a millisecond time scale. When the target jumps suddenly from one fixed position to another, the instruments see a long succession of behaviors. The error at first jumps to a large value; then the spot accelerates toward the target, reaches a peak velocity, decelerates, and wobbles back and forth a few times until it finally comes to rest almost centered on the target.

The man doing the tracking perceives very little of that. He sees the target jump and "instantly" corrects the error, feeling proud of his reflexes. As traffic-safety educators know too well, a person is not likely to sense his own reaction lags. They are less than the minimum significant time interval for the associated control organization.

All of this leads to a conclusion about behavior. If we think of behavior, as we normally do, in terms of the perceived results of muscle forces, then every changing aspect of that behavior reflects a corresponding change in reference signals, the reference signal just slightly leading the perceptual results of action. If the reference signal stops changing, the perceived behavior freezes, right there.

Control-system Dynamics

Human control systems are adapted to a natural environment in which disturbances come and go not suddenly, but with some typical maximum rate of change. Our control systems have acquired a speed of error correction just fast enough to prevent natural disturbances from having significant effects on what we perceive and control. These special adaptations can be measured by applying disturbances that appear or disappear much more rapidly than their natural counterparts do and by using electronic instruments to record changes of output that occur too fast for the human observer to notice (because, of course, he is organized as his subject is). By such means the *transfer function* of any control organization can be measured: the differential equation which describes the detailed time course of error correction.

The transfer function of a control system may reveal that it senses not just some quantity, but also the rate of change of that quantity. The system's output may be driven not just by the magnitude of the error, but also by the rate of change of error and time integrals of the error. These added details represent the modifications which must be added to any sensitive control system in order to compensate for the destabilizing effects of intertial masses, time lags inside and outside the system, and special characteristics of the controlled quantity. Such transfer-function studies are of interest mainly as ways of understanding how the system achieves the performance it demonstrates, or for designing new control systems. They can also be misleading, for the complications they reveal can hide the main features of organization which must be the first targets of investigation.

A perceptual signal may be a complex time function of sensory events, but the central significance of that signal can be seen only when a steady-state condition has been reached—after the transient terms in the differential equations have died away or become insignificant. Since that steady state is set by the reference signal, we are also talking about the significance of the reference signal in terms of a steady-state external quantity.

In this model we limit the description of behavior to such steady-state descriptions—and that is very nearly the same thing as saying that we will choose a time scale of observation appropriate to the system under study. This does not mean that change cannot occur. It only means that we cannot deal with changes that occur too fast. That is no real limitation—neither can the system we are studying. Except in the few cases in which we already understand the main features of a control system, however, it will be a few years before the added details to be obtained from transfer-function studies can help more than they confuse understanding.

One potential confusion needs to be warded off before we leave the subject of control-system dynamics for good. There are control systems which deal explicitly with time functions—in which a steady magnitude of perceptual signal stands for a constantly changing quantity, or for the cumulative effects of a series of events: derivatives or integrals, in other words. Those time functions *are* the central significance of the perceptual signal in such cases, and the "transient terms" we are averaging out would then be derivatives of those time functions. Thus, we are not eliminating rates of change or cumulative effects as controlled quantities, but only those time-dependent changes that are part of the interior design of a particular control system.

LEADING QUESTIONS: CHAPTER 5

1. Will a control system that is 1,000 times as sensitive as another control system respond to a given disturbance 1,000 times as strongly? Assume that the less sensitive system has a loop amplification factor of 10 (see pp. 63–64).

2. The word *level* in *reference level* means amount or degree or state of some given perception. How would you describe your reference level for the distance between your eyes and this page?

3. When you unlock a door, what is the reference level for the relationship between key and keyhole? Is that relationship capable of smooth variation?

4. When you want to hear some music, is your reference level for that perception set high (violent, piercing, overwhelming perception of music) or low (barely audible perception of music) or somewhere between? Can

you think of instances of this whole range of reference levels for "hearing music" evidence by other people's behavior?

5. Can you cause tea to exceed your reference level for sweetness by adding sugar to it?

6. What is your reference level for the state of another person's attentiveness when you are talking? How do you correct errors?

7. Someone says, "You're not listening to me." If that statement is false, what error is created, and relative to what reference level of what perception? If the statement is true, what error, etc.? If you respond at all, does that not imply an error?

8. Why is a statement like "Egg production was much less in 1920 than it is today" a conversation stopper? Does it call for any response at all?

9. Does the term *error* in feedback theory imply a value judgment? What would happen if all error signals were arbitrarily and permanently set to zero in the brain?

10. Can your sense of self-esteem be a controlled quantity? What are some means for controlling it?

6

A Hierarchy of Control Systems

The control-system model in the last chapter is a unit of organization. Behavior as a whole results from the operation of many such units at once. Many control systems may act simultaneously on the same environment yet remain independent—for example, one system might control the sum of two quantities while another simultaneously and independently controls the difference between them. Even when interactions occur (the control actions of one system tending to alter the controlled quantities of other systems), those interactions may be treated as any ordinary disturbances are treated. Each system can simply adjust its own output to cancel such interactive effects. There is another mode of interaction, however, which we will now consider, a mode in which one control organization is part of a larger one and hence not at all independent of it.

Figure 6.1 is a hierarchical model of the tracking situation that has been our central example so far. Since we are now definitely inside the behaving system, the muscle-tension control system can be explicitly included, so we have a three-level model.

This complex-appearing diagram will unravel if approached systematically. Starting at the top, we accept as given a reference signal standing for the overall goal relationship of spot *on* target. The signal representing the actual relationship comes in from the left; it results from three steps of visual information processing. The resulting error signal enters the "output function," a neural computer that derives the appropriate reference signal for stick position (as

70

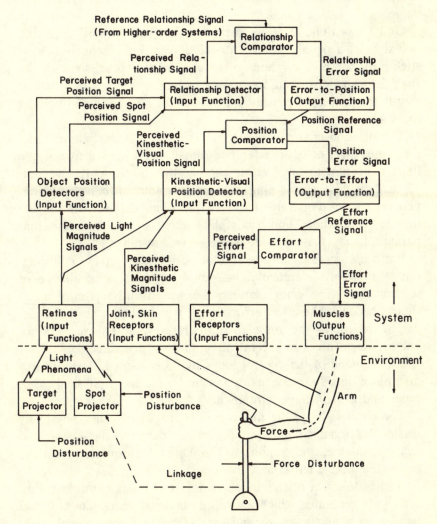

FIGURE 6.1. *A three-level control-system model of a person in the tracking situation.*

kinesthetically sensed) from the relationship error signal. For a given initial amount and direction of relationship error, the resulting position reference may be far to one side, implying a much larger change than actually required, but when the steady state is reached, the reference signal will have returned to just the right value.

Going down one level, we see a "position comparator" receiving two signals: a signal standing for the current kinesthetically-sensed stick position and the reference signal. The perceptual signal is derived by two steps of information processing, the first of which is simply the process of sensing the state of the arm and hand holding the stick.

The position error signal is converted by another "output function" into a set of effort reference signals (here shown as a single line) that enter a set of effort comparators that also receive perceptual signals representing the second state of muscle-tension. (There is one comparator for each tiny fiber that is part of "the muscle" as a whole, and a complete set of signals for each comparator. In fig. 6.1 only one example is shown.)

For each amount and direction of position error there is a magnitude of effort reference signal, implying a required degree of sensed effort. The error between the sensed and reference effort signals becomes the effort error signal, which enters the *first order output function*—the muscle. Actually, several muscles are involved, since forces in several directions are generated.

So far, none of the control loops has been closed. The closures take place outside the behaving system by means of physical properties and laws in the environment.

The shortest loop, the first-order feedback path, lies physically inside the organism; the muscle-tension detectors lie inside and near the muscle, and respond to mechanical deformations that occur as the muscle tenses and changes shape.

As a side effect of the action of this first-order control system, forces are generated which act on the bones to cause the arm and hand as a whole to move and exert forces on the control stick. Skin pressure and joint-angle detectors generate neural currents that represent these byproducts of muscle tension, and these neural signals (together with effort signals which also carry position information) enter the *next level of input function,* a neural computer which creates a signal standing for kinesthetically sensed position (or better, "state"). That closes the feedback loop for the second system.

Motions of the control stick which result as byproducts of controlling kinesthetic position are mechanically and optically linked to the tracking spot of light. Both the target and the spot are imaged onto the subject's retinas where light detectors convert local light intensities into neural currents representing light intensity. (I am ignoring some complications here.) The intensity signals reach neural computers which sort out objects, the spot and target, and the object signals are again processed by the final neural computer to yield a signal representing the distance between the objects, for that is the relationship in question. This completes the last feedback loop.

The behavior of this three-level system could be carried out by a single control system suitably designed, but we are aiming here not for a sufficient model, but a correct model—one that not only accomplishes the same result that the human being accomplishes, but does it in the same way. We cannot ignore the fact that first-order control systems do exist; the model cannot simply bypass them. We cannot ignore the obvious division of the brain into levels of different complexity; therefore we must at least try to build the model with similar levels. And most important, we cannot ignore direct experience, which tells us that we can perceive the distance between two objects only if we can perceive the objects, and we can perceive the objects only if we can distinguish different local light intensities. We must try to represent the fact that perceiving the objects depends on perceiving light intensities but not vice versa. We must try to account for the fact that kinesthetic position control is sometimes seen by itself, *not* in a tracking situation, or else we must restructure the entire model for every slightly different situation, which would be like having no model at all. The model will have levels.

A practical (that is, evolutionary) reason for levels of control can be seen by considering some different kinds of disturbances and how they are corrected by the three-level system. The system is organized to correct for the effects of disturbances at the lowest level (and hence at the highest speed) possible, thus reducing the error-correcting difficulties for higher-order systems.

The little hammer used to test knee reflexes acts by stretching the tendon in the knee, just as if the attached muscle had suddenly lengthened. The jerk that follows is a first-order error correction which comes too late to prevent the disturbance from acting. This reflex requires only a tenth of a second or less to begin, showing that first-order control systems are *very fast* (even if not always quite fast enough). Any disturbance of effort, then, can be resisted if it does not start and stop within a few tenths of a second. An example might be the disturbance due to kinetic energy stored in a moving limb which, when the order is given to stop moving, would act like an effort tending to continue the movement. The first-order systems counteract this disturbance by producing a surge of effort in the other direction which abruptly absorbs the kinetic energy and incidentally decelerates the limb to a stop. This function of first-order control was noted by Taylor and Birmingham (1948; quoted from a review by Fitts [1951]); this is a description of a short, rapid, tracking movement as in our example:

> . . . For approximately the first 0.07 sec. force in the direction of motion was applied at an increasing rate, then it was applied at a decreasing rate for another 0.07 sec., then braking force was applied at an increasing rate during the next 0.10 sec., and finally the negative force was applied at a decreasing rate for the last 0.19 sec. of the response (p. 1321)

This movement began and ended, therefore, in 0.39 second. Without fast, short, control loops, that would have been impossible— yet this motion was employed to make a spot track a target.

Disturbance acting at the level of muscle tensions are counteracted by control systems which operate at that level. The next level of disturbance might involve interference with the immediate consequences of muscle tensions; for example, stickiness of the control lever which might prevent the movement from taking place properly even if the correct net effort is applied. This stickiness (or any equivalent mechanical interference) would prevent the kinesthetic sense of position from changing as it should when the usual effort is applied. The resulting kinesthetic error would result in a change in the effort reference signal, increasing it until the applied force overcame the stickiness (or other interference). This correction could not be quite as fast as the adjustment of effort itself, for it would involve the whole process of effort-adjustment plus other processes of perception and comparison, as well as added physical relationships. However, in the final steady state (say, one-half second later), the kinesthetic error would be erased by means of the readjustment of the effort reference signal.

Still another level of disturbance can interfere with the spot motion directly without affecting the kinesthetically sensed stick position. A loose linkage, for example, would permit the spot to move somewhat without any corresponding stick motion, and of course a movement of the target would have an equal disturbing effect on the perceived relationship of spot to target. The resulting error (either cause) in the highest-level system would result in a change in the position reference, and hence a change in the effort reference. The resulting changes in force and position would take up the slack in the linkage and restore the correct relationship (with the target stationary or moving), but this would be the slowest error correction of all.

Now try to imagine all levels of disturbances acting at once, with the target in slow but erratic motion being one of the disturbances. Each control loop continually changes its output so as to keep its own perceptual signal near its reference signal's magnitude; only the highest system receives a constant reference signal. A higher system acts not by operating muscles, but by varying the reference signal for a lower-order system, using the entire lower-order system as part of its output function. Only the first-order system actually produces forces that cause external effects, yet the feedback loop for all systems passes through the environment of the whole collection. The fact that the feedback loop always passes outside the behaving system means that there is always a behavioral experiment that can be applied to investigate the system's properties at any level of organization.

Meanings and Neural Currents

In figure 6.1, the various signals and boxes carry identification labels; their significance is not, however, just what it may seem. The neural current standing for the distance between the target and the spot, for example, (the "perceived relationship signal") carries no label in the brain; it is just a neural current, and its magnitude varies as the target-to-spot distance varies. It represents that distance —*is* that distance as far as the brain is concerned—only because of the computing functions that lie between the signal and the light-detectors in the eye. If the computing functions in those intervening boxes were to change form, then the same neural current would represent some *other* aspect of the external world, perhaps a meaningless one. In that case the reference signal's meaning would change accordingly for now a given magnitude of that same neural current would represent the reference condition of a different controlled quantity. Nonsensical controlled quantities are just as easy to control as sensible ones—or are all controlled quantities, in a fundamental way, nonsensical?

In a somewhat sneaky way, I have defined the target-spot relationship as the perceived distance between these objects. This was done for a purpose that will now become evident. When the spot is *on* the target, that distance is *zero*. Hence the reference signal entering the highest-order system to specify spot on target has a magnitude of zero. Any non-zero perceptual signal constitutes an error; we do not need a comparator, it seems! (Let the reader solve the problem of distinguishing *right* distances from *left* distances—two systems are required. We will stay on the right side of the target here.)

In a way this trick of definition is not the only answer to the inevitable question, "What sets the highest reference signal?"—but it is the easiest answer. Lack of a reference signal has precisely the meaning of a reference signal of zero, which in turn implies a specific perceptual situation, not the lack of a perceptual situation. A zero reference signal means only that the control system will act so as to prevent the corresponding perceptual signal from appearing, and that in turn means holding some objective (even if abstract) condition in the physical world constant.

There is a difference, however, between lack of a reference signal and presence of a reference signal that just happens to have a magnitude of zero for the time being. If the reference connection exists, the reference signal might be different from zero on another occasion, as, for example, when I whispered to the subject, "Now keep the spot three inches to the right of the target."

If we imagine that for a distance of one inch from target to spot, the perceptual signal will have a magnitude of 10 impulses per second, then the subject's reaction to my request is obvious: he adjusted the reference signal from higher-order systems (at the top of fig. 6.1) to a magnitude of 30 impulses per second.

Models and Models

The complex notion of a distance relationship has thus been reduced to a one-dimensional and practically meaningless neural current. One's first reaction is to feel that some vital essence has been left out, but in fact nothing has been left out—except all of the higher-order systems. The magical essence is *not* in the pictured systems of figure 6.1. They are only a part of the process in the brain which converts abstract concepts and goals into specific instructions for behavior—make *this* happen, make *that* happen. Neither *this* nor *that* is the same thing as the reason for which *this* and *that* have to be created in perception. The model in figure 6.1 shows (in principle) how one can get from the name of a relationship as a verbal goal to a model of the relationship as a specific reference signal that can direct a specific perceptual result.

I don't mean to beg the real question which is, how does meaning get attached to neural currents in the unspecified higher systems? I think it is safe to guess that we will find precisely the same situation at every level: simple signals standing for the state of ever-more-complex external entities. The complexity is not to be found in the neural currents which we experience as the real world; it is in the layers of neural computing devices that derive one set of signals from others, the existence and nature of which computing devices we do *not* experience. . . . Do we?

It would be best, I think, to put off any further entanglement in this difficult subject until after the actual model (of which fig. 6.1 is only a brief sketch) is developed fully. Then, at least, we will all know what aspects of experience are supposed to be contained in it and which are left out. There is, however, one more matter to consider which may cause many raised hands to lower again, at least for a while.

In figure 6.1 there are two models, one of the physical world outside the behaving system and one of the world inside. The "environment" portion of the figure 6.1 has the same degree of reality as the "system" portion, although I admit that the model of the behaving system above the line may change more than the physical environment one below it. And if the behavioral model can provide the same amount of descriptive and predictive power as the physical model (given proper adjustments), we may have to be satisfied, finally, with not knowing whether it is "really" true, though at the least we will some day know that it is *as* true as the physical model (my current highest reference signal).

A Look Ahead

The next eight chapters are concerned with an attempt to construct a preliminary model of human behavioral organization as it would exist after learning is essentially complete. This model consists of a hierarchical structure of feedback control organizations in which higher-order systems perceive and control an environment composed of lower-order systems; only first-order systems interact directly with the external world.

The entire hierarchy is organized around a single concept: control by means of adjusting reference-signals for lower-order systems. This is almost certainly an oversimplification, if only because the control systems are all nonlinear to some extent. There may well be other modes of control such as adjustment of parameters of control systems. The simple structure I offer here appears to have considerable explanatory power, but it should be thought of only as a preliminary sketch made for the purpose of suggesting research that will lead to further development of the model.

I was aware long ago that I could not hope to construct a completely correct model, so I aimed instead at a model that would be as complete as possible, not begging any questions and not leaving conceptual gaps which could be used as excuses for failures of the model. The conjectures in the rest of this book will often go beyond what can be defended by experimental proof. The purpose of such conjectures is not to give the impression that I have some private pipeline to Truth, but to make the model as specific and as complete as can be done. To the extent that the model has been carried to completion, covering all aspects of behavior, subjective experience, and brain function, every attempt to apply the model will test it and, where it fails, point to what needs modification.

Only a complete model that is supposed to apply all of the time and in all circumstances can really be tested by experiment. If one limits the scope of a model, failures of prediction or explanation can always be attributed to effects of what has been omitted. Even worse, a model which leaves out important aspects of behavior is a standing invitation to conclude that those other aspects are unimportant, illusory, or nonexistent, as "scientific" psychologists have apparently done with awareness, volition, thinking, and most other aspects of inner life. A model that deals only with a narrow range of behavior or experience invites fragmentation and compartmented thinking. Furthermore, one never knows what failure of fragmentary models means in terms of what to do next.

Of course this model is *not* complete. I am not acquainted with all possible varieties of behavior and experience, and I have only a rudimentary acquaintance with the vast literature on brain function and structure. The model is simply as complete as I could make it at this time. I have not deliberately avoided *any* issue I was aware of. Many readers who have better knowledge than I have in the many fields touched upon will see where improvements, additions, and corrections can be made with little effort. I hope they take that attitude rather than one of armchair criticism of errors. Errors that do exist, I think I can claim, will at least be honest, not silly, or due to hasty thought or unexamined prejudice.

The hierarchy described here through chapter 13 is meant to cover only performance. As will be seen, it is possible to account for a great variety of behaviors in terms of a structure having unchanging characteristics, even behaviors commonly taken to require learning or adaptation. After the basic hierarchy has been described and related (as well as I can) to existing knowledge, the model will be extended further, first by introducing a theory of learning and then by introducing memory. In the course of this latter exposition, a place will be provided for awareness and volition as specific phenomena not covered by the model of the control hierarchy, and then, through analyzing imagination as a variety of memory phenomenon, a way will be shown for wholly subjective experiences to take place—as they undeniably do.

Those who are familiar with the kinds of abstract models that abound in the social sciences may not immediately recognize that this model is quite different in form and content from other models that also employ block diagrams. This model is not intended to be abstract. It is supposed to be a start toward a literal block diagram of the functions of the human nervous system. I expect many parts of this model to be traced to specific physical structures—eventually, when the model has been sufficiently improved, *all* parts except, perhaps, awareness. None of what follows is intended to be a representation of situations, influences, relationships, or interactions taking place in a social milieu or any such externalized imaginary locale. It is intended to describe the organization that is responsible for such representations. This is a model of a human being, be he subject, experimenter, or theorist. It is not a model of what one person sees others doing, but a model of one individual at a time. Nevertheless, it does not depend on the specific experience that individual has had, or the specific behavior he happens to be doing, or the specific structure of goals and perceptions that distinguishes him from other persons. Insofar as the model is correct, it describes every individual in every culture doing or thinking or experiencing anything. When specific content is put into this model, it becomes a specific individual. Left unspecific, it describes —I hope—the human nature of every person.

REFERENCE

Fitts, P. "Engineering Psychology and Equipment Design." In *Handbook of Experimental Psychology,* edited by S. S. Stevens. New York: John Wiley 1951.

LEADING QUESTIONS: CHAPTER 6

1. Can you find a way to create a tactile sensation of pressure on the palm of your hand? Can you create it without also creating sensations of effort? Can you create sensations of effort without producing the sensation of pressure on the palm of the hand? Which perception is lower in the hierarchy? Does the relative ranking ever reverse?

2. You have been captured by an alien monster, a psychologist from Jupiter. In order to obtain oxygen to go on breathing, you are required by him to solve a certain number of algebraic equations every day. Does this necessarily place breathing higher in your own hierarchy than solving algebraic equations?

3. You are driving a car. Can you name a disturbance which in no way affects the car or its relationship to the road, but still requires you to use the steering wheel to correct it?

4. Starting with the goal of buying a quart of ice cream, can you construct a descending series of goals ending with the goal of tensing a specific muscle to a specific degree? For example: in order to buy ice cream I must go to a place that sells ice cream. In order to go to a place that sells ice cream, I must . . . .

5. A fever results from a rise in the brain's reference level for sensed body temperature. How does this explain the chill that goes with a fever? One may feel either hot or cold. Which feeling would go with a rising reference level, and which with a falling reference level? What could be altering that reference level?

6. How is wanting something related to reference levels for perceptions? How can a person stop wanting something he wants?

7

First-order Control Systems: Intensity Control

The central nervous system is bounded by a set of output devices, the muscles (and glands), and by a set of input devices, the sensory nerve endings. Everything outside a normally operating nervous system that can affect the flow of information into it must act by stimulating sensory nerves at its boundary; every effect the nervous system can have outside itself results from neural currents reaching its boundary from inside. A model of the behaving system is therefore a model of processes that take place inside the boundary, all else being the environment of the behaving system (even if sometimes contained within the same physical envelope).

In this chapter we will define and analyze a set of negative feedback control systems that lie just inside the boundaries of the central nervous system. In effect, a second boundary will be defined, such that all control systems in this set lie inside the overall boundary, but outside the new boundary, in a shell completely surrounding (topologically) the remainder of the nervous system. When these first-order systems in this outer shell have all been accounted for, they will become the total environment which the remaining systems can sense and affect, for the first-order systems are the only means by which the inner parts of the nervous system can interact behaviorally with what lies outside the nervous system. That being the case, the only environment with which the inner systems can interact *is* the set of first-order systems.

The Basic Spinal Feedback Loop

The shortest feedback loops known are those involved in the *spinal reflexes*. We will be concerned here only with the most behaviorally important of these, the reflexes that are intimately associated with muscle action. In the following discussion the various parts of these reflexes will be identified and named as components of a feedback control system. The basic spinal motor reflex is the *tendon reflex*, shown schematically in figure 7.1.

A reference signal (the reason for the use of this term will become apparent) reaching the spinal motor neurone excites the motor neurone to produce a train of impulses passing down the so-called final common pathway, the motor nerve through which all behavioral acts are initiated. When these impulses reach the muscle, the muscle contracts, stretching the attaching tendon and stimulating the Golgi cells, sensory receptors clustered on and

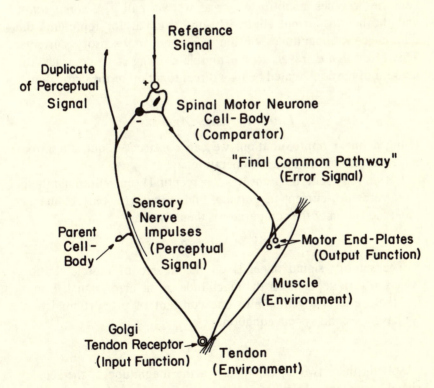

FIGURE 7.1. *The basic first-order control system; the tendon reflex loop.*

near the tendon. A train of sensory impulses is thereby started, that pass through a sensory nerve and reach the same motor neurone where the process began. A closed loop exists. Disturbances propagate around this loop in about 1/20 second (typical): about 1/10 second, therefore, will be the least significant time interval for this system.

The neural current generated by the tendon receptors normally affects the spinal motor cell in the inhibitory sense. Thus, according to the neural-current convention, this connection bears a minus sign. The reference signal is actually the composite of many converging neural currents, some negative and some positive, but since the other input to the neurone is inhibitory, there can be no effect on the motor neurone unless the net reference current is positive. Therefore the reference signal is assigned a net positive value, greater than or equal to zero.

With this value assigned to the input currents, the spinal motor neurone becomes a subtractor, or as we will call it, a *comparator*, and the neural current emitted by this comparator represents the difference in magnitudes of the reference and sensory currents. This *error signal* travels to the muscle causing it to contract, the amount of tension created being a direct function of the error signal.

Linear-Feedback Analysis

Using a linear approximation, we can construct a quick approximate analysis of this system's operation.

Let p represent the sensory- (perceptual) current magnitude, r the reference-current magnitude, and e the error-current magnitude; the action of the comparator is then given as:

$$1. \quad e = r - p.$$

The sensory signal depends on the degree of muscle tension, which in turn depends on the magnitude of the error signal. Lumping these effects together into one constant of proportionality, k, we have a second system equation:

$$2. \quad p = ke.$$

Solving these two equations for p, the magnitude of the sensory signal or perceptual signal, yields:

$$3. \quad p = \frac{kr}{1+k}.$$

In the typical spinal control loop, the reference signal r may have a value of hundreds of impulses per second during a normal act, but the error signal emitted by the motor neurone will be at most 10 to 20 impulses per second: nine-tenths or more of the reference signal is canceled by the inhibitory sensory feedback. This implies a normal value for k in the equation above of about 10, so that

$$p \approx \frac{10}{11}\, r.$$

This elementary treatment (which is more general than it may seem) reveals a fact of utmost importance about these spinal control loops: They act so as to maintain the perceptual signal at nearly the same magnitude as the reference signal. This result remains essentially true despite a variety of changes which, without the feedback to the subtractor neurone, would drastically alter the sensory signal.

Suppose, for example, that the rested muscle responds energetically enough to give k a value of 20. Without the feedback, we would expect, from equation 2 alone, to see a doubled magnitude of muscle tension, and hence of perceptual signal, for the same reference signal as before. *With* the feedback, however, the perceptual signal is 20/21 of the reference signal, which is only 5 percent greater than before. Working backward around the loop, we can see that this result occurred because of a drop in the error signal driving the more sensitive muscle (the muscle tension thus remains about the same) and that the drop in error signal is exactly accounted for by the slight increase in sensory inhibition. Since perceptual and reference signals were originally almost in balance, a small rise in the perceptual signal can cause a large drop in the error signal: That is the essential logic of feedback control.*

The Line of Command

Consider what this analysis means about the traditional idea of the command signal. The usual notion is that higher centers in

---

*This algebraic analysis, besides assuming linearity, assumes stability in the sense that the transient terms in the differential equations describing this system die away so rapidly that we need consider only the steady state part. Since behavior normally *is* stable, this is justifiable. Only on the time scale on

(continued on p. 86)

the brain create patterns of neural signals that command certain patterns of movement via the muscles. This interpretation is somewhat weakened by our finding that the signal which actually drives the muscle can change (as the muscle's state of fatigue changes) independently of the command signal. The feedback, of course, is responsible for this; there is nothing mysterious going on. The actual muscle tension still remains about the same and correlates with the command signal—the reference signal in the feedback analysis.

A further and much more serious weakening of the traditional view comes about if we introduce arbitrary disturbances into this system. As has been done many times, we could arrange to add tension to the tendon in addition to that generated by the muscle, by mechanical means. In terms of the system equations, this means rewriting equation 2 so that the perceptual signal depends on the sum of the effects of the error signal on the muscle and the added tension disturbance, D:

$$\text{2a.} \quad p = ke + cD,$$

where c converts a given amount of tension in pounds to impulses per second of perceptual signal. From this equation alone we would expect a change in disturbance, ΔD, to result in a change in perceptual signal, Δp, of magnitude

$$\text{4.} \quad \Delta p = C \, \Delta \, D, \text{ where } \Delta \text{ means "the change in."}$$

With the feedback present, the two system equations given for the magnitude of the perceptual signal change, equation 3 becoming:

$$\text{3a.} \quad p = \frac{kr}{1+k} + \frac{cD}{1+k},$$

or in terms of the effect of a change in disturbance, and with r constant,

$$\text{3b.} \quad \Delta p = \frac{C \, \Delta \, D}{1+k}.$$

The feedback reduces the effects of a disturbance on the perceptual signal by a factor of $1 + k$ (or about 11 in our typical system).

---

which transient terms can be ignored is it legitimate to use simultaneous algebraic equations as is done above.

This happens because there is a change in the muscle tension opposed to and almost equal (in effect on the perceptual signal) to the disturbance.

The muscle tension itself varies over a wide range without any change in the reference signal. This implies directly that the brain does not control patterns of muscle tensions: it affects muscle tensions, but these effects can be overridden by natural events (such as loads on the limbs) which can stretch the tendons or relieve the tension on them.

There is, however, one quality which *is* reliably controlled by the reference signal: the *perceptual signal*. We have seen that this signal is maintained by feedback action at a magnitude that nearly cancels the reference signal at the comparator neurone, which means that the magnitude of the perceptual signal remains close to that of the reference signal; it "tracks" it. Even disturbances that might tend to affect the perceptual signal fail to have any serious effects on this tracking as long as they do not overwhelm the system. Of all the variables in this feedback situation, only the perceptual signal is directly and closely dependent on the reference signal. Perception is controlled *with reference to* the reference signal.

This fact of perceptual control is made even more obvious when we bring in the fact that the sensory signal magnitude is not directly proportional to tension on the tendon, but to the logarithm of that tension (Granit 1955). If the sensory signal varies directly with the reference signal, as feedback forces it to do when the reference signal changes magnitude, then tendon tension must be varying as the antilogarithm of the reference signal. This property of feedback systems is the heart of analogue computing.

The relationship of perceptual and reference signals will remain nearly the same even if the muscle's sensitivity to error-signal stimulation changes radically. Clearly the way in which the tendon tension depends on the reference signal is *not* determined primarily by the muscle's properties, but by the properties of the sensory endings involved in the feedback loop. Since tendon tension is a direct measure of forces tending to move the skeleton, this same analysis shows that forces applied to the environment are related to the reference signal by the properties of the sensory endings and not (to a first approximation) by the properties of the muscles. Wiener presented essentially this analysis in 1948.

The effective chain of command runs from the reference signal, backward through the sensory endings, to the physical quantity that directly stimulates those endings. All control-system engineers think this way about inorganic control systems. The same point of view is valid—for the same reasons—in thinking about these organic control systems. The effective cause-effect path is not the obviously apparent one.

While this idea of *control of perception* is still fresh, here is a fact about spinal reflex loops that is now highly suggestive. Each nerve fiber carrying sensory feedback signals to the spine divides just after it enters the spinal cord. One branch is the one we have already considered, the one that goes to the motor neurone. The other may carry neural currents to other destinations, but the most interesting are the numerous cases in which this branch turns upward and becomes part of the tracts carrying sensory information toward the regions from which the reference signals originate. There is the strong suggestion that the reference signals come down saying, "make it feel like *this*," and a few tens of milliseconds later the perceptual signals proceed back upward, "feeling like *this*." As a side effect, forces are exerted on the external world.

Secondary Modes of Control

There are two complications to deal with before we can expand this treatment to include *all* first-order systems: interconnections among control systems, and a second chain of command that bypasses the spinal motor neurones, the *gamma efferents*. Feedback analysis offers interpretations of both.

I shall deal here with only one kind of cross connection between control systems; the same analysis can be extended to the rest but that is not essential here. There are many pairs of reflex loops known involving muscles which extend and retract a limb, or create other approximately opposed forces. A perceptual signal in one control loop may divide, with one branch reaching the spinal motor neurone of the opposing reflex loop with the opposite sign. This is often spoken of as preventing conflict between opposing muscles. That is too teleological an explanation even for my permissive tastes and misses the point. The point is that *the sign of feedback is preserved* by this arrangement so that *each* loop uses *both* muscles in its control actions. Conflict is certainly not prevented, as one can demonstrate at will by "making a muscle"—that is, opposing the efforts of biceps and triceps with a high level of (conflicting) muscle tensions. Cross connections simply require enlarging the concept of what is a control system at this level to include two or more muscles.

The Gamma Reference Signal

The gamma efferents are fibers carrying signals directly into the muscles. Owing to their apparent origin in the reticular formation of the brain, and to current conjectures about the role of this formation in "arousal," it has been generally accepted that these fibers carry signals controlling the sensitivity of reflex loops at the spinal level. Aside from the fact that the sensitivity of *any* nonlinear system changes with signal magnitude, this interpretation is not necessarily correct—in fact the data seems to show the opposite change in sensitivity that is commonly ascribed to gamma efferent action. The effect actually recorded is closer to addition and subtraction than a change in slope of a response curve, the usual meaning of *sensitivity* in engineering. Apparently this term connotes "threshold" in physiology, but systems seldom operate near their thresholds.

Magoun (1963) gives a table relating the sensory response to stretching of a muscle while various gamma-efferent signals are artificially injected (both positive and negative in their effects). Plotted as a graph, the data are given in figure 7.2.

Near the origin the effect does seem like a change in sensitivity (slope), but for amounts of stretch near the middle of the range, the curves tend more to be parallel, indicating simple algebraic addition of gamma effects and stretch effects on the secondary signal. At larger amounts of stretch, the slopes actually show opposite sensitivity effects to those near the origin; a sufficient overall linear approximation would be three *parallel* lines, indicating an additive effect.

The actual mechanism of gamma-efferent action, summarized by Gibbs (1970) in a servomechanism-analysis setting, is somewhat complicated but not beyond analysis at this preliminary level. The gamma efferent fibers reach *muscle spindles,* tiny specialized muscle fibers scattered throughout muscles. Each muscle spindle has in its center a few muscle cells that contract when excited by (positive) gamma-efferent signals. Wrapped around

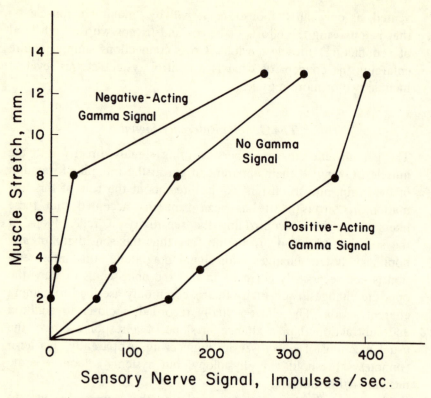

FIGURE 7.2.   *Effect of facilitating (positive-acting) and disfacilitating (negative-acting) gamma efferent signals on the stretch-reflex length detectors. From data given by Magoun.*

these spindles near their centers are *annulospiral endings,* which fire when the muscle spindle elongates, and are suppressed when a gamma-efferent signal shortens the spindle by causing the internal muscle fibers to contract. When the *main* muscle contracts, the whole imbedded muscle spindle is shortened.

The sensory signals generated by the annulospiral endings follow paths leading into the spinal cord and terminate on motor cells that are involved with the same muscle: they excite these motor cells (instead of inhibiting them as the tendon receptor signals do).

Tracing around the closed loop of cause and effect in figure 7.3, we see that the feedback is negative. A stretch of the main muscle elongates the muscle spindle, which excites the annulospiral ending and thus the motor neurone, causing the main muscle to contract and shorten. The initial stretch is opposed by the subsequent

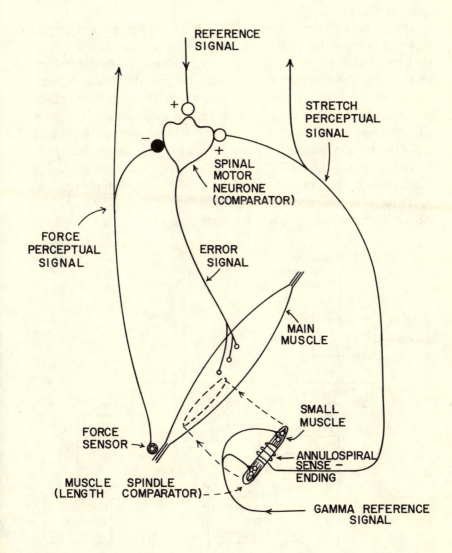

REFERENCE
SIGNAL

STRETCH
PERCEPTUAL
SIGNAL

+

−

SPINAL
MOTOR
NEURONE
(COMPARATOR)

FORCE
PERCEPTUAL
SIGNAL

ERROR
SIGNAL

MAIN
MUSCLE

SMALL
MUSCLE

FORCE
SENSOR

ANNULOSPIRAL
SENSE −
ENDING

MUSCLE   SPINDLE
(LENGTH   COMPARATOR)-

GAMMA REFERENCE
SIGNAL

FIGURE 7.3.

shortening; hence the feedback is negative. If the muscle is already contracted, relieving a stretch will tend to allow the muscle to shorten more, but that reduces the exciting signal from the annulospiral ending and relaxes the muscle somewhat: again, negative feedback.

The gamma-efferent signal biases this feedback toward greater or lesser tension by adding an extra effect on the length of the muscle spindle. In effect, there is a mechanical comparator here, so that the annulospiral signal represents the difference between stretch of the main muscle and contraction of the muscle-spindle muscle cells. The first-order control system thus contains two comparators, one neural (the spinal motor cell) and one partly mechanical (the muscle spindle). Figure 7.4 shows this schematically.

This diagram (figure 7.4) is completely equivalent to figure 7.5. The result is that the effects of gamma-efferents simply add algebraically to the effects of the reference signal previously discussed and introduce no basic new considerations.

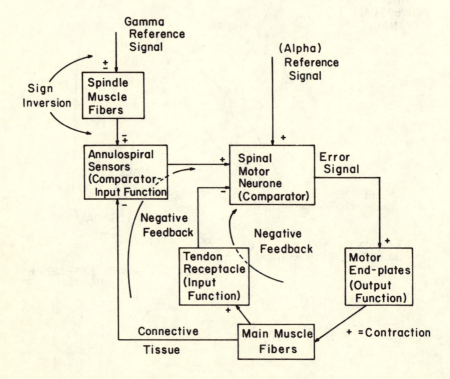

FIGURE 7.4.   *Block diagram of first-order control system, showing parallel negative feedback loops.*

The annulospiral ending responds strongly to rate of change of muscle length, having a much smaller response to steady-state conditions. I have considered here only the steady state. In this linear approximation the rate-of-change component simply adds damping to the control system, slowing changes in its response and thus adding stability. The rate of change component would not be affected by an additive gamma efferent effect. Though this linear analysis is certainly not a wholly accurate picture, it will serve for a while.

The First Order of Organization

The schematic diagram (figure 7.1) with which we began shows one motor neurone, one sensory ending, and one muscle fiber. In

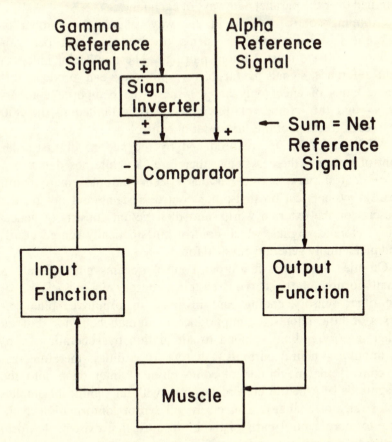

FIGURE 7.5. *Equivalent diagram of first-order control loop, showing alpha and gamma signals as reference signals.*

fact, each element must be duplicated hundreds of times to represent the situation even for a small muscle's control system, because there is one motor neurone for each contractile muscle cell in a whole muscle and corresponding feedback paths from an equally large collection of proprioceptive sensory receptors.

The fact that a muscle acts as a whole on its attachments to the skeleton serves as a natural way to group these control systems. All the comparator neurones that send error signals to the muscle can be grouped into a *composite comparator* emitting an error current measured by summing all the neural currents going to the same muscle. A large set of reference signals enters this composite subtractor, as does a large collection of perceptual feedback signals. The characteristics of this composite control system should be expressed in terms of average neural currents summed over the parallel pathways of each kind.

Grouping control systems in this way reduces the number of different first-order control systems involved in overt behavior to about 800 (at most, without pairing). The number of independent reference signals is far larger, but they can produce different kinds of effect only at 800 sites—the composite comparators—and the number of different effects is limited to the 800 degrees of freedom of this first order of control.

All behavioral acts are produced by the actions of first-order control systems; these systems, therefore, are interposed between more central parts of the nervous system and the environment. Central systems act on first-order control systems and not on the muscles or the external world, and their action consists of generating reference signals which control kinesthetically sensed effort, and incidentally generate physical forces.

On the input side, first-order control systems employ only a small portion of the nervous system's sensory endings. Some of the other sensory endings are involved in primitive spinal reflexes of little interest or importance in human behavior, but *all* other sensory endings respond to stimulation by generating trains of impulses—neural currents. All sensory endings, therefore, act to convert the magnitude of some physical interaction into the magnitude of a neural current (with or without significant emphasis of rates of change). Conversely, all sensory information available to more central parts of the brain must first exist in the form of these primary neural currents.

The set of all sensory endings wherever located can be called the set of *first-order input functions*: "input" because of the direction of travel information into the system, and "function" because the relationship between neural signal magnitude and external event defines the functional significance of a given sensory ending (the physical shape, mode of action, or materials of construction are irrelevant in an organizational model).

First-order input functions are interposed between the physical environment and higher-order organizations in the brain. Hence the set of all first-order perceptual signals emitted by first-order input functions is the only environment that higher systems can respond to; higher systems do not and cannot respond directly to physical stimuli.

We have now defined the entire "shell" of first-order control systems and input functions surrounding the remainder of the nervous system. A boundary has therefore been defined separating first-order systems and functions from higher-order systems and functions, similar, except for the kinds of variables involved, to the boundary between first-order systems and the external world. Across this inner boundary pass two sets of neural currents: (1) a set of perceptual signals on their way inward (some under direct control via the muscles), and (2) a set of reference signals on their way outward to first-order comparators.

Experiential Significance of First-order Perceptual Signals

Any one first-order perceptual signal can vary only along one dimension frequency (see Granit 1955, for extensive discussion of this fact). This means that however the associated input function is stimulated, only one dimension of that stimulation can affect the perceptual signal: the *intensity of stimulation,* without distinction as to the cause or kind of stimulation. The perceptual signal from a touch receptor does not reflect whether the cause is an electric current, a touch, or a chemical poisoning, or whether a touch occurs to the left or right of the exact receptor location.

If this is true, it is even more apparent that a first-order perceptual signal reflects only what happens at the sensory ending: the source of the stimulation is completely undefined and unsensed. If any information exists about the source of the stimulus, it exists only distributed over millions of first-order perceptual signals and is explicit in none of them.

The significance of any one first-order perceptual signal is therefore extremely limited and local; this applies even in the eye, although using our higher levels of organization we "know" that light can come from distant objects. There is no information in any one first-order visual signal to indicate the origin of the light which the input function absorbs: the source can be fluorescence inside the eyeball or an exploding star a hundred million years removed in space and time, with no change in the character of the perceptual signal.

All information contained in first-order perceptual signals is therefore information about what is happening to the associated input functions and about nothing else. Furthermore, this information is one-dimensional, indicating only how much effect is occurring. It may be that differences in the amplitude or duration of individual impulses, which can differ from one input function to another, can tell higher centers something about the place where the signals originated at the boundary of the nervous system, but that is only a hint, not data about causes distant from the organism, and we will not have to rely on that kind of information to build a successful model, so it cannot be essential.

One can apparently sense one's experiences as if no levels higher than first order existed. Werner (1948), for example, conducted some experiments in "synaesthesia" (substitution of one sense for another by mistake; these experiments, incidentally, may be worth repeating in the light of this model). One of his experiments involved inducing normal subjects to concentrate their attention on sensory experience so intensely that the

> sensation of color or [audible] tone pervades the body so searchingly that there is no longer any optical or tonal "matter" and the subject is at a loss to tell the modality [kind] of sensation. We are justified in designating this level of experience as a synaesthetic level. It is a "sensorium commune," a generalized sensorium, an undifferentiated sense, the primitive basis for the development of the specific phenomena of the several fields of sense. (p. 97)

Werner also quotes a subject reporting one of the effects of taking the mind-altering drug mescaline: "I think that I hear noises and see faces, and yet everything is one and the same. I cannot tell whether I am seeing or hearing. I feel, taste, and smell the sound. It's all one. I, myself, am the tone." (p. 92). Apparently one of the effects of this consciousness-expanding drug is to force one's awareness to the lowest levels of his organization, an effect that makes one wonder about the appropriateness of the term "mind-expanding." It may be that the universe seems to expand when the observer contracts.

It is not necessary to enter a special state of mind to notice the existence of first-order perceptions in experience. Once one realizes what he is *not* looking for, he can see them isolated with little effort. First-order perceptions are *not*, as Werner realized, what we normally call sensations; they are, rather, the dimension of experience along which all sensations can vary, and along which all sensations are alike. They represent only intensity, the sense of how much of any sensation is present. If one simply attends to two different sensations—say, a sound and a light—and tries to describe to himself what makes them different, he will soon see not how they are different but how they are the same. One is an intensity of this kind, the other an intensity of that kind, and both share the property, directly perceived, of intensity. All sensations share that property, the elementary dimension of variation. All attempts to analyze a single perception into its component parts end with the awareness that the parts of all pure sensations appear to be of the same kind: They are anonymous intensities.

Awareness of experience at this level is, in this model, conscious perception of first-order perceptual signals. It is *not* awareness of elementary stimulations, for any number of different kinds of stimulus-events could cause the input functions of first order to emit the same intensity signals; electrical stimulation of a warmth detector feels like warmth, not like electricity, and a carefully aimed touch with a needle-point will feel like warmth, not like a needle-point touch. "Warmth" is how a particular first-order perceptual signal impresses higher-order systems. And at first order, without the benefit of these higher-order interpretations, *all stimuli feel alike.*

Thus in matching the levels of this model to conscious experience, I identify the first-order perceptual signals as *intensity* signals.

REFERENCES

Gibbs, C. B. "Servo-Control Systems in Organisms and the Transfer of Skill." In *Skills,* edited by D. Legge. Baltimore: Penguin Books, 1970.
Granit, R. *Receptors and Sensory Perception.* New Haven: Yale University Press, 1955.

Magoun, H. W. *The Waking Brain.* 2d ed. Springfield, Ill.: Thomas, 1963.

Werner, H. *Comparative Psychology of Mental Development.* Chicago: Follet, 1948.

LEADING QUESTIONS: CHAPTER 7

1. Can you perceive first-order effort-intensity signals? Try tensing different muscles. What is *similar* each time? (The *amount* of effort.)

2. Can you perceive the way in which a loud sound is like a bright light or like a pungent smell? How would each be experienced at the low end of the intensity scale?

3. Can you raise and lower the total effort-intensity in an arm independently of motion or position of the arm? Hold this book in one hand. Can you vary the total effort-intensity without altering the net upward forces supporting the book?

4. In order for a sound to have a detectable pitch, it must have a detectable loudness. Is the reverse true?

5. In order for an edge to be visually detected, there must exist detectable brightness. Is the reverse true?

Second-order Control Systems: Sensation Control or Vector Control

We have now separated from the rest of the central nervous system a specific set of control systems concerned with the control of sensed effort-intensity, together with all sensory endings that are not involved in a first-order control system. This means that we have accounted for all means whereby the central nervous system can produce forces affecting the environment outside the nervous system, and for all means whereby external physical quantities impinging on the nervous system give rise to sensory neural currents. Now we will look at the remainder of the central nervous system—the brain proper—to find another layer of control systems. The object will be to define a set of control systems that is hierarchically superior to the first-order systems, and which at the same time is as close to the level of first-order systems as possible. The general goal for the next few chapters will be to continue the process we have begun of isolating sets of control systems that in some way have similar relationships to the external world and to do so in such a way that all such systems, known or hypothetical, are accounted for by the definitions. The picture to be developed here is perhaps optimistically neat, but considerable evidence exists in support of at least the general relationships to be discussed as we progress from this new order of control, second order, to the highest order about which I am willing to venture even a guess, the ninth order.

The general relationship proposed in this chapter between second-order control systems and first-order control systems puts the second-order systems in control of first-order systems. There may be many hundreds of second-order systems active at the same time and operating essentially independently of one another, but they all produce overt behavior by means of sending reference signals to first-order systems (thus producing patterns of forces involving many or all of the skeletal muscles of the body), and they all receive information from sets of first-order input functions. (A first-order input function is a sensory nerve ending, nothing more, but the general term is used to permit uniformity of language throughout the model.)

We will discuss first the input portions of second-order control systems, after which the output portion will be described, and finally the whole system in relation to behavior.

Second-order Input Functions

The input function of a second-order control system is, I propose, a collection of synapses and interconnecting nerve fibers which acts as a neural computer. I will propose a relatively simple kind of computation as being appropriate at this level. The quantities that affect this input function are neural currents that come from first-order input functions; some of those first-order input functions are involved with control of muscular effort so that those currents represent sensed effort. Other neural currents come from first-order input functions that respond to pressure, light, sound, vibration, deep touch, surface touch, balance organs, taste buds, olfactory organs, and so on. The list of quantities that give rise to first-order neural currents is long, and the division into "senses" is, as we will see, rather arbitrary at that low level.

The neural currents that reach a second-order input function can be thought of as analogous to the physical quantities that affect first-order input functions. Even a single first-order input function, a sensory nerve ending, can be caused to fire by many different physical effects acting separately or together; the first-order neural current that results is therefore representative of a combination of effects. In the same way the second-order input function is affected by many first-order neural currents, and a signal leaving the second-order input function would therefore represent some combination of effects of the first-order currents. The second-order input function therefore has the form of a many-to-one relationship; this, as just pointed out, is also true of first-order input functions, although the fact is not quite so clear there.

A signal leaving a second-order input function in the form of a neural current represents a second level of sensory abstraction in the nervous system. Whereas each first-order input signal could be thought of as an analogue of some basic physical effect, each second-order signal, depending for its magnitude as it does on the magnitudes of many first-order signals and hence ultimately on many physical effects, is the analogue of a *derived quantity*—a quantity that cannot be observed in any one of the physical effects, and whose existence and magnitude must be derived from sensing many different local physical effects.

One of the simplest ways of combining neural currents to represent a derived quantity is to add their magnitudes. In the brain stem where the neural computers are located to serve as second-order input functions, there are strong suggestions that the summation of first-order neural currents is indeed a likely property of these networks. The nerve fibers carrying neural currents from first-order input functions terminate in well-defined volumes of the brain stem known as *sensory nuclei*. Each fiber reaches such a nucleus branch. Recall that at such a branch, the neural current before division is simply reproduced in each branch with the same magnitude (in impulses per second). Many of the branches so formed may reach the same destination, the cell body of a nerve that is part of the nucleus (Ranson and Clark 1947). The number of branches carrying current from a single source to a single cell body clearly determines the weighting of that signal; the more branches, the more the original signal will contribute to excitation or inhibition of the receiving cell. Since a single receiving cell body receives neural currents from many different first-order current-carrying fibers, the current ultimately generated by this cell will be proportional to the weighted sum of the different signals reaching it. (The term *proportional*, of course, is meant only approximately.)

Negative weightings as well as positive appear to occur: some incoming first-order neural currents terminate at Renshaw cells, which then relay the signal into the sensory nucleus proper, but with an inhibitory effect.

Associated with every different kind of sense is a sensory nucleus somewhere in the outer portions of the brain. There is an auditory nucleus receiving first-order signals from the sound receptors, a vestibular nucleus receiving signals from the semicircular canals and from many effort-control systems associated with the neck and eyes, and so on. In many of these nuclei, there appears to be a pattern of connections whereby a signal leaving the nucleus returns branches to neighboring cells to inhibit them; these are important and well-known connections, and they tend to cause interactions among the various signals leaving second-order input functions, but I will not try to take these effects into account. I feel that such attempts are best left for future modifications of the model.

The picture I will use for second-order input functions is therefore relatively simple. A given second-order input function receives neural currents from a number of different first-order sources and combines them by weighted summation to produce a single neural current that leaves the second-order input function. This would be called the *second-order perceptual signal.* As we will see when the picture of the whole second-order control system is completed, this signal is, in fact, the controlled quantity of a second-order control system. Whether this signal corresponds to any single entity in the external world is of secondary importance: it may or it may not (see fig. 8.1). As far as any potential control system of this order is concerned, this would be the signal that would be compared with a reference signal, and any variations in output would be such as to keep this signal from changing. If the signal happens to correspond to any identifiable variable in the external world, that variable would necessarily be held constant by the same control action.

A Useful Interpretation of Second-order Perceptual Signals

A weighted sum of first-order intensity signals can be called a *vector,* with each signal being a component of the vector along one axis of the coordinate system. We are dealing here not with geometric space, however, but with a very large collection of independent variables, so the first-order "space" in which these vectors exist has an uncomfortably large number of independent coordi-

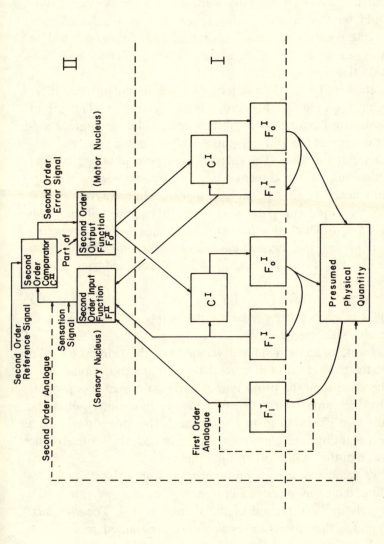

FIGURE 8.1. *Second-order control system shown in relationship to several first-order control systems and one uncommitted first-order input function. Dashed lines with arrows indicate correspondence of perceptual signals to parts of physical model of hypothetical external world.*

103

nates. It is an n-dimensional space, and n in a huge number. Before I guess at how such vectors appear in experience, I would like to expand on this concept, because I think it will be useful.

The "origin" of this coordinate system is $(0, 0, 0, 0, \ldots, 0)$: the state occurring when all intensity signals are zero. A "coordinate axis" would be traced out in this space by one single intensity signal varying between zero and maximum. That defines a "straight line" in this perceptual space, regardless of its significance or geometry outside the nervous system.

As a set of physical stimulations changes in magnitude, there will be changes in many first-order intensity signals. The set of such signals contributing to a given second-order perceptual signal will thus present a shifting pattern of magnitudes to the second-order input function. The second-order perceptual signal that results, however, is one-dimensional. It can vary only in magnitude and hence cannot possibly provide a different representation for every different pattern of intensity signals. There will be many ways in which this pattern can change *without changing the magnitude of the perceptual signal of second order;* these ways are the key to understanding what a weighted sum means in perceptual space.

To see what this invariance implies, let us plot two signals at right angles to each other (reducing the number of dimensions to a manageable size, see figure 8.2).

It is possible to draw a slanted vector from the origin of s_1 and s_2 so that the projection of s_1 onto the vector is proportional to k, and at the same time the projection of s_2 onto the vector is proportional (by the same factor) to 1. Thus we have interpreted the weightings as a direction in this two-space. This direction is fixed when the weightings are chosen: it is determined, therefore, by the organization of the second-order input function.

Any two vectors s_1 and s_3 can be projected onto the slanted vector; adding their projected magnitudes gives the weighted sum of the signals in the direction of the slanted vector. The weighted sum of s_1 and s_2, therefore, locates a point on the slanted line.

Generalizing to many dimensions, we can now interpret the pattern of weightings characteristic of a given second-order input function: It determines a *direction* in the multidimensional first-order perceptual space. All combinations of first-order intensity signals are thus added in terms of their components in this one direction. The magnitude of the second-order perceptual signal represents the length of a vector along this line of projection obtained by adding all the projected (weighted) contributions from the first-order signals.

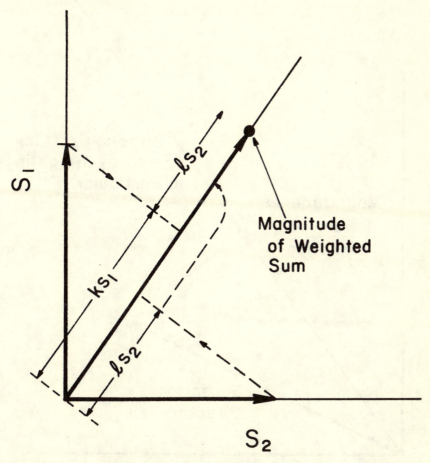

FIGURE 8.2. *Weighted summation of intensity signals (S_1 and S_2), interpreted as projection of orthogonal intensity-vectors onto a given line in sensation-space.*

All of this can be simplified considerably by visualizing the vector sum of all first-order signals; this sum represents one vector having a certain direction and length. The weightings of which we have spoken simply project this vector onto the direction determined by the organization of the second-order input function. It is shown in two dimensions in figure 8.3.

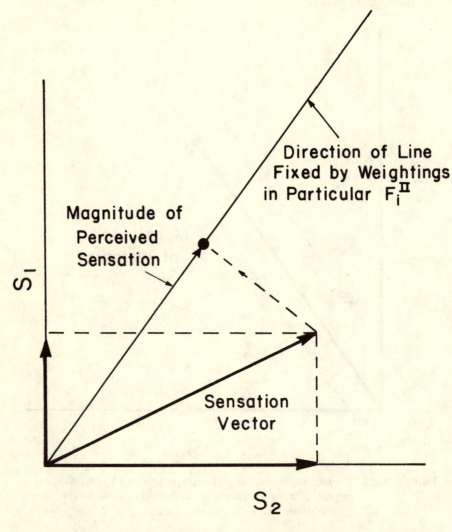

FIGURE 8.3.   *Sensation-vector shown as vector sum of two intensity-signals (S_1 and S_2). Response of a particular second-order input function shown as projection of sensation-vector onto a particular direction-line in sensation space, the orientation of the direction-line being fixed by the weightings given to the individual intensity-signals by the second-order input function in question.*

106

In the case of kinesthetic control systems of second order, this projection concept has a direct physical meaning. An arm and hand have some twenty-seven independent motions. Thus, weighted intensity signals from tendon, muscle, joint, and skin receptors can represent efforts in twenty-seven different and independent directions in first-order perceptual space. This means that twenty-seven different second-order arm-hand control systems may act simultaneously without serious interactions if their input functions are optimally designed. Some of these "directions" can represent flexion at joints, and some can represent rotations in ball-and-socket joints. Together, of course, these motions have the result of placing the hand-arm combination in specific orientations and positions in physical space, but we have not yet reached the level where that can be accomplished under feedback control. All that second-order kinesthetic systems can do is control in one direction, independently of what other second-order systems are doing, and that direction is *not* a geometric "direction." It is a vector in twenty-seven-dimensional kinesthetic space; arm position in conventional three-dimensional space is a construct of a higher level than the one we are considering here.

Experiential Significance of Second-order Vectors

In the brain stem and upper spine are many sensory nuclei; they have been associated experimentally with various modalities of sensation (Ranson and Clark 1947). Each sensory nucleus tends to receive signals from particular kinds of first-order input functions, but there is much overlap.

If we think of the set of all first-order perceptual signals as defining the totality of first-order perceptual space, then these various second-order input function collections, the sensory nuclei of the spine and brain stem, define groups of directions in that space, subdividing it into regions. These regions represent, I believe, what we experience as *sensations,* the least step upward in complexity from intensities.

Within each region, there are many second-order vectors, their directions fixed to the same extent that the weightings of first-order perceptual signals are fixed (see chap. 4). Each different weighting results in a second-order perceptual signal that is consciously perceived (if consciously perceived) as a particular quality of sensation. When the first-order vector lies in the direction defined by one second-order input function, we experience the maximum amount of that sensation relative to others. All other input functions receiving the same set of first-order signals will respond less because of the angle between their directions of maximal sensitivity and the direction of the total first-order vector. "Pure" sensations can result only if the directions defined by various second-order input functions are at right angles in this *n*-space, so that when the intensity-vector is aligned with the direction defined by one input function, its projection onto the other direction approaches zero.

In many cases, intensity signals from different kinds of sources reach the same groups of second-order input functions—sight, sound, kinesthesia, and balance signals may thus all contribute to a single sensation signal. In such cases we still experience a single quality of sensation, but it is not as easy to classify. The sensations of speech, for example, involve sound *and* effort; without the effort component one would still experience *sound* sensations but not those he associates with *speaking*.

The division of sensations into five "senses" is therefore rather arbitrary; many sensations cross the boundaries. The "taste" of a steak is recognized as maximum when a whole array of intensity signals is present, including tastes, smells, temperatures, efforts of biting, and even (sizzling) sounds all in just the right proportions. Only then is the steak-vector aligned perfectly with the direction that yields the maximum second-order sensation one calls "the taste of steak."

Second-order Output Functions

I identify the output functions of second-order control systems with concentrated masses of neural interconnections in the brain stem called *motor nuclei*. These nuclei are similar in location, size, and appearance to the sensory nuclei which I am suggesting embody second-order input functions. They differ, however, in the sources of signals that reach them and the destinations of signals that leave them.

Entering a typical motor nucleus are neural currents descending from higher-order structures in the brain, and also "collateral" neural currents that branch off from the signals leaving second-order input functions. The output signals produced in these motor nuclei follow pathways which terminate in the motor cells of the spinal cord: these output signals, clearly, are the reference signals for first-order systems.

The signals entering second-order output functions may have either inhibitory or excitatory effects. As pointed out earlier, the kind of feedback that is present does not depend on the signs of various signals inside a system but only on the overall sign of an effect propagated all the way around a feedback loop to the starting point, including the portion of the path that lies outside the nervous system. If the reflected effects are opposite to the initial disturbance, the feedback is negative. Many combinations of signs in the various functions in the control loop will leave the feedback negative as it must be to account for the general properties of behavior, and this means that reference signals may have either positive or negative signs, as may input signals which are compared with the reference signals. The only case that is wholly forbidden is one in which both the reference signals and the input signals have negative signs, because no nerve cell can respond to a totally inhibitory input. In most circumstances we can expect reference and input signals to have opposite signs, so that subtraction occurs. The sign of the error signal, in terms of its effects on first-order systems, will depend on which signal is subtracted from which, and even after that is determined there remains the possibility of inversion of sign by a Renshaw cell before the output of a second-order system finally reaches the place where it will serve as a first-order reference signal.

Second-order Comparators

In the anatomical region where second-order control systems exist, the reticular formation is found. This structure may contain comparators for second-order systems, but there are great complexities to the connections in the reticular formation, and it might be a mistake to assign so elementary a role to what goes on there. This important collection of computing functions may be involved in modes of control that I do not consider in this model, such as adjustment of the sensitivity of control systems, or in the governing of which control systems are to be operating at a given time. I do not feel competent to judge how the reticular formation ought to enter into this model, and so, whatever the disadvantages, I will simply pretend that it is not there.

The comparison function required for second-order control systems is adequately represented in the convergence of branches of second-order input signals from the sensory nuclei with descending signals from higher systems entering the motor nuclei. This does not permit visualizing a separate comparison function, but the output from the motor nucleus will be a function of the algebraic sum of these two kinds of inputs to the nucleus, and that is sufficient for our purposes. The descending signals are properly situated to serve as reference signals for second-order systems.

The organization of second-order comparator/output functions does not have to be complex, as we will see. We have already taken into account the comparison function, and have identified the signals from higher centers as reference signals, so only one aspect of the output functions still needs to be discussed and that is the selection of sign and destination of the outgoing first-order reference signals. This is best done in the context of overall organization of second-order feedback loops.

Second-order Feedback Control

Suppose we already have a second-order perceptual signal and reference signal entering a second-order output function with opposite signs, and that these signals converge on common neurones so that their effects partly cancel. This gives us a potential error signal, and the problem now is how this error signal could be routed to first-order control systems as a reference signal so as to create a negative feedback loop.

Suppose we can arbitrarily connect the error signal to any first-order comparator we like: The result will be a change in muscle tension, most likely. As a result of this change, there will be physical effects that alter many first-order intensity signals, some being kinesthetic intensity signals and some being of other types. If these changes have *no* effect on the second-order perceptual signal in question, we assign a weight of zero to that connection (or just don't make it). Assuming that there is an effect, the result can only be an increase or a decrease in the one-dimensional second-order perceptual signal, and hence an increase or a decrease in the error signal with which we started.

This means that we need only choose the *sign* of the connection to the first-order comparator. Fortunately there is a choice, for many first-order reference signals reach first-order comparators via a short interneurone, a Renshaw cell, which generates inhibitory effects on the motor neurone. If we need an inversion of sign, we need only select a reference-signal path that involves such a sign inverter.

The error signal from the second-order output function can branch into many paths, all carrying duplicates of the same error signal (see chap. 4). These paths can reach many different first-order comparators, though even with the sign chosen correctly for negative feedback in most of these paths, the amount of feedback that results from first-order actions will vary from the maximum possible to scarcely any. The amount is determined by the effects of each muscle on the total first-order intensity vector and on the projection of that vector onto the direction fixed by the second-order input function in question. The total effect of all muscles (activated by duplicates of the second-order error signal) on the second-order perceptual signal is the sum of all these projected effects. As long as the net projection has the correct sign for negative feedback, and sufficient net magnitude, the perceptual signal will be made to track the reference signal.

Thus any sensation can be placed under direct feedback control if (and when) there is a combination of muscle tensions that can affect its magnitude in the right direction. A taste we experience can be intensified by efforts in the muscles of mouth, jaw, and tongue; a sound we utter can be controlled in several dimensions (loudness, pitch, timbre) by use of the muscles of the diaphragm, larynx, throat, mouth, tongue, and jaw.

Disturbances

The effort-intensity signals generally are an integral part of such controlled sensations. They represent the directly controlled component of a sensation vector; there are also indirectly controlled and uncontrolled components. The indirectly controlled components are those intensity signals immediately affected by the muscle systems, but which are not involved in first-order control systems. The uncontrolled components arise from effects from external and independent sources in the environment which can alter the first-order vector independently of the organism's own effects. These uncontrolled components therefore may act as *disturbances* of second-order control systems. If a second-order control system can alter the first-order vector in a direction opposite to the effects of the disturbance, control can be maintained and the second-order perceptual signal can be prevented from changing significantly. A given disturbance may act in such a direction in first-order space so as to disturb many second-order perceptual signals at once, but each second-order system needs to act only in the direction that counters the component of the disturbance projected onto its own direction of maximum sensitivity, which is fixed by the weighting factors in that second-order input function.

The effort outputs commanded by a given second-order system are selected so as to have the right directions of effect, but not necessarily so as to be free of effects in other directions as well. This means that the action of one second-order control system can—and probably does in most cases—have disturbing effects on other second-order systems. Such disturbances are indistinguishable from externally generated ones, for they too can only increase or decrease the perceptual signal. Hence if direct conflict is avoided, it is possible for many second-order systems to share control of many first-order systems quite independently of each other. Strong interactions among systems (verging on direct conflict) can make stabilizing of the whole array difficult, however. We may suppose that the more serious mutual interactions have been weeded out by evolution or learning, since adult organisms have little apparent difficulty with instability.

The Second Order of Organization

We have now isolated a second shell of systems lying just inside the first order of organization. Inside this shell is a diminished remainder of the brain; outside it, constituting its environment, are the first-order systems and input functions.

From the inner volume of the brain comes a set of second-order reference signals. Passing inward are duplicates of the second-order perceptual signals that are also involved in second-order feedback control systems. We may also allow for the existence of second-order input functions that are *not* involved in control loops, but which simply create sensation signals that are sent inward, uncontrolled.

There may also be first-order intensity signals that bypass second-order systems, but here we have to be careful not to confuse anatomical organization with functional organization. Some first-order perceptual signals go directly from the spine to the sensori-motor area of the cerebral cortex, apparently bypassing structures lower in the brain, but tracing of feedback loops shows that these higher-order loops are *functionally* second-order loops; they fit exactly the picture developed so far. This does not rule out order-skipping perceptual signals, but it does show that we must look first at organization and only then at geometrical relationships in the brain.

It is easier to predict a low probability of order-skipping reference signals, even at this low level. If, to pick a convenient collection of systems, all twenty-seven degrees of freedom of the hand-arm system are under control by second order systems, then there is no way to inject an independent first-order reference signal without having its effects canceled as the second-order systems react to the resulting disturbance. Thus even if such order-skipping reference signals did exist, there would be little they could accomplish, and therefore we may assume that they no longer exist after all these millenia of evolution.

Sensations and Reality

This is a good opportunity to emphasize a "philosophical fact" that emerges from this theory: perceptual signals *depend on* physical events, but what they represent *does not necessarily have any physical significance* (fig. 8.1). The taste of fresh lemonade, for example, contains an easily recognizable vector, derived from the intensity signals generated by sugar and acid (together with some oil smells). However unitary and real this vector seems, there is no physical entity corresponding to it. The juxtaposition of sugars, acids, and oils in one common volume does not create any special entity there, and there are no significant chemical reactions in the glass of lemonade. That is, the mere intermingling of these components has no special physical effects on anything else, except the person tasting the mixture. The only significant consequence of ingesting these components together is to provide something for the lemonade-taste recognizer to recognize.

This means that we would be much safer in general to speak of sensation-*creating* input functions rather than sensation-*recognizing* functions. To speak of *recognition* implies tacitly that the environment contains an entity to be recognized, and that all we have to do is learn to detect it. It seems far more realistic to me to speak instead of functions that *construct* perceptions, with the question of external counterparts to these perceptions being treated with much skepticism. Indeed, an organized approach to physics which takes the arbitrariness of human perceptions into account *at all levels of observation* would seem to me a most powerful way of deepening our physical concepts of reality.

That speculation, however, takes us considerably outside the field of this book, so we will get on with the business at hand, the next higher level.

REFERENCE

Ranson, S. and Clark, S. *The Anatomy of the Nervous System.* Philadelphia: Saunders 1947.

LEADING QUESTIONS: CHAPTER 8

1. Why is it that a color sensation like *purple,* which corresponds to no single wavelength of light, seems just as real as the color sensation *green,* which can correspond to one wavelength?
2. If a humidity meter is (unintendedly) affected by temperature, to what does the meter-reading correspond in the physical environment?
3. If the temperature-sensitive humidity meter is used as the sensor of a humidity-control system, will the meter-reading be stabilized? (Yes.) What is being controlled?
4. From a reductionist point of view, is there any such thing as chocolate corresponding to the taste of chocolate?
5. Can you think of a situation in which a sensation of sweetness can be affected by a muscular effort?
6. How does picking up a fresh egg involve control of pressure sensations?

Third-order Control Systems: Configuration Control

Many perceptual signals from second-order systems split into two branches, much as the kinesthetic perceptual pathways divide when they enter the spinal cord. As in the first-order systems, the perceptual signals travel to comparators, here to complete the second-order control loop, and duplicates of these signals pass upward (inward in our concentric-shell visualization) to higher-order systems. The reference signals *from* higher-order systems directly control some of the second-order perceptual signals going *to* higher-order systems, and uncontrolled second-order perceptual signals also travel toward the inner parts of the brain.

The pathways leaving second-order input functions, the sensory nuclei of the brain stem and other functionally similar structures, go to two nearby destinations: the cerebellum and the sensory nuclei of the thalamic region, the midbrain. In these two regions the sensation signals converge and enter another stage of information processing. From these same general regions come the reference signals for second-order systems. We may therefore expect to find third-order control systems in the cerebellum and in the thalamus and its immediate surroundings. (There is another more remote location in the cerebral cortex which I will discuss later.)

The behavioral role of the cerebellum appears to concern a host of kinetic coordinations which are largely carried out without the need of, or apparently the possibility of, conscious awareness, Most of the experimental data about the functions of the cerebellum are in the form of negative observations—observations of disturbances of behavior that result from cerebellar damage, and subjective reports are obviously of no help here. Electrical stimulation experiments have been conducted, but the results are very difficult to interpret. One finds observations such as "exaggerated postural reflexes," "disturbance of equilibrium," or "incoordination of movements," but nothing specific enough to characterize the kinds of variables under control by the cerebellum in the way most needed here. The importance of subjective reports in identifying brain functions is nowhere as evident as in the lack of functional knowledge about the cerebellum.

One class of symptoms of cerebellar damage is the appearance of several types of tremor. Tremor is, in control-system terms, not a mode of behavior but a sign of instability. All control systems can oscillate if they become unstable. The *frequency* of oscillation, however, can provide at least some information, for the higher the order of control involved, the more slowly must the control system act, and hence the lower must be its frequency of oscillation when it verges on instability.

When first-order systems become unstable (as when muscles exert too much effort), "clonus" oscillations are seen, at roughly ten cycles per second. Second-order instability, as in the tremors of Parkinsonianism, involves groups of muscles and is of lower frequency, around three cycles per second or so. Third-order instability is slower still, slow enough that it can be characterized as "purpose tremor" or "over-correction." Certain cerebellar damage due to injury or disease can result in over- and undershooting the mark during actions such as reaching out to grasp something, either in a continuous self-sustained oscillation or a slowly decreasing series of alternating movements.

The low frequency of oscillation of unstable cerebellar behavior clearly shows that the feedback loops are of higher than second order. The fact that there are no intervening perceptual organizations seems to support the identification of at least some cerebellar loops as third-order loops (see Eccles 1969).

A Sketch of Cerebellar Systems

The general structural arrangements in one well-studied part of the cerebellum, the vermis, appear approximately right for third-

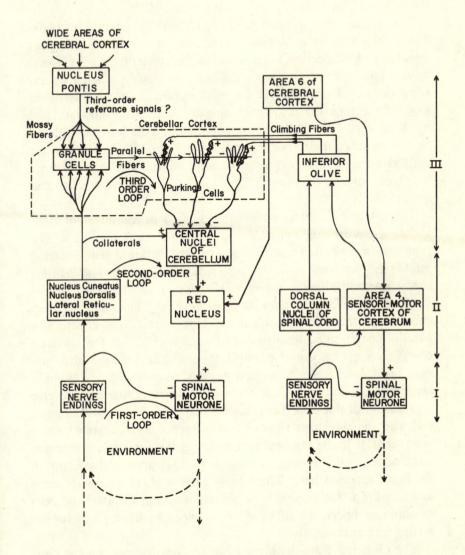

FIGURE 9.1. *Relationship of first, second, and third-order systems (conjectural), showing relative position of cerebellum as a third-order system.*

117

order systems. Figure 9.1 represents my selection of a few systems that seem clearly described, the diagram being derived from Ranson and Clark (1947) and Eccles, et al. (1969).

The reader should refer to Eccles' and his coauthors' book, *The Cerebellum as a Neuronal Machine,* to appreciate the great regularity of connection to be found in the cerebellar cortex (outer layer), and also the enormous difficulty of tracing out the underlying circuits. Unfortunately for our purposes, all the microelectrode work reported dealt with single impulse transmission, and so there is no hint of the nature of the computations carried out by the regular matrix of excitation and inhibition which these authors have shown so clearly. If only, while the electrodes were in place, measurements of input and output frequencies had been made!

The cerebellar cortex is represented, without a number of complicating features, in figure 9.1 inside the dashed rectangle. The principal organization is a regular array of Purkinje cells (looking something like beets). Two types of fibers, *climbing* and *parallel* fibers, interact with the *leaves* (dendrites or input extensions) of the Purkinje cells. The parallel fibers generally have an inhibitory effect, and the climbing fibers a strong excitatory effect. The parallel fibers inhibit long rows of Purkinje cells, but the climbing fibers each excite just one Purkinje cell. The parallel fiber signals arise from cells connected to the *granule cells* lying in a layer just inside the cerebellar cortex. These granule cells receive a profusion of duplicated copies of second-order perceptual signals and also signals which I take to be reference signals from higher-order centers in the cerebral cortex; hence the comparison function must occur in this region, at least in part. It apparently occurs in the input function here, which is as good a place as any. Ranson and Clark (p. 334) show these signals reaching the Purkinje cells as climbing fibers, which would be a more familiar place for inserting reference signals.

The climbing fibers with their one-to-one mapping on the Purkinje cells effectively make a non-cerebellar structure (the *inferior olive* of the brain stem from which these fibers arise) an integral part of the cerebellar cortex. The inferior olive receives second-order perceptual signals from spinal and midbrain nuclei (input functions of second order) and also from area 4 of the cerebral cortex, a "misplaced" second-order system that will be mentioned again. Thus, the inferior olive is also an input function of third order, but as far as I can tell it receives no reference signals from higher-order systems (unless the pathway from area 4 has been wrongly identified). All reference signals apparently enter via the granule-cell layer.

The outputs of this system are the fibers extending downward from the Purkinje cells. Most of them reach either central nuclei still within the cerebellum or a separate layer of cells in other motor nuclei. Their effects are uniformly inhibitory. The central nuclei, which receive positive excitation from fibers branching off the mossy and climbing fibers on their way to the cerebellar cortex, emit positive signals to motor nuclei of the brain stem. I have shown only the red nucleus. These motor nuclei are output functions of second order, since they emit first-order reference signals.

The central nuclei of the cerebellum thus appear to have the right connections for second-order comparators, and the outputs of the Purkinje cells are the second-order reference signals. As I earlier warned, the organization is not quite as neat as even the simplified-form model, but there is still a strong family resemblance.

The quantities controlled by these third-order systems seem to be primarily kinesthetic in nature, although auditory and vestibular (balance) information also seems to reach the cerebellum. One cerebellar defect results in "decomposition" of limb movements; in a grasping motion, the joints extend or retract one at a time rather than, as in normal action, together. A function of the cerebellum is clearly to manipulate many vector-effort reference signals at once, and thus to create coordinated patterns of otherwise independent efforts. *To control is to sense:* The cerebellum must *perceive* those same patterns.

Thalamic Third-order Systems

Experimental evidence about functions of *thalamic* third-order systems is far more direct, which is why I spend no more time on the cerebellum even though its structure is better known and is highly suggestive of *how* some third-order systems may accomplish what they do. A series of direct thalamic stimulation experiments with cats (Hess, 1957) shows the function of third-order systems quite clearly, and function is the crucial issue in this model, not structure. Many different structures can effect the same function.

Hess sank electrodes into the thalamic regions of the brains of 300 cats (ten electrodes in each cat) and found upon using these electrodes to inject electrical impulses that those regions governed *position control*.

By varying the amount of stimulation to a given electrode (in amount of current per impulse or, more physiologically, the frequency of the impulse-train), Hess was able to produce smoothly graded reversible changes in the cats' limb positions, head positions, and even whole body configurations. For example, by varying the frequency of the stimulating pulse-train, Hess could cause a cat's head to swing to any position from straight ahead to far to one side. One frequency corresponded to one *position,* not to a motion or to an effort. Other sites of stimulation produced other kinds of position control: extension or retraction of limbs, rotation of the head on the axis of the neck, opening and closing of the eyelids, and even such complex effort-configurations as " 'assuming the position' and urinating."

Hess emphasized that these were not just "movements." Each position was under continuous control at all times, the head or limb involved being actively maintained in the current-controlled position even against disturbances. He noted and emphasized the essential role of the *perceptual* parts of the thalamus in this organization of behavior; his experiments left no doubt that a feedback loop exists.

Despite a lack of awareness of feedback theory, Hess performed his experiments thoroughly enough to tell us much about these third-order systems. He found, for example, where the filtering occurs that is essential for preventing too rapid a response and hence instability: it occurs in the *perceptual,* not the output, parts of the thalamic control system.

Using low-frequency impulses (around 8 per second), Hess showed that these impulses injected into sensory nuclei resulted in smooth control of a lowering of the head. The same impulses injected into motor nuclei caused the same kind of action, but head-lowering occurred in steps, one step per impulse, eight steps per second.

The same data hint strongly that there are *neural integrators* involved, and that the motor impulses were entering prior to these integrators in the third-order output function. The stepwise response to each impulse was not a brief downward jerk of the head followed by a return to the initial position, but a staircase motion. Each impulse caused the head to lower slightly and stay in the new position. This suggests that each impulse entered a neural integrator (see chap. 4) which in turn emitted a repetitive train of impulses at a rate proportional to the *total number* of stimulating impulses up to that time.

When electrodes in the sensory paths were used to destroy small areas around their tips, the effects were opposite to those produced upon stimulation (but of course no longer reversible, I presume). The exact locations of all 3,000 electrodes, by the way, were later determined by dissection.

Hess' cats tell us that one more class of controlled quantities of third order is *bodily configuration.* Another kind of experiment with brain-stimulation reveals that such position-control systems are in a different location as well: the sensori-motor area of the cerebral cortex. In the preceding chapter I mentioned that some second-order systems are to be found here, being functionally identifiable as second-order control systems by the fact that they receive first-order intensity signals and emit first-order reference signals. The third-order systems in this same area are located next to these second-order cortical systems, including the same area 6 indicated in figure 9.1.

Stimulation of the motor part of these "voluntary" third-order systems produces behavior that neurologists have long considered paradoxical. In general, a train of electrical pulses injected here causes movement, say of a limb retracting or extending. It does not, however, always cause the *same* movement even though the electrode is not moved, which is the reason this phenomenon has been termed the "instability of the motor point."

Ranson and Clark (1947) describe the phenomenon this way, citing Ward:

Ward . . . was able to show that the character of a movement of a limb following stimulation of a given fixed cortical point varied with the previous position of the limb and head. Stimulation of a given point of the motor zone controlling foreleg movements, for example, caused the contralateral [opposite side] foreleg to assume a "final position," making whatever preliminary adjustments that were necessary to attain it. Depending on the position previous to the stimulation, the limb might begin its approach to the final position with protraction or retraction, movements exactly opposite in direction. [P. 304]

T. C. Ruch (1951) proposed a complicated theory to explain this paradox, based on uneven fatiguing of Betz cells in the motor center, some of which cause extension and some retraction. The concept of position control, however, offers a much more functional explanation. The human observers of this phenomenon have been paying attention to the wrong level of their *own* perceptions. They have been viewing the action from the standpoint of fourth order (next chapter), rather than third order.

The third order variable is not motion, but configuration. If investigators of the instability of the motor point had done as Hess did, and varied the frequency of stimulation while carefully recording the results, they would have realized that the final position reached by the limb was the crucial fact, not the transient movements required to get there after sudden application of the electrical stimulation. The electrical stimulus in effect acts as a reference signal for a third-order configuration control system, a given frequency clearly specifying one state of that configuration. The transient motions are incidental, reflecting only a sudden change in the reference signal. Only the steady-state condition tells us what the system does.

We have now more or less identified three locations in the brain for third-order control systems, all concerned with control of bodily configurations. The midbrain, however, contains third-order sensory nuclei receiving many different kinds of second-order sensation signals concerned with hearing, vision, smell, taste, touch, and other sensations. In various circumstances human beings are able to control configurations of many different sensations, and it is not unreasonable to think that more third-order control organizations may exist in the midbrain regions. The sensory computers, not the motor connections, define what is controlled, so if it appears that a third level of sensory processing occurs in the general area of the midbrain, the existence of corresponding third-order control systems is all but guaranteed.

Other Third-order Structures

One of the more important perceptual computing centers is found in the geniculate body and the colliculi, which lie right against the thalamus; this is an important stage of *visual* information processing. At least two other stages precede it, however, in the retina itself. First-order retinal signals generated by rods and cones absorbing light enter into a computing network while still in the retina. It may be at this layer of the retina where second-order visual signals are created representing, for example, gradients, edges, and small-area illuminations. If I am counting levels properly, therefore, the visual centers near the thalamus should be the third order of visual input function.

The signals emitted by these input functions enter into feedback loops governing eye and head position and are also involved in kinesthetic control systems—voluntary hand-eye coordination. It is most attractive to believe that a collection of third-order systems exists clustered together and that all such systems perform a similar class of computations, as one would guess they must if they are to interact properly.

Stimulation of the visual cortex of the brain creates signals like those in the perceptual paths from third-order visual systems (which are also inputs to the visual cortex). Such stimulation gives rise in human subjects to perception of *forms*—not always familiar because of the random stimulation, but still describable by the subject as *stars,* blue, green, and red *disks,* colored *balls,* radiating gray *spots,* long white *marks,* moving *shadows,* black *wheels,* and so on (Penfield and Roberts 1959). These can be called *visual configurations,* or elementary examples of that class of perceptions.

The term *configuration* can, with careful definition, become more than a pun relating third-order kinesthetic systems and third-order visual systems. We can define a configuration as an invariant function of a set of sensation vectors, thus implying particular computing properties common to these different input functions: They abstract invariant relationships so that the third-order signals will change only if sensation vectors on which they are based change in certain ways. Kinesthetically, this might mean that a hand-body configuration would be perceived as the same despite varying levels of effort and despite changes in orientation of the connecting arm relative to the body. Visually, it might mean perceiving the separation of two points as constant regardless of the direction of the line joining them in space and regardless of the amount or color of illumination.

The auditory system begins with nerve endings in the spiral organ of Corti, the auditory structure that sorts sounds along a one-dimensional line as the lens of the eye sorts light waves onto a two-dimensional surface. There is, to extend the parallel, a small muscle attached to each eardrum which controls the sound energy entering the ear, just as the muscles of the iris control light energy entering the eye. The first-order intensity signals travel through the cochlear nerve to the cochlear nuclei, second-order auditory input functions in the upper brain stem. The signals leaving this nucleus would represent various sound sensations, such as pitch, timbre, and loudness.

The second-order perceptual signals travel from the cochlear nuclei to what should be the third-order input functions, the superior olivary nuclei and the nuclei of the trapezoid body. Here, however, they do not stop, but branch, the main path turning upward toward the geniculate body next to the thalamus. The olivary and trapezoidal nuclei, therefore, may be further parts of auditory second-order systems, or a set of third-order input functions.

The second-order signals finally terminate in the geniculate body and inferior colliculus, described as being in the main path to the cerebral cortex. Stimulation like that from the fibers leaving these third-order input functions (and entering the auditory cortex) is reported by Penfield and Roberts (1959) to give human subjects the conscious impression of ringing, humming, clicking, rushing, chirping, buzzing, knocking, or rumbling—auditory configurations composed of various auditory sensations in random arrangements. A more natural set of sensations might lead to perception of phonemes, or the sound-shapes typical of different musical instruments or human voices, or the other configurations of auditory sensations that form recognizable invariants of hearing-space.

If this force-fit of definitions to neuroanatomy should withstand more rigorous tests than I can give it now, we will have some guidelines for future experiments with this level of the brain. One of the difficulties always encountered in such experiments is the impossibility of limiting the effects of stimulation to just the connections being studied, or for that matter to just the neurones intended to be stimulated. The presence of negative feedback loops creates effects that act at the very point of stimulation, a fact that will become even more important when brain function is studied in terms of continuous neural currents. The better we are able to understand the functional organization, the more readily will we be able to understand and allow for these effects.

This model of third-order perception suggests an interesting experiment which has not as far as I know been done. If injecting impulses into a human brain at a given point gives rise to a particular sense of configuration, then according to theory the presentation to the subject of an objective stimulus matching his description ought to result in natural perceptual signals appearing in that same location and, using the stimulating electrode as a detecting electrode, should yield an indication that correlates with presence and absence of that objective stimulus, but not with a greatly different one. This would be a direct test of the theoretical postulate that one perception goes with one pathway in a given brain.

Experiential Significance of Third-order Perceptions

Visual configurations can be what we term *objects*. If one looks around, he can perceive his surroundings as sensations—colors, edges, shadings, points—but it is difficult to avoid noticing how these sensations cling together to make forms. These forms are highly invariant with respect to many kinds of sensation-changes, even those that occur when the object-configuration rotates or becomes nearer or farther away. When we notice a solid real object, we are experiencing the output of a very sophisticated third-order perceptual function, one capable of ignoring all changes in its input sensation signals except a certain narrow class of changes. The invariance of the sense of "chair" when a chair is seen from different angles does not have to imply that the brain "compensates" for the rotations; it means basically that the configuration signal remains constant while the chair appears to rotate, and this can be accomplished if the third-order input function represents the set of sensation vectors in a way that is independent of the spatial coordinate system. That is characteristic of tensor notation.

If invariant objects are invariant because certain types of changes are ignored, then we have to account for the (often overlooked) fact that we can also see the differences when we observe a chair from different angles. The chair signal may not change, but there is certainly an orientation signal that does change quite noticeably. Visual configurations include many types of invariants, not just objects. The spaces between objects are perceived as distances. The appearances of lines and edges yield a sense of relative orientation. Combined visual and proprioceptive sensations from the two eyes yield depth signals associated with all parts (but mainly the central part) of the visual field. Other combinations yield size perceptions. What we express in serial language as "the big chair cattycorner on the far side of the room" is probably perceived at third order all in parallel: big *and* chair *and* cattycorner *and* far *and* side *and* room. And these elements, I am supposing, are all third-order perceptions, derived separately by as many third-order input functions operating simultaneously. . . . We postulate boldly, promising to repent in the laboratory.

Phonemes are probably auditory third-order perceptions, for they consist of simultaneous occurrence of several pitches, together with hiss and buzz sensations. Phonemes are certainly invariant with respect to many kinds of sensation changes, such as low or high register or irrelevant voice overtones, but if the pattern of sensations changes in the right way, one phoneme disappears and another distinctly different one takes its place. Syllables, too, may be included in third-order perceptions, for although they consist of a string of phonemes we hear at least *some* syllables as essentially single sounds: ha! For this to happen the sensation signals from the first phoneme must be stored briefly so that for a moment the sensations of both phonemes are simultaneously present at the third-order input function. Such storage is easily accounted for by what is termed *after-firing* of the receiving cell body; the cell has to continue generating neural current for only a tenth of a second or so after the input currents have ceased, well within the observed range for some neurones.

To account for discrimination of all the phonemes of a spoken language, we need fewer than 100 third-order input functions, each perceiving a different invariant among the sound sensations. Considering that in a midbrain nucleus there are some 10,000 cell bodies per cubic millimeter, each with fiber extensions that can potentially interact with thousands of neighboring cells, a mere hundred phoneme-recognizers is a trivial computing function. I would not hesitate to design 100 such computers, given a few cubic millimeters of nuclear brain tissue and 100,000,000 years.

There is a class of experiments that can suggest some details of third-order input function organization. For example, some perceptions of third order appear to be mutually exclusive, as in the staircase or cube illusions and the Gestalt example of a vase that turns into two faces when figure and ground are reversed. The computers involved in perceiving these configurations evidently can emit several signals with different meanings—but only one at a time. Attneave (1971) has proposed that criss-crossed inhibitory connections found in most sensory nuclei may account for this mutual exclusivity; such an arrangement would suggest ways of testing whether perceptions that are conceptually similar are detected by computers that are spatially close to each other.

Control

Third-order control is the control of configurations. A given reference-signal magnitude determines one magnitude of the configuration signal, which in turn represents, we suppose, the state of some static collection of sensations on the continuum of states corresponding to the continuum of magnitudes of the configuration signal. Sometimes many configurations can be seen in the same collection of sensations; then we usually experience all the configurations at once. Mutually exclusive pairs are rarer than non-exclusive sets. When many configurations can be perceived at once, they can often be *controlled* simultaneously (with practice) and even independently. A man can create an expressive intonation of voice, a phoneme, a posture, and a facial expression all at the same time, and think nothing of it.

Some third-order configuration-control acts are elementary and require only a few systems; a frown, for example. Some are so complex and multidimensional that one may require years to learn to control them perfectly; a ten-finger atonal chord on a piano, with the proper note voiced, for example.

However complex third-order perceptions may become, they cannot represent more than the present-time collection of sense objects that exists right now; these perceptions span time only accidentally and incidentally. A creature possessing no more than these three levels of control could correct only those errors that could be corrected by simultaneous adjustment of a set of vector forces—a single effort toward a fixed position. If application of that effort failed to correct the error, the error would remain until the environment changed. A three-order organism having reference signals provided by heredity rather than higher-order systems could not choose one state of configuration rather than another as a means of coping with changing conditions; its "choice" of reference configurations, however wide and complex the selection, would at best represent a program appropriate to the average environment over the past several hundred millenia: an "instinctual" program, in other words. Human systems need higher levels of organization, not simply more complex capacities for control of configurations.

REFERENCES

Attneave, "The Superior Colliculus." *Scientific American* 225 (1971): 63–71.

Eccles, J. C. "The Dynamic Loop Hypothesis of Movement Control." In *Information Processing in the Nervous System,* edited by K. K. Leibovic, pp. 245–69. New York: Springer-Verlag, 1969.

Eccles, J. C., Ito, M.; and Szentagothai, J. *The Cerebellum as a Neuronal Machine.* New York: Springer-Verlag, 1967.

Hess, W. R. *The Functional Organization of the Diencephalon,* translated by T. R. Hughes. New York: Grune and Stratton, 1957.

Penfield, W. and Roberts, W. *Speech and Brain Mechanisms.* Princeton: Princeton University Press, 1959.

Ranson, S. W., and Clark, S. L. *The Anatomy of the Nervous System.* Philadelphia: W. B. Saunders, 1947 ed.

Ruch, T. C. "Motor Systems." In *Handbook of Experimental Psychology,* edited by S. S. Stevens. New York: John Wiley, 1951 ed.

LEADING QUESTIONS: CHAPTER 9

1. Clench your fist hard while you are looking at it. What sensations and efforts are involved in maintaining this configuration?

2. Do the skin sensations and muscular efforts seem to be part of the clenched-fist configuration? Relax the efforts while maintaining the same visual configuration. Does it now give a different impression?

3. Look around the room for intensities and sensations: intensities as lightness and darkness, and sensations as edges, shadings, colorations. Now look around to notice shapes, locations, distances. Could the second part be done if no sensations could be detected? Is the reverse true?

4. Can you concoct a configuration consisting of sensations of texture, temperature, effort, and taste?

10

Fourth-order Control Systems: Control of Transitions

From here on, as help from experiments with the brain diminishes, the development in this book will lean more and more toward finding plausible definitions. The emphasis will turn more toward an analysis of direct experience, that same world of appearances that is normally taken for granted in the design of scientific experiments. The uncritical acceptance of appearances and the unconscious assumption that perceived properties of the external world are *objective* properties is the basic reason for the lack of the brain experiments that would be most useful here. Hence, even though we may have to use general observational data and subjective perceptions, the result will point out experiments that need to be done and data that needs informed reinterpretation.

Perception of Change

Some parts of the brain responsible for the fourth order of control and perception must be between the thalamus and the inner layer of the cerebral cortex—of that we may be reasonably sure because, as we will see in the next chapter, there is good evidence for localization of the *fifth* order of control systems in this layer of the cortex, and circumstantial evidence seems to require an intermediate level of systems. (This does not rule out "misplaced" systems of fourth order.)

The most elementary example of fourth-order perception is also the easiest to identify: without it, movies and television would not work. When a human being is presented with two related configurations in sequence, within a short enough span of time, he perceives a new entity of experience not present in either configuration alone: *change*. A continuing string of configurations is sufficient to provide the experience of movements, changes in shape, approach and recession, spinning, velocity, and many other types of change that define *transitions* from one state of the third-order world to another.

In the form of perceived motion, this phenomenon has been well studied in the visual realm. Koffka (1935) for instance, writes,

> It is a well known fact that a paper [by Wertheimer] on visual motion was the beginning of Gestalt psychology. . . . Wertheimer's paper and a number of publications which followed it dealt chiefly or exclusively with stroboscopic motion, i.e., the case where perceived motion is produced by stationary objects. . . . it has been proved beyond a doubt [citing Wertheimer, Cermak and Koffka, Duncker, Brown, van der Waals, and Roelofs from 1912 to 1933] that as far as stroboscopic dynamics are concerned there is no difference between stroboscopic and "real" motion, i.e., perceived motion produced by actually moving objects.

It is significant that for motion to be perceived, the change from one configuration to another must be neither too slow nor too fast. Too fast, and different configurations appear simultaneous; too slow, and the sense of motion is lost. The second hand on a clock rotates at a rate near the lower limit of perception— the minute hand gives no sense of motion, and a hand that would make the full round in 1/10 second would verge on a stationary blur. The range of this perception's "magnitude" is such that it would match the dynamic range to be expected of a neural signal, bounded on the lower end by statistical fluctuations (noise) and on the upper end by the maximum number of impulses per second that a nerve cell can generate—between 1,000:1 and 10,000:1, say. The sense of motion associated with a given configuration, therefore, *could* be represented by a single neural signal, or a small set of parallel signals, as required in the model.

One of the fourth-order perceptions appears to be the experience of time. Koffka cites Brown's (1931) experiments in which factors influencing apparent velocity were shown to have unequivocal correlation with judgments of time intervals; that is, mere changes in general illumination produced changes of almost 25 percent in subjectively perceived time flow (time flows faster in the dark). This is a difficult riddle since velocity is formally defined as rate of change of position with respect to time. One does not, however, experience time by itself, but only in terms of the duration of transitions—only in connection with other perceptions. There is a psychological relativity here that is tied closely—suspiciously closely—to Einstein's (1950) theory of special relativity, in which, as Minkowski put it (roughly), neither space nor time retain a separate existence, but only a union of the two remains. In human perceptual space, a string of consecutive configurations leads to a subjective impression that is clear and familiar, but which makes time itself into a special way of perceiving changing configurations. I am still baffled by this phenomenon, but once we can begin putting experiments at this level into the whole framework of the model, we may be able to see more clearly whether time has separate perceptual existence or is just another of those unfortunate verbal will-o'-the-wisps one chases.

Perception of change is not restricted to the visual field. For example, just as in the visual field a moving point of light may be simulated by lighting a string of bulbs one at a time in rapid succession (a trick that advertisers know only too well), a similar sense of change may be created in the auditory field by playing successive notes rapidly on a musical instrument (a glissando). A series of closely spaced tactile stimulations may be felt as a touch moving on the skin (a crawling bug); and a series of temperatures may be sensed as "warming" or "cooling."

Nearly any perception of the first three orders, in fact, may apparently be detected at fourth order as *change*. The phenomenon I am calling here the "perception of transitions" may explicitly involve rates of change of any perception of intensity, sensation, or configuration. This fact was noted by Notterman, Filion, and Mandriota (1971) in an article in which they explored the thresholds of detectability for translational (visual) motions, expanding lines and circles, changes in illumination, and changes in auditory intensity. There was some confounding with other orders of perception (configuration, for example), but pure rate-of-change detection was clearly shown.

Some of the discussion by the above authors is worth reproducing, if only to show that a zeitgeist is abroad:

> The behaving organism responds not only to the static magnitudes of stimuli exciting different sensory systems, but also to the manner in which these magnitudes vary as a function of time. The time derivatives of stimulus magnitude are determined partly by the environment itself . . . and partly by the feedback consequences of the organism's own immediately prior behavior. As with any other closed loop system, one must assume not only that changes in the momentary value of a discrepancy . . . are detectable, but also that changes in the rate at which the discrepancy [error] is being reduced to zero are detectable. If these two changes were not detectable, then the detecting and correcting entity, whether electromechanical or biological, would tend to overshoot or to undershoot or to oscillate about its mark. Despite the behavioral implications of these principles, no description of the general capacity to perceive changes in stimulus rate seems to be available.

Besides showing that others have noticed the same "obvious" phenomena with which we are concerned in this chapter, the excerpt brings up another point of importance: the difference between *perceptually explicit* and *unperceived* functions in behavioral control systems.

The *perception* of rate of change in this chapter is the first appearance of time variables that are explicitly experienced. The steady-state condition of a fourth-order perceptual signal represents a constantly changing state in lower-order perceptions. There is considerable evidence, however, that rate-of-change signals occur even at first order even though we experience only what seems to us a proportional representation of external stimulus magnitudes. Thus, for control systems of lower orders we must think of rate-of-change signals as being part of the dynamic design of the control systems and *not* as the controlled quantity. This point of view is automatically ensured by adopting the time scale appropriate to the level being discussed and considering the steady state of the perceptual signal. Perceptions are being defined throughout this model by asking the significance of a perceptual signal when it is being maintained at the same magnitude as a fixed reference signal.

When we reach fourth order, we find that a constant impression is given by continuous change. Other time functions might possibly be similarly represented—acceleration, for example—but that is a proposition to be settled by experiment.

Control of Transitions

Any perception of change can, given the objective means, be placed under feedback control by a fourth-order control system. When a dancer moves fluidly from an erect stance to a prone position, not only the starting and finishing configurations of the body are under control, but the speed and organization of the transition as well. The speed of each movement is precisely regulated; the fall of an arm is not an accident of gravity but an arduously practiced example of rate-of-change control. A racing driver about to negotiate a turn at the limit of adhesion controls his speed by judging the rate of expansion of objects in his foveal vision and the radial speed of peripheral objects, juggling braking and acceleration to keep these fourth-order perceptions rigidly at the level he has learned is necessary. Even a horse has fourth-order control systems; he plods up a hill pulling a cart at a steady pace, and plods down the other side (all efforts reversed) at the same speed.

These are all examples involving time, but I strongly suspect that this is too narrow a view of fourth-order behavior, especially considering our apparent lack of time sensors. A more general concept of transitions that may prove valid is that of *partial derivatives* (perhaps with time as a parameter in the perceptual computations). A partial derivative is roughly the same as the proportion of change of one variable with respect to a change in another variable: $\Delta X{:}\Delta Y$. It would seem that some such computation is required in order to establish a motion in a particular direction or along a particular curve in space: a baseball player running to catch a fly ball is controlling the apparent path of the ball relative to himself; it has been conjectured that he keeps the ball apparently *rising* at a slow rate until the moment he catches it. This implies not only time changes but space directions.

If we think of control of transitions as the control of motion along a curve (in any perceptual space, not just visual space), the concept of fourth order is considerably broadened, including the way in which a person makes one configuration turn smoothly into another, and the way in which many perceptions vary in proportion to others—as one might anxiously judge the rate of rise of water level in a bath in proportion to the rate of increase in temperature as hot water is added. Usually time *is* a parameter, for it usually makes a difference how fast the curve is traversed, but in many cases the time element is not controlled. If a basketball player is running to intercept an opposing player who has the ball, he adjusts his own speed of running in proportion to that of the opponent to keep the line joining them shortening without changing direction. The captain watching the swelling image of another ship is trying to avoid the same perceptual situation. Such actions may involve higher-order considerations, but perhaps not.

Brain Experiments

Penfield and Roberts (1959) report that stimulation of the *second somatic sensory area of the cerebral cortex* results in the "desire to move" or a "sense of movement." Of course we cannot tell whether the system in question was at the point of stimulation or simply received the resulting neural signals some distance away, nor does the term *movement* guarantee that rate of change was the essence of the controlled event.*

I believe it was Penfield who noted a specifically fourth-order effect of brain stimulation in or just beneath the cerebral cortex: the patient reported that the current caused the visual image of the doctor to seem to be approaching rapidly, even though there was obviously no actual movement. This may be an example of a fourth-order perception experienced in isolation from its normal precursors of configurations, sensations, and intensities.

Fourth-order output functions must contain time integrators (chap. 4) to create constantly changing third-order output signals in response to steady error signals. Thus we would expect the relevant parts of the brain to be heavily populated with closed loops of neurones, so-called reverberating circuits.

*It is somewhat naive to assume that the part of the brain stimulated is the part in control of the observed effects, a fact that weakens all "localization" experiments. As Baldwin (1960) noted, excision of an area of the brain that produced memories on stimulation does not eliminate the ability to remember the same events. One cannot stimulate "one area" of the brain, for the resulting signals may go *anywhere*. Nevertheless, we have to use all the hints available.

Fourth-order Behavior

At fourth order—and not before—we reach the level of organization required to execute a controlled movement, to create a rising or falling tone of voice, to trace out a path in space, or in general to control a smooth transition from one configuration, sensation, or intensity to another. This kind of control is to be contrasted with third-order control, in which transitions to a new state (implied by a suddenly appearing reference signal) occur as fast as the control systems are capable of acting. Controlled transitions must necessarily be slower than third-order corrections would be, primarily to prevent instability. The result will be that the third-order reference signals, the means by which fourth-order systems adjust the magnitudes of their own rate-of-change perceptual signals, will never change so fast as to cause appreciable error in third-order control systems.

References

Baldwin, M. "Electrical Stimulation of the Mesial Temporal Region." In *Electrical Studies on the Unanesthetized Brain,* edited by E. R. Ramey and D. S. O'Doherty. New York; Hoeber, 1960.

Brown, J. F. "On Time Perception in Visual Movement Fields." *Psychologishe Forschrift* 14 (1931): 233–48. [Koffka's reference]

Einstein, A. *The Meaning of Relativity.* Princeton; Princeton University Press, 1950.

Koffka, F. *Principles of Gestalt Psychology.* New York; Harcourt and Brace, 1935.

Notterman, J. M., Filion, R. D. L., and Mandriota, F. J. "Perception of Changes in Certain Exteroceptive Stimuli." *Science* 173 (1971): 1206–11.

Penfield, W., and Roberts, L. *Speech and Brain Mechanism.* Princeton; Princeton University Press, 1959.

Leading Questions: Chapter 10

1. Anyone who owns a television set knows what a ricochet sounds like, since *all* bullets ricochet on TV. The configuration involved at any instant is a pattern of pitch sensations and a buzz sensation. What change in perception is involved?

2. It is known that vision blanks out when the eye jumps from one point of fixation to another. The world does not appear to move, although the visual field changes. Why is there no sense of movement? Why *is* there a sense of movement when the eyelid is pulled to move the eyeball mechanically?

3. Focus on your own finger and move it slowly sideways. Now the background *does* give a sense of motion. Why? If the background contained *no* configurations, familiar or unfamiliar, could that sense of motion occur?

4. What auditory change perception is commonly perceived as approach? Is there a comparable visual perception?

5. "Toppling" is the rate of change of what configuration?

6. How could you tell without looking that your hand is approaching a hot burner on the stove? Without the ability to detect change, could you always avoid being burned?

11

Fifth-order Control Systems: Control of Sequence

If we imagine that the perceptual signals of all levels through fourth order somehow can become objects of awareness, we can ask at this point what the world looks like to this brain. Movement and rate of change can be detected; there are objects and arrangements and static patterns that can be seen; each configuration decomposes into a variety of sensations; and with each sensation is associated some average degree of intensity. The organism can cause configurations of its own limbs to change at controlled rates, can maintain static configurations against disturbances, can control the magnitudes of sensations (which we sometimes call vectors), and can at least control the intensity of its own effort signals.

What we have, however, is still a very elementary organism, no matter how complex its equipment for handling variables for these four levels may be. It can control its own position and some external configurations; it can control movement. Nothing more. It cannot, for example, select one movement instead of another; if any organisms exist with only four orders of control system, the reference signals for movement must originate either from stimuli, or from genetically transmitted and stored information. We cannot even say that this organism is skilled, for although it can make configurations change at controlled rates, it cannot select when or in what combination to produce these changes.

Neurological Evidence

The next step in the model takes us once again to a new class of perceptual quantity and introduces the control systems which generate the reference signals for motion. We are looking for the systems that do what Hess did when he slowly varied the frequency of electrical impulses and made a cat's head swing smoothly from one side to the other. There is neurological evidence for the nature of this next level of control; the kind of behavior associated with it is strikingly different from all lower-order behaviors.

Brain-stimulation experiments provide a direct hint. Bickford, Dodge, and Vilhein (1960) report the results of injecting electrical impulses into the region just below the precentral cortex, where we might expect to find the next level of organization. This particular experiment was done in a woman's brain, while she was awake. When impulses were injected in the range of one to eight per second, an endless variety of repetitive movements of the extremities occurred, beginning a few seconds after stimulation began and persisting for a few seconds after the last electrical impulse. Some of these repetitive movements involved just a finger or a hand; others involved movements of two or more limbs, such as rubbing one foot against the other. In one case the subject began rotating anything held in the hands, by inching the fingers around the edge of it. An increase in frequency of the stimulating impulses increased the frequency and intensity of the actions. Forcible attempts to stop the actions were resisted, and sometimes when one sequence was blocked another would begin in its place. As we would expect from this model, the kind of action depended on where the stimulation was injected; one signal generally caused one kind of behavior.

The kind of behavior seen here specifically involves control of sequences; the inching of the fingers along the edge of a piece of newspaper requires opening and closing the fingers, moving the hands toward and away from each other alternately. There is clearly something more involved than just movement, for successful execution of these actions requires producing the configurations and movements in the correct sequence. The sequence in which one hand releases the paper, moves over, grasps it, and then the other hand does the same thing, determines which way the paper will move in the hands. The same movements put together in a different sequence would result in tearing the paper.

There is good behavioral evidence that the brain structures just beneath the cerebral cortex, in the "limbic system," are essential for the execution of sequential behaviors, or for perceiving the difference between one sequence of input patterns and another. Pribram (1960) says explicitly, "Limbic system function is . . . conceived to be related primarily to the mechanism of the execution of complex sequences of action."

Control of Sequences

Experientially, it seems that a sequence is always a sequence of lower-order elements, and that there is no intermediate step between presentation of elements and recognition of a sequence. The two configurations A and B are perceived as one sequence when presented A,B, and as a different sequence when presented B,A. The sequence *fast, slow*, is perceived differently from the sequence *slow, fast*.

I propose, therefore, that the fifth order of control system in this model should be associated with perception and control of the sequence in which lower-order perceptions occur. This would mean that five orders of control system are required to produce the simple behavior we call walking.

For control to exist, at least in the terms of this model, we must try to conceive an organization that can sense the state of a sequence, and produce a signal indicating that a particular sequence is in progress. The perceptual signal emitted by a fifth-order input function will not *be* a sequence, but will stand for presence of a particular sequence. Since this must be a one-dimensional signal if unambiguous control is to be achieved, we must ask about the dimensions of the space in which sequences exist; that is, the ways in which what we call a sequence can change.

A sequence is a string of distinct elements. One way in which such a string can be altered is to change the order in which some of the elements occur. In short sequences composed of few elements, especially those in which elements occur one at a time (as in a telephone number), any change at all may destroy the sense that a particular sequence is occurring. Other sequences, in which less critical information is involved, may still be partially sensed even though some elements are missing or interchanged; for instance, the string of (spoken) letters, "Mississppi." One perceives that as not quite the same as "Mississippi," but the error in the sequence is small enough to permit nearly the same sense of the sequence.

Every sensory modality can be involved in perception and control of sequences. A melody is a sequence of pitches; a chord progression is a sequence of pitch configurations; the bouncing of a ball is a sequence of rising and falling motions; tying the shoelaces requires execution of a sequence of movements and kinesthetic configurations.

The brain-stimulation experiments which have been done at this level suggest something more about the sequences which are perceived and controlled at fifth order: they are *unitary*. That is to say, they are short, stereotyped, and well learned. One word for such elementary sequences is *event*, and I like this term because it expresses a subjective fact about short and familiar sequences, a fact that is consistent with the way this model deals with all perceptions by means of one-dimensional signals. When an event begins, a person immediately, or shortly thereafter, gets an impression of a particular event in progress, and this impression remains throughout the event. Take the sequence of kinesthetic perceptions involved in a golf swing: there are actually many configurations and many different motions involved in taking a swing at a golf ball, but one does not perceive them separately unless he is deliberately paying attention to the details. Rather, one senses "the groove," the swing as a whole from start to end. Or another example: the pianist executing a difficult phrase is producing a very complex series of configurations and motions, but it often happens that when there is an error he cannot say which detail was wrong without reviewing the sequence in memory or playing it again; he has detected an error at fifth order, but was not paying conscious attention to the lower-order details.

The very fact that we perceive experience broken up into familiar events, for many of which we have names, indicates that there is a definite mode of perception involved. The sense of *the same thing continuing to happen* as the event proceeds indicates, according to our basic postulates about perception, that one event is detected and reported in the form of one signal. The fact that events depend for their constancy on the sequence in which the details occur, regardless of speed in many cases, indicates the kind of input functions that must be involved, devices that receive some set of signals and produce outputs as a function of the order in which the signals occur, with a maximum output for one and only one sequence.

A reference signal sent to a sequence control system specifies that some particular sequence is to be made to appear in perception. Initially, that sequence is *not* occurring, so there is an error that causes the output function to act. As the sequence progresses the output function of this system must produce reference signals for motion and configuration controlling systems in the correct order. The fact that stimulation of the brain can cause repetitive execution of sequential behaviors implies that the output function is like an automatic code generator; it is organized like a shift register or a paper tape reader to produce the detailed reference signals leading to the perceived event, and if the error signal persists—that is, if the reference signal is maintained—the sequence of output signals simply repeats. If error is detected, a common response is to halt the sequence and start over, or finish out hastily and then repeat it.

One class of events which human beings sense and produce is of special interest: words. A spoken word can be considered as a particular sequence made up of phonemes (third order) and diphthongs (fourth order). At fifth order we have just enough mechanism to allow producing the coordinated actions of jaw, tongue, vocal cords, and diaphragm necessary to generate a word as a unitary sound event, and to perceive that a word has been spoken. Because of the assumptions basic to this model, we have to assume that if a person has a speaking vocabulary of 30,000 words, he possesses 30,000 fifth-order control systems for uttering those words; if he can recognize as familiar 150,000 words, he possesses 150,000 input functions of fifth order devoted to just that one task, and as many more for recognizing written words, although those may be dealt with at third order as unitary configurations.

Since these numbers seem a little outrageous, it may be well to pause a moment to consider how a word-recognizing input function *might* be organized, just as a check of feasibility, and not as a guess as to how it is actually done. The task is made rather easier than it might otherwise be by the fact that we have signals available (from lower-order systems) which stand for the major units of speech: in principle we only need sixty-odd third-order signals to represent all phonemes an English-speaking American can recognize as different, plus a few fourth-order systems to recognize common transitions from one phoneme to another, such as *oi*. Given the signal for the three phonemes in the word *juice,* how might a computer be designed, working in terms of neural currents, which would emit maximum signal when these signals occur in the sequence *j, oo, ss?*

We will take advantage of another known property of some synaptic connections, namely, that some cells will not fire until several input signals are present; that is, some cells have a high threshold, so that in effect a constant is always subtracted from the sum of input currents.

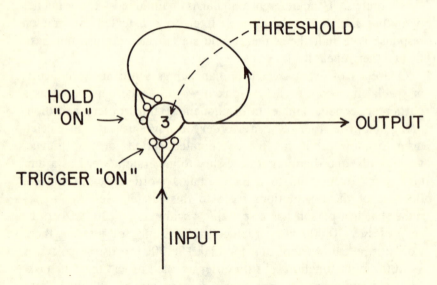

FIGURE 11.1.

First, we need to construct a storage element which can be turned on or off by input signals and will stay in whatever state it was left. The simplest type one could construct on the basis of the neural-current model would be a one-neurone version of the neural integrator, a cell with output fibers that loop back to excite the same cell. Just for schematic convenience, let us say that every storage cell has a threshold of three units, and that all input signals carry a signal of one unit of magnitude. When a path branches, *each* branch carries one unit of signal. (See fig. 11.1)

This storage cell receives an input signal which branches into one, two, or three copies of the same signal. Its "recirculation" loop (I won't call it a "feedback" loop for obvious reasons) may also branch into one, two, or three copies of the signal. Let us set up first the storage element receiving the third-order signal from the third-order input function that recognizes the phoneme *j* (I'm not trying to follow any formal linguistic convention here). We want this signal always to commence the recognition process, so we let this input have three branches. An input signal, then, will cause the cell to begin firing, and the recirculation loop produces a strong enough input signal by itself to maintain that firing indefinitely. The input signal standing for *j* turns this element on, and this element will stay on indefinitely afterward.

The second phoneme to be recognized will be *oo*. When the signal appears standing for *oo,* we want to turn on a second storage element, but if, and only if, the first one is already on: this condition means that the second element will turn on only if *oo* occurs *after j.*

Therefore we take a copy of the recirculating signal from the first storage element and connect it with a weight of *one* to the second element, and we give the *oo* signal input a weight of two: furthermore, we give the second element's recirculation path a weight of only two, so the second element will neither fire nor maintain itself in the on state unless the first element is also on (see fig. 11.2).

Next, the storage element for the *ss* phoneme is constructed; it is identical to the second, and receives a copy of the recirculating current from the second element. The third element will not turn on until both *j* and *oo* have occurred. We will take a copy of the signal from the third element and call this the perceptual signal emitted by this word recognizer, since the last signal will appear if, and only if, the three phonemes occur in the order *j, oo, ss.*

Finally, we need a way to reset this circuit to its initial stage after an output signal has been generated. The easiest way is to take a copy of the output signal and run it back to storage element number one with an inhibitory connection. This will halt the neural current in element one. Since a signal from element one is needed to keep element two on, element two will also turn off, and that will finally turn off element three and the output signal will disappear (see fig. 11.3).

It may be starting to become clear just why a model in which

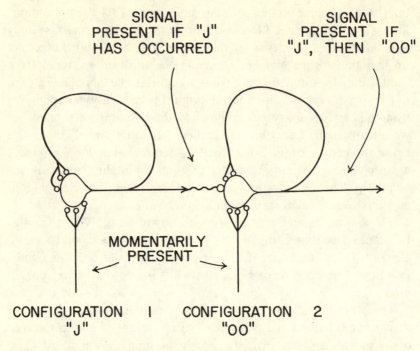

FIGURE 11.2.

signals are one-dimensional leads to a very parsimonious model in terms of the number of neurones required, even though there appears to be a great wastefulness in terms of the number of individual systems required. Also, I hope it is beginning to be-

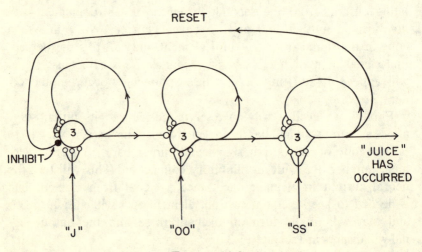

FIGURE 11.3.

come evident why the idea of definite orders of perception is attractive; the above little circuit happens to be set up to recognize the word *juice,* after the individual phonemes have been detected, but it could represent the circuit for recognizing any three-phoneme word. All that distinguishes one word from another, as far as this circuit is concerned, is where the signals come from; these happen to come from the third-order systems that respond to *j, oo,* and *ss,* but the signals would look exactly the same if they came from third-order systems responding to *b, uh,* and *g.* This means that for the general task of recognizing spoken words on the basis of the sequential order of phonemes, one needs a collection of structurally identical, sequence-recognizing circuits. Obviously the circuit above could be extended to respond to sequences of any length. We could make the operation even more realistic if we added a summing neurone which received copies of all of the recirculating currents. As the sequence progressed, this sum signal would get larger and larger as each storage element in turn went to the *on* state, and for incomplete sequences a person would have at least some perceptual signal.

The main point is not how clever we could be in designing fifth-order, sequence-recognizing circuits, but how few neurones are required: just one per phoneme in a word. If we assume for discussion six phonemes per average word, this would mean that a recognition vocabulary of 150,000 words would require a maximum of 900,000 neurones (better design would require far less), and this number of neurones would occupy something like 150 cubic millimeters, or 1/6 cubic centimeter of brain tissue. Six-fold, or sixty-fold redundancy would still be quite sparing of neural capacity. Furthermore, one very puzzling phenomenon would be taken care of by this model without strain: if someone says "gilp," the listener knows immediately that this is not any word he knows: he simply gets no recognition signal from *any* fifth-order system.

Summary

In summary, I am proposing that the fifth level of organization in the brain consists of systems for detecting and controlling the sequence in which lower-order quantities occur, singly or in groups. Production of a specific sequence-event requires sending a reference signal to the fifth-order system specifically organized to produce that event; perceptual signals generated by fifth-order input functions (whether involved in a negative feedback control system or not) represent the fact that a given event is in progress or has occurred but are themselves simply one-dimensional signals, not sequences. Brain-stimulation experiments show that a regular uncoded train of electrical impulses injected into the regions of the brain where we might expect fifth-order systems to reside does in fact cause the execution of short, simple sequential behaviors.

REFERENCES

Bickford, R. G., Dodge, H. W., Jr., and Vihlein, A. "Electrographic and Behavioral Effects Related to Depth Stimulation in Human Patients." In *Electrical Studies on the Unanesthetized Brain,* edited by E. R. Ramey, and D. S. O'Doherty. New York: Hoeber, 1960.
Pribram, K. H. "A Review of Theory in Physiological Psychology." *An. Rev. Psych* 11 (1960): 1–40.

LEADING QUESTIONS: CHAPTER 11

1. Recall your actions in getting dressed this morning (or every morning). How many distinct events can you recall? Is there any event that is not composed of controlled movements and key configurations in a particular sequence?

2. People learning a foreign language often complain that native speakers run their words together. What is the problem in terms of fifth-order perception?

3. Eeyore, Pooh Bear's donkey friend, was given a broken balloon and an empty pot for his BTHTHDY. The episode ended with Eeyore happily putting the ballon in the pot, taking it out, putting it in, etc. Was Eeyore putting the balloon in and taking it out, or taking it out and putting it in? Does a grandfather clock go "tic-toc, tic-toc" or "toc-tic, toc-tic"?

4. By the way, how does the theory of fifth-order explain how we can recognize "BTHTHDY"?

5. The opening event of Beethoven's Fifth Symphony (the V-for-victory theme) is composed of two sound configurations and a change. What are they, and what would happen to one's recognition of that event if the same configurations and the change occurred in a different sequence? Why do I not call their sound *sensations?* How would it sound if the change were not perceived as such?

The Brain's Model

The five levels of perception which have been more or less defined in the past few chapters consist of signals which have been derived from the interaction of physical quantities and sensory endings through five successive steps. Under the basic postulate of perception (that all perceptions are neural signals and are all that is available to awareness), these signals constitute an analogue model of the external world. Let us drop back to first-order input functions, to see what this means.

A first-order input function can be defined as a set of sensory receptors which always respond at the same time (the most likely tie being physical proximity). The signal emitted by this first-order input function is produced by a physical quantity, and the magnitude of the neural current depends on the intensity of stimulation. Whatever the relationship, whether linear or nonlinear, it can be said that the neural current is an analogue of the physical quantities.

Analogues in the precise sense meant here, however, must always be stated so that it is clear what is an analogue of what: a neural current which arises because of contact of the hand with an object is not an analogue *of that object;* one neural current simply does not have enough degrees of freedom to represent every important aspect of the object. Rather, the neural current is the analogue of the magnitude of the physical effects that are causing the neurone to fire, in this case the magnitude of pressure, or deformation of tissues.

147

Saying that the neural current is an analogue of an external quantity like pressure means that there is a one-to-one correspondence between the magnitude of the neural current and the magnitude of the physical event: the analogue is *quantitative*. It would be possible, knowing the relationship between external variable and neural current, to use the magnitude of the neural current as a meter reading to indicate the state of the external quantity. In fact, the relationship between a first-order neural current and the quantity of which it is the analogue is precisely the same as the relationship between the pointer position on a meter and the quantity which the magnitude reading is supposed to represent. The meter and the apparatus feeding current to it are functioning as the first level of perceptual interpretation in the brain: they respond to the magnitude of some physical quantity and present the result in the form of a number.

As mentioned much earlier, the brain can experience only the environment that is represented in this first-order analogue of the quantities at the first-order sensory interface. The set of all such first-order signals, then, is the reality with which the rest of the brain deals: it is a first-order model of something lying outside the nervous system. Being of first order, it represents that external world as a set of magnitudes, and we know entities that can vary only in magnitude as quantities or numbers. A given signal is like an algebraic symbol: it has a fixed identity, but can take on any magnitude over a range, a continuum, of magnitudes. All that can be known about the external world is implicit in this first-order model.

The second level of perception has as input the signals which are analogues of intensities of stimulation. The resulting second-order perceptual signals are therefore analogues of quantities implicit in the first-order signals. One might say that the second-order input functions convert certain quantities from being implicit to being explicit. It must be realized, however, that there is nothing in principle that makes any particular implicit function of first-order signals more "real" than any other: there is an infinity of ways to combine first-order signals to yield second-order signals, and every one of them would, in this model, provide a signal that could be perceived as a part of "objective reality."

What gives all second-order signals something in common is not the choice of first-order signals to be combined, but the type of transformation that is applied to sets of first-order signals to convert them into second-order perceptual signals; to convert them, that is, to sensations or vectors. Every weighted sum of first-order signals yields some vector, some sensation signal. Such signals have in common with each other the fact that they are derived from the first-order analogue by a certain type of quantitative process.

If first-order signals are analogues of environmental intensities, (the local magnitudes of physical interactions with sense organs), to what do the second-order signals correspond? Of what are *they* to be considered the analogues? A very interesting possibility is suggested if we look at a linear approximation to the way in which an external reality might be related to two first-order and one second-order systems.

Suppose there are two quantities in the external world, and that both of them affect each of two first-order input functions. This means that the intensity of stimulation at each first-order sensor is an ambiguous indicator of the magnitudes of the two quantities, q_1 and q_2. Let q_1 be connected by a scaling factor a_1 to the first sensor, and q_2 be connected by a scaling factor b_1 to the same sensor, so that the first-order intensity signal emitted by that sensor is

$$s_1^1 = a_1 q_1 + b_1 q_2$$

In the same way, the scaling factors a_2 and b_2 determine the contributions from q_1 and q_2 to the second sensor, so the other first-order intensity signal is

$$s_2^1 = a_2 q_1 + b_2 q_2$$

Now let us sum the two signals s_1^1 and s_2^1 in a second-order input function, but using carefully chosen weights: let the first signal be weighted by a number proportional to b_2, and the second be weighted negatively by a weight proportional to b_2. The result will be a second-order signal s_1^2 (superscripts indicate order and are not exponents):

$$s_1^2 = (a_1 b_2 - a_2 b_1) q_1 \text{ [note that } q_2 \text{ does not appear]}$$

Because of the special way the weights were chosen, the second-order signal is a function of q_1 *only,* and is unaffected by variations of q_2. In effect the second-order weighting can be adjusted to produce a signal analogous to the magnitude of a quantity once removed from the sensory interface. The first-order signals each stand only for the magnitude of total stimulation from all sources at each input function; the second-order signal we have just created stands for quantities *which are an immediate cause of the first-order input intensities.* The fact that this *can* be done may mean that it *is* done by the nervous system.

This does not prove, of course, that real nervous systems work this way; certainly they would not be able to do a precise sorting out of independent causes of intensity signals, just because the systems are not linear. But such a process is *possible,* and furthermore we know that what are loosely termed *sensations* seem to correspond to physical properties of the external world that are not uniquely represented at any one sensory ending: a temperature sensation, for example. Temperature is not, strictly speaking, a quantity that can be sensed. All the first-order temperature sensors can respond to is the flow of heat across their boundaries, in or out. Yet when one feels warmth, he is feeling something that the physicist can show is one of the variable attributes of matter, and if one can sort out the intensity signal from the kind-of-sensation signal, he will see that the sensation of warmth is reasonably invariant with respect to which sensors are responding to it and with respect to many other intensity signals that may arise at the same time from touching a warm object.

We may be permitted to guess, then, that second-order perceptual signals are analogues of variable attributes of the external world, simple physical attributes which can also be measured, in most cases, by physical instrumentation. The weighting that takes place at a second-order input function sorts out one attribute from another even though the effects at first order are mixed together. The vector efforts of which we spoke in chapter 8, derived from effort-intensity signals by appropriate weighted summation, are simply attributes of a particular part of the environment and would be analogues of directed forces.

Now the brain contains two models, the second derived from the first. The first model represents the external world as a set of individual magnitudes, pure numbers. The second model represents the first model as a collection of variable attributes, of sensations or vectors.

The third level of perception receives "stimuli" in the form of sensation signals, and perhaps also of intensity signals. The resulting third-order perceptual signals are again derived from lower-order information by a particular type of transformation, one that yields invariants of a more sophisticated kind. Each third-order signal represents the "location" of some elementary configuration along the path that constitutes its continuum of change. The signals of third order, then, are analogues of still another aspect of the external world—perhaps, to pick one possible example, one characteristic of an object, the same object that was represented at second order as a collection of simple attributes and at first order as a collection of overlapping intensities. A step upward in the hierarchy of perception corresponds to a step outward in the complexity of external organizations being analogized in the brain. The brain's model of reality now includes the basic characteristics of configurations. If a person were to acquire a new third-order perceptual transformation, he would suddenly see a new configuration spring into objective existence in the world outside him, as one suddenly perceives a disguised pattern. Of course, we believe that the pattern was there all the time, but that is a trivial observation: all possible patterns, useful and useless, are there all the time. We perceive, however, only in terms of the patterns which our third-order systems are organized to construct from lower-order information.

Fourth-order input functions add to the model the things we call change and motion. When external entities move relative to others or relative to the sensing organs, the configurations which are models of them change, and at fourth order those changes themselves become entities in the model. Coordinated changes become paths through the environment, or directions, or simply rates of change. Not until the model reaches the fourth level of organization do the changes in the lower-order parts of the model become perceivable parts of the model.

Finally, at fifth order, changes of configurations of sensations made of intensities become grouped into new space-time entities that we call events or sequences. These take their place alongside all the other elements of the brain's model of reality and represent reality in a way dictated once again by the intervening perceptual transformations.

The brain's model of reality, as far as consciousness is concerned, *is* reality—there is nothing else to perceive. The behavior of this model is the behavior of reality; when one acts to affect reality, he is acting so as to affect this model, and he has no inkling, save for physics, of what he is really doing to the external world in the process of making his brain's model behave in various ways. He cannot sense the neural networks that cause the implicit properties of one model to be represented explicitly at a higher level as a different kind of model; he perceives only the consequences of these transformations. What we are doing in this book is adding to our brains' models a new model, one which represents the transformations that we cannot perceive. This process of making a model of the brain's model is not infinitely regressive, any more than it is infinitely regressive to define, say, a well-formed function in logic as a relationship between two well-formed functions. The model may be recursive, but it is not regressive.

The higher levels of organization with which we will now attempt to deal—not, I am afraid, with complete success—live in an environment composed of the five levels of models already defined. As has been true at every level, the next higher level possesses outputs that enter this environment and cause it to change, and the next higher level also possesses input functions such that these changes result in altered perceptions. There is feedback, and since we do not observe the symptoms of positive feedback, it is negative and stable. Not every perceptual signal is necessarily under feedback control, but those that are under control must be controlled with respect to reference signals as usual. That is the model we are committed to for the time being, and we will stick to it as long as possible. To do less would invite irrelevant criticisms.

LEADING QUESTIONS: CHAPTER 12

1. If intensity, sensation, configuration, change, and sequence are *created* by human perceptual functions, does that imply that no external reality exists?

2. How are the observations of physics limited by the nature of the first five orders of human perception?

3. Reductionists insist on describing behavior in pseudo-objective terms: for example, "the organism made a jumping movement." What levels of perception are being taken for granted, and what levels are being ignored? What specific level of perception is employed by an observer making the above statement?

4. A scientist tells a visitor in his laboratory, a layman, "Read that unlabeled meter for me, will you?" Will the visitor say, "Three point two disintegrations per second" or will he say "three point two"?

5. When would the word *Mississippi* most likely be perceived as a configuration, and when as a sequence event? Why do we read faster than we can listen?

13

Higher Levels

We now pass from classes of perception that can be seen as exterior to ourselves to those which seem to be inside ourselves—from the world of "physical reality" to the world of "subjective reality." This model makes no special distinction between these subdivisions, however; they are matters of training, convention, and convenience as far as we are concerned here. *All* levels are "inside"; of what lies outside our sensory endings we know next to nothing. The level we are about to consider is a transitional one, for certain of its aspects seem easy to conceive of as aspects of the solid, real, lower-order world, while other aspects strike us more as conceptual in nature.

Sixth-order Control Systems: Control of Relationships

Consider a typical behavioral experiment. A subject learns to repeat a list of words. After an interval he is tested for recall. Later the same experiment is repeated, but this time a second list has to be learned between a new initial list and the later recall test. It is found that learning the intervening list interferes with recall of the initial list. This phenomenon is named *retroactive inhibition*, and takes its place as a scientific fact. Clearly the experiment consists of observable events in the sense of our model: the question is, what has been learned about an organization of higher level than events? Does this experiment help us construct another level in the model? Not in any obvious way.

One could go on looking at other types of events in the hope of seeing the nature of the next level up. One could try experiments involving lights, bells, visual images, and other stimulus events and requiring speaking, writing, bar-pressing, pointing, and other response events. A long list of experimentally defined facts would result. But the facts would show no unifying principle common to all these experiments, and we would still see no hint of the nature of the next level of organization. And we never would, as long as we failed to notice what is most obviously common to all these experiments.

The common factor is not in the experiments but in the *experimenter*. What is the experimenter perceiving or trying to perceive in all these experiments with events? He is trying to see *relationships* among the events. He is looking for cause-effect relationships, exclusive-or relationships, implication relationships, space-time relationships, statistical relationships, or even just associative relationships. To do this he must obviously possess the ability to perceive and control relationships, and that is the nature of *his* next level above the event level of organization.

The experimenter's own point of view is the factor we are looking for. The experimenter perceives and manipulates relationships but is not necessarily aware that he is doing so. He is looking at events outside himself, and when he perceives a relationship, it, too, seems to reside outside himself. His own ability to see events in terms of relationships may go unnoticed because it is part of himself, not an attribute of the observed events. Yet that ability, not its specific application to specific events, is what we must incorporate into our model. More than that: any experimenter who fails to make that ability part of his model of himself will fail to notice evidence of its existence in his subject and will never think of doing experiments concerning the subject's ability to perceive and control relationships. He will deal with relationships as if they were "objectively real" parts of the outside world, laws connecting some events to other events. Sometimes he may find these relationships very puzzling, as the term *retroactive inhibition* might suggest, simply because he does not see them as subjective interpretations imposed as much by his own perceptual organization as by the reality he believes himself to be studying.

The sixth order of perception and control in our model is hypothesized to concern relationships, those invariants that appear in collections of independent events and lower-order perceptions. A perceived relationship results from the response of a sixth-order input function to some collection of lower-order perceptions. When those perceptions provide an example of the appropriate invariant within some range of similarity, the relationship is perceived to an appropriate degree. By adjusting lower-order reference signals and thus altering perceptual inputs (both controlled and indirectly controlled), a sixth-order system creates and maintains whatever degree of the particular relationship it is being told (via its reference signal) to perceive.

Controlling a relationship perception may or may not have external significance. Placing a lens and a piece of paper in a specific relationship to the sun does appear to have significant consequences detectable by independent means. Placing the lens against one's forehead and uttering a curse has significance only in the perceptions of human beings who have learned to perceive those simultaneous and sequential events as an example of a special relationship.

Purely empirical studies of behavior tend to concentrate on studies of relationships among events (or motions, configurations, etc.). Such studies often result in essentially inexplicable results, simply because they cannot take into account any higher-order considerations. Not only is there no easy way to tell whether a given observed relationship really has objective importance (as opposed to statistical significance), but if an experimenter's point of view is limited to the relationship level *as a matter of principle*, he cannot help missing higher-order organizing principles that govern the subject's behavior and thus explain *why* certain relationships are seen. Indeed, if he notices indications of higher-order organization, he is likely to reject them as anthropomorphisms, scientific errors on his part.

Not all experimenters, of course, so limit themselves. In the past twenty years, there have been many illuminating studies of the higher-order processes we are considering here. An example of a specific study involving sixth-order systems, which will also serve as an entry into higher-level systems, is the work of Bruner,

Goodnow, and Austin (1956). These authors were studying *concept attainment*, a term which we will see encompasses many levels in our model, as well as involves subjects we cannot deal with until later, learning and memory.

Common to one set of these experiments was an array of eighty-one cards, each bearing a design made of a limited set of lower-order elements. Around the edge of each card could be a single, double, or triple border line; on each card could be one, two, or three identical geometric shapes, the shapes being either squares, pluses, or circles. In addition, the shapes could be printed in green, red, or black. Bruner, Goodnow, and Austin conceived this situation as consisting of four attributes (border, color, shape, and number of shapes), each with three values. The subjects' task was to discover a concept exemplified by a "focus card" indicated by the experimenter, through the subjects' pointing at supposed positive instances of the concept and receiving a "yes" or "no" answer from the experimenter.

Three general types of concepts or categories were defined. A *conjunctive* category was defined as the conjunction of attributes each with some value, as *three red circles*. The authors describe this as the conjunction of *three* (shapes), *redness*, and *circles*, which is the logical *and* relationship.

Their *disjunctive* category "may be illustrated by that class of cards . . . that possess three red circles *or* any constituent thereof: three figures, red figures, circles, three red figures, red circles, or three circles." This collection is simply the logical *or* relationship: *three* or *red* or *circles*, which expression is true in formal logic if at least one element is present.

The third class of concept was the *relational* category, "a specific relationship between defining attributes." Since the other two classes of concept are specifically the logical *and* and the logical *or*, it seems safe to say that what Bruner et al. mean by a concept is what I mean by a relationship. There is, however, some difficulty in accepting that appearance without more critical analysis.

In the array of cards there seem to be four attributes, each with three values. The authors are led to conclude that the array contains 255 different conjunctive concepts, apparently on the basis that each attribute can have any one value while the others cycle through the remaining possibilities, and so on, leading to 81 four-attribute concepts, 108 three-attribute concepts, 54 two-attribute concepts, and 12 one-attribute concepts. If this analysis were correct, we would have to conclude that the relationship level in our model includes elements from the sensation level as well as the configuration level, and that a different relationship must be perceived for every different combination of lower-order perceptions. That would make the meaning of *relationship* trivial. There is, however, good evidence that the number of relationships is not nearly as large as seems to be the case in this experiment.

According to the authors' analysis of the best systematic strategy, isolating one concept requires a minimum of four steps (using the "conservative focusing" strategy, p. 87). If 255 categories really existed, however, the minimum possible number of steps using the maximally efficient binary partitioning approach would be 8 ($2^8 = 256$). According to the results, it seems that only four steps are really needed, and thus that there are 16 items involved ($2^4 = 16$). The null case is excluded, leaving 15.

We can see that there are really only 15 items by looking at the structure of the task. Because of the rules of the experiment, any configuration could be eliminated from consideration by showing that a *change* in its constituent sensations made no difference. (If I stretch a point by calling color a configuration, try to see it my way as an invariant derived from any specific color sensations.) The kind of change made no difference, however: changing from three borders to two or to one, changing color from red to black or to green. Picking a new card that differed from the initial focus card only in the value of one attribute, therefore, constituted a binary test, not a three-way test: relevant if the experimenter answered "no," and irrelevant if the experimenter answered "yes." The authors themselves point out this feature of the test strategy. The result is that this test could have only one of sixteen outcomes, each involving some number of relevant and irrelevant attributes.

We can now see that the term *concept* does not bear a simple one-to-one correspondence with the sixth level of perception in our model. It covers a mixture of perceptions from several levels, at least as it was employed in this experiment and was thus operationally defined. However, what the subjects were required to *do* in order to accomplish their tasks did include the steps needed to isolate one of the fifteen non-null relationships involved; the means for doing this involved manipulating sensations simply because that was the only method available. Subjects had no way to indicate that they were ignoring attributes. The relationships isolated were not specific to the many different examples of each relationship that could be found in the array; they were simply the fifteen non-null *forms* of conjunctive (*and*) relationship among four elements.

There was in fact no need for subjects in this experiment to perceive the target relationship. The task could have been successfully carried out strictly in terms of sensations, as I will show in a moment when we discuss the strategies employed. This point emphasizes a difficulty I have repeatedly found when trying dutifully to relate this model to the work of others. All too often good research is spoiled for my purposes by the fact that common-sense terms have dictated the very experimental variables themselves. *Concept* is simply not a scientifically useful term; it has evolved from ages of theorizing in a haphazard fashion. Even Bruner, Goodnow, and Austin comment on the controversy over the nature of concepts and adopt only a working definition, which, as we have seen, is not entirely consistent with itself. There is no reason to assume that just because people have been concerned with the term *concept* for a long time, it has some inherent meaning. I expect that many serious problems will be resolved when terms like this are simply allowed to die of old age, or are redefined more usefully in terms of models.

A direct investigation of "relationship-attainment," by the way, could get out of hand very quickly unless one severely limited the field of possibilities and provided strong hints. Even if only logical relationships were the target, the numbers get huge. With two variables, there are 16 logical expressions possible. Four variables raise the number to 65,536, and with five variables the number of different expressions is 4,294,967,296! No human being would be likely to find a target relationship among five variables by any empirical method involving examining positive and negative instances of the relationship.

Bruner, Goodnow, and Austin were not so much interested in the nature of concepts as in strategies of concept attainment, as influenced by the type of concept to be attained. A *strategy* as they define it is a regular structure visible in the process of decision-making. Thus they see a level of organization of behavior transcending any we have discussed so far. In their own words, "It is only when one departs from the analysis of individual acts-at-a-moment that the sequentially coherent nature of problem-solving becomes clear." We have been considering behaviors which, although manipulated to create and maintain perceived relationships, are still unitary acts or fixed sequences of acts treated as units: "acts-at-a-moment." We have seen nothing involving *decision-making*. That term, like the term *strategy*, is one way of speaking about the next level of perception and control in our model. Problem-solving is only one of many evidences of the nature of this level.

Seventh-order Control Systems: Program Control

I am looking for my damned glasses. First I go *into* the bedroom (relationship). I look *at* the dresser. I *pick up* a shirt and look *under* it. The glasses are not there, or anywhere else in the bedroom. Next, the bathroom: *on* the bathtub? No. *On* the sink? No. *In* the wastebasket? No. On to the living room. *Under* the newspaper? Ah! End of program. Now back to the main program: to read the newspaper I put down in order to find my glasses.

Executing the program called "looking-for-my-glasses" involved, in retrospect, a definite list of relationships brought about one after the other in sequential order. Yet the program is *not* a list. It is a *structure*, and at the nodes of this structure are tests or decision points. There was no way I could have predicted the list of relationships, or at what point the list would terminate and a new sort of relationship-list would begin to unfold (when the glasses turned up).

Programs can be hierarchical in nature, in a way that has nothing to do with the hierarchy of perception and control we have developed so far. One element in the example above is the action of looking in the bedroom for the glasses. If they are found, the program branches to a different program. But looking in the bedroom involves a structure of decisions, too. I scan around the room, looking for things that glasses could be under, or for the glasses themselves. I don't know which item will pass the test first, but when one does, I halt the scanning subprogram and institute the picking-up-and-looking-under program. I may utilize these subprograms a dozen times before giving up and leaving the bedroom to search the next room. Even picking up and looking under could involve a program. Picking up a stiff piece of cardboard requires a different set of lower-order acts than picking up a limp undershirt that happens to have one end caught in a drawer.

The essence of a program is what computer programmers call a test, a branch-point, or an *if*-statement—a point where the list of operations being carried out is interrupted and some state of affairs is perceived and compared to a reference state of affairs. Is A equal to B? Is a logical statement now true of the environment? Has some key event now occured? Has a configuration achieved a predetermined shape, or an intensity a predetermined value? Sometimes such tests form a "tree", one test leading to a choice of succeeding tests without further intervening operations. The choice points may form a network, the outcome of each test determining the path, open or closed, that will actually be followed through the network, but the network, not the particular path followed, being the organization in question. Thus many different sequences of relationships can be examples of a single program structure, just as many different event combinations can exemplify a single relationship, and many different sensation sets can exemplify a given configuration.

A "strategy" such as one of those investigated by Bruner, Goodnow, and Austin can easily be expressed as a program through the use of a flow diagram. One advantage of a flow diagram is that a person need not specify how each operation is to be performed, and so need not say what machine is to be employed in executing the program. As human beings we can see that the same program exists even if different means are required to perform the operations in different instances. Notice that this program works even though the target relationship is never mentioned. It *could* be perceived after the program has ended.

I will not try to diagram the other strategies in the Bruner, Goodnow, and Austin book, partly because some of them become rather complex, but mainly because another trio of experimenters (Newell, Shaw, and Simon, 1963) has already done this sort of program simulation of thought processes for many years far better than I can. Of all the computer simulations of thought processes, I think that theirs was the first to make use of human behavior and subjective reports as a guide to what should be programmed. Rather than trying to develop mathematical generalizations to rep-

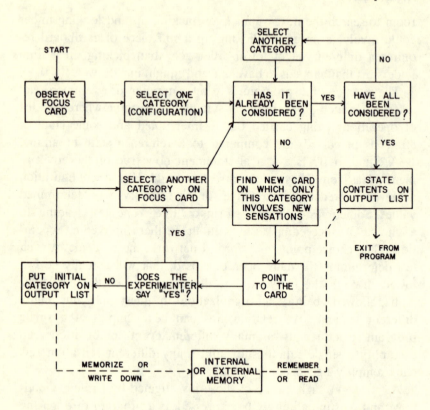

FIGURE 13.1.   *Flow diagram of conservative-focusing strategy. After output list is complete, the elements may be examined to see what conjunctive relationship is exemplified.*

resent their own subjective or commonsense experiences (as many modelers do), these men did behavioral studies in which they asked human subjects to describe all their conscious thought processes as they struggled to accomplish goals such as proving logical identities. The experimenters extended this approach and produced the first successful chess-playing program.

The programs these men developed were hierarchical structures in which higher-level programs evaluated key consequences of program operation and on that basis selected goals for lower-level programs to accomplish. In this way their structure was much like our model, although we are placing all program structures at one level in the model. The feedback control organization of our model shows up clearly: the perceptual function is represented by evaluation processes which detect the presence or absence of critical parameters; comparison is embodied in if-statements in which the result of evaluation is compared with some desired outcome of the evaluation (the reference signal). The output function which responds to errors consists of the set of operations that can be performed on the "objects" being evaluated.

These programs were, as I said, many-leveled. Their hierarchical organization offers a strong temptation to compare the organization of programs to the organization of behavior; indeed, if one does not ask where perceptual entities come from or how they are appropriately manipulated (a problem for organisms, but not for computers), one can create program-like models that do correspond in their behavior to many interesting aspects of human and animal behavior.

Furthermore, since human beings can recognize programs (building a house, going shopping, looking for glasses), it is possible to see the program-like aspects of any behavior, even if the behaving system itself does not have a program level of organization. This is called computer *simulation*. One can simulate the behavior of a lever or a spinal reflex in a computer even though neither one involves programs in its operation. Tacitly involved in all such simulations, however, are many levels of human perceptual interpretation; after all, a computer simulation of a lever does not have one end that rises when the other end falls; rather there are two lists of numbers, one of which increases in value as the other decreases. A human being must interpret these lists of numbers if he is to perceive them as positions of two ends of a lever, or he must build into the computer some artificial perceptual processes that will present the numbers as line-drawings—which still must be interpreted by human perceptions. The computer cannot *be* a lever.

I am very gingerly approaching an interpretation of seventh order organizations which I know will be controversial in some quarters. I am saying, in effect, that our own seventh level of organization is in fact computerlike, and that reality as seen from this level is much like a computer simulation of reality.

I am not sure how to deal with perceptions at this level. If I were to follow the pattern laid down at lower orders, I would assert that one perceives the existence of a program-like structure at this level, compares it with a reference structure, and on the basis of the error alters the lower-order relationships, and so on. But that doesn't seem properly to fit the way programs work: they involve perceptions, but the perceptions are part of the if-then tests that create the network of contingencies which is the heart of the program. Perhaps a level is missing here. If what follows is slightly ambiguous, therefore, be assured that this is not because of a simple blunder but because of genuine indecision. Thinking about thinking is somewhat paradoxical.

Let us suppose, then, that there is a "program point of view," without saying precisely what that point of view is. This point of view goes, I believe, under another name: *rationality*. It is at this level that we think in a logical, deductive manner. I do not necessarily mean formal logic here; programs can be organized to obey any imaginable rules. At the program level we have not only deduction but supersitition, grammatical rules, expectations about the consequences of behavior in the physical world (models), experimental procedures, mathematical algorithms, recipes for cooking and chemistry, and the strategies of business, games, conversation, and love-making. Bruner, Goodnow, and Austin used the same terms: "In dealing with the task of conceptualizing arbitrary sequences, human beings behave in a highly patterned, highly 'rational' manner." One man's rationality may be another man's insanity, but that is only a matter of choice of programs. A program level is as necessary for a systematic delusion as it is for a physical theory; sometimes the difference is not readily evident simply because both "make sense" from the seventh-order point of view.

Uses of Language

I must pause here to point out what may be another missing level. Consider the "looking-for-glasses" program. As *executed,* no intervening levels were needed. The program level had only to issue reference signals to appropriate relationship-controlling systems, which then in turn brought about all the necessary lower-order events, motions, configurations, and so on. As *described,* however, no actual behavioral events in relationship were involved: instead, I presented *word* events in relationship.

There are two ways I have considered the use of words, one not requiring a new level and the other requiring it. The first approach says that words are simple perceptions like any other perceptions save for the ease with which they can be manipulated, and that they act on memory to evoke associated perceptions that are *not* words. Higher-order systems would then perceive the objects, events, relationships, and so on evoked by lower-order perceptions into which the words have been transformed. This is the view I presently favor.

The second approach to words is to introduce a specific symbolizing level, where words (or any other symbol-perception) can be translated into perceptions and where the inverse translation can also take place. According to this proposal, the program level would deal specifically with symbols and would actuate lower-level behaviors by sending reference symbols to the new level, which would match them by present-time *non*-symbolic perceptions. My chief reason for rejecting this level is parsimony, a secondary reason being that I believe I often execute programs without use of any symbols at all, as when I tie shoelaces. That situation could be viewed as a limiting case of symbolizing, in which a perception is used as a symbol for itself. (Any perception can be used as a symbol for any other perception anyway— why not the "identity transform?")

If words or symbols are treated simply as ordinary perceptions, as I prefer to do, then in effect we are saying that symbol-handling processes begin at lower order with special perceptions receiving special treatment, but nevertheless treatment in terms of configurations, changes, events, relationships, and programs, like all perceptions. We do know that associative memories can be built and that human memory shows associative properties sufficient to explain "encoding" and "decoding" processes relating word perceptions to other kinds of perception. But these, although perhaps the best reasons for not including a specific symbol-handling level, are not the reasons that impress me the most. Treating words as simply another class of perceptions (perceivable at many levels) seems to explain a kind of communication difficulty that is as annoying as it is hard to comprehend.

Verbal communication can be analyzed in two ways. One way converts words and word relationships into perceptions (by whatever means) as the communication proceeds, while those perceptions are viewed from higher-order points of view to see what the speaker "means." Thus if I say, "The cow jumps over the

moon," the listener provides himself with a cow-configuration
and a moon-configuration and makes the cow-configuration move
so as to execute a jumping event that causes the cow to describe
a trajectory relative to the moon that could be called "over."
If the listener is young and naïve, he may be surprised and de-
lighted at this novel idea.

The second way of analyzing verbal communication is to deal
with words directly, using a word-handling hierarchy, never con-
verting them into perceptual meanings until all word processing
is finished. A person applies verbal and logical rules to the words,
which lead to the production of more words that can also be processed in the same way, and he arrives at the conclusion, "Don't
be silly—a cow is too weak to jump over the moon. You see, a
circumlunar trajectory requires a certain minimum launch
velocity to establish a Hohmann transfer orbit, and considering
the mass of the average cow . . ." blah, blah, blah. Of course
this irritating analysis is correct. It leads one to construct an
image of a stupid cow making an ineffectual leap carrying it
perhaps three feet toward the moon before it falls back, breaks
a leg, and has to be shot (some people tend to go *beyond* the
words in "decoding," another fact that makes me favor the memory hypothesis).

Symbols employed in this way can be a powerful tool, for the
right programs of symbol manipulation can generate statements
which, when converted to reference perceptions, prove to be
matchable by perceivable entities. That is the essence of science.
In that case the programs become models of processes we cannot
observe directly—useful if not necessarily deathless models.

Unfortunately, human beings often forget that symbol-manipu-
lating *does* take place in their heads, and they fail to test their
programs against direct experience at all the intermediate stages.
When that happens, word manipulation carries them out over an
empty abyss. Words lead to other words, but all links with direct
experience are left behind. One can then easily find himself
chasing what may prove to be a ghost: what is the "real" meaning of *intelligence* or *concept* or *vicarious mediation* or *quark*?

The misuse of symbol-handling programs creates a great deal
of difficulty. If a policeman hears someone call him "pig," he
may realize that the perception evoked by this noise has nothing

to do with his perception of himself, and conclude that the speaker has simply made a mistake. Or, he may substitute the name of a class ("hippie") for the person before him, and use this symbol together with the symbol "pig" as elements of a word-handling program leading to results that demand violence. Likewise, a demonstrator shouting "Power to the people!" may have no image in his head corresponding either to *power* or to *people*, but only a logical structure that tells him what these noises bid him to do. In all too many ways, our lives are run and sometimes ruined by the consequences of performing programmed manipulations of words. Consider the uses of *communism, capitalism, freedom,* or *peace-with-honor*. A bridge of word manipulations freed of perceptual meanings can be built *from* anywhere *to* anywhere. When the intervening words cannot be matched to any nonverbal experience, one can only ask why the person engaged in this process wanted to reach the destination. Enough— let us proceed with the main development.

In 1960 still another trio of authors published a book on a behavioral model: *Plans and the Structure of Behavior* by Miller, Galanter, and Pribram. These authors specifically recognized the program level as a specific kind of behavioral organization and were the first to investigate it in a wide variety of situations. The core of their model was the so-called TOTE unit of organization.

TOTE stands for Test-Operate-Test-Exit. In these authors' view a TOTE unit involves *Testing* for some condition by comparison with an Image (reference signal in our model), performing an *Operation* (output) affecting the condition being tested, Testing again, and so on until the Test is passed, at which point control *Exits* from this program and goes to another one. This simple unit of organization by no means exhausts the kinds of networks possible in seventh-order organizations of our model, nor does it account for categories of perception and lower-level kinds of control systems that do not operate in terms of programs. But it correctly embodies the essence of negative feedback control of perceptual inputs, hierarchical organizations in behavior, and the role of reference signals in directing behavior.

Insofar as these authors applied their model to aspects of behavior that are probably actually involved in programlike behaviors, their book constitutes a starting point for the investigation of our seventh-order systems. Those whose interest is in giving content to this model would do well to begin with *Plans*, for it is as close to a textbook of seventh-order behavior as now exists.

We are not concerned here, however, with amassing examples of specific behaviors, but with sketching in possible levels of organization in an overall attempt to build a functionally complete model. We must go on now, because there are still regularities in behavior not accounted for with the levels so far defined.

Eighth-order Control Systems: Control of Principles

We must now perform once again that peculiar backing-off process I call "going up a level." What end is served by carrying out any particular program or group of programs? Bruner, Goodnow, and Austin comment: "Our subjects were quite clearly 'trying to succeed,' and the task obviously aroused achievement needs and other extrinsic motives . . . the 'act of getting information' takes on broader significance. It may mean to the subject, 'I am a bright fellow,' or 'I'll show this psychologist.'"

Such higher-order considerations could, of course, be viewed as evidence of higher-level programs still within the seventh level of organization. One could always think of *a* program that exemplifies "I'll show this psychologist." The key to seeing a higher-order organization behind this motive, however, is to find a motive that cannot itself be expressed as a program—which could be seen in many different programs.

A start toward understanding the nature of eighth order can be seen in Newell, Shaw, and Simon's concept of *heuristics*. A heuristic is not an exact procedure or an algorithm, although examples of a heuristic can be expressed as precisely defined programs. Rather, a heuristic is a *principle* adhering to which tends to make programs run more smoothly. In writing their theorem-proving programs and chess-playing programs, Newell, Shaw, and Simon were working with procedures so complex that no straightforward program could possibly succeed. In a game of chess, a computer could be programmed to explore all possible outcomes of each move and thus, it seems, play infallibly. But Newell, Shaw, and Simon cite Shannon's estimate, that "there are something like 10^{120} continuations to be explored, with less than 10^{16} microseconds available in a century to explore them." The straightforward if-then approach of programming obviously will never be feasible for a chess program *or* a human brain.

What enables machines or people to play chess is a set of general principles that help pick specific programs or strategies. Following a principle does not guarantee that any particular lower-level event will occur. Sometimes one has only the satisfaction of knowing that in defeat he was at least able to demonstrate the principle properly! It is the nature of heuristics to be fuzzy at the program level, to be somewhat statistical in nature, to be a little too general for the actual situation. One heuristic employed in chess playing of all kinds is the maxim, "Develop strength in the center of the board." *Strength* is an elastic concept, as is what one considers the *center* of the board in a given situation. Sometimes developing too much strength at the center can leave one vulnerable to instant defeat. But this is a good general rule, which has favorable effects over a large number of games.

Heuristics are employed in nearly every complex human endeavor. In football a team may have a game plan, but the plan is not a specific program like a diagramed play. A businessman may approach a conference having a general idea of how to sell the opposition on his specific proposal, but he cannot say beforehand what specific form this general plan will take. A mathematician constructing a proof uses many fixed and programmable algorithms, but governing the transitions from one step of the proof to the next are generalized and rather hazy rules he has picked up through sheer experience and possibly could not even articulate. The hardest steps in a mathematical proof are those which occur between the lines.

We have words referring to principles—*honesty, perseverance, simplification*, and so on—but all these words can do is point to the perception intended, by suggesting lower-order situations in which human beings can perceive such principles. Principles are perceived and controlled at a level higher than the level at which logical or grammatical sentences can be constructed. Perhaps they include what Chomsky refers to as "deep structure" in grammar, or a higher level of deep structure. But they include far more than that.

Among other possibilities, eighth-order perceptions must include whatever it is that enables programmers to write programs.

However many levels a program contains, it always contains a highest level of executive program, and even if that program directs self-organizing activities of lower levels in the program, it cannot reorganize itself without ceasing to be able to reorganize anything: something else (the programmer) has to write the executive program. Something of the same relationship must exist between the programmer and his own seventh-order systems as exists between himself (at eighth order) and the machines he programs. The main difference is in the operation codes he works with!

We are skirting the edge of learning phenomena here, which will be dealt with in the next chapter. Certainly we are talking about one aspect of learning, the kind of learning that can be learned. But our system so far cannot modify its own structure; it cannot learn to do anything *new* at any level. If eighth-order perceptions amount to principles that can actually result in assembly of programs that solve problems, those principles must be selected from the set that is known already, and their application must involve the manipulation of program fragments that also have already been learned.

Eighth-order systems perceive and control what I call principles. This means that the purpose of selecting and operating any given set of programs is to make or keep a principle true. Perceiving principles is not merely a matter of passive observation; to perceive that honesty is the best policy is in effect to accept that principle as an eighth-order reference level, which in turn implies governing one's behavior to prove continually that honesty is in fact a principle that is perceivable in one's lower-order behaviors. We have to recognize that principles are not basically sentences or evaluations obtained through logical deduction, but directly perceived *facts*. Once we have learned to perceive in terms of some particular principle, we become able to see the state of that principle in all our lower-order perceptions having to do with it, and we can then learn to behave in such a way as to control that state. Perhaps a "hardened criminal" perceives honesty just as other people do, but his reference level for that perception is different. He controls honesty in order to keep it at a rather low level.

Eighth-order systems can operate in conditions where no program can succeed because the situation is too complex to handle by an exact algorithm, however flexible it may be. They can also operate in conditions where there is a high noise level which prevents even workable programs from working properly all of the time. This does not mean that eighth-order systems are statistical in nature. What it does mean is that eighth-order systems may be constructed to extract signals from noise by means such as synchronous detection (looking only when a signal is expected), or by other averaging methods. Such an organization would be in keeping with the requirements of a system that deals in generalizations which may be valid only over many instances of a given lower-order kind of behavior. One such situation is found in scientific laboratories: I think the function of eighth-order perception and control in science is almost self-evident.

One last comment: Perhaps one reason that we do not yet have a computer program that is a chess master is the fact that programs do not, and perhaps cannot, contain the ability to perceive the heuristic being employed by the opponent. Is this lack merely a question of not having written the right program, or could it be that machines intended to be operated by stored networks of contingencies lack the proper kind of components? What say the programmers and machine designers?

Ninth-order Control Systems: Control of System Concepts

I have chosen a fuzzy term to fit a vague idea in this attempt to define one final level of behavioral organization. The motive for even trying to do so may reside at this very level: a feeling that this model will not qualify as a *complete system* unless it can account for why we choose one set of reference principles rather than another. As the reader may have detected, I have steadfastly refused to settle for the answer, "Because we have been rewarded for doing so"; that is not a model but a substitute for a model. Eventually I will have to give in and speak of learning, the kind that is related to "reinforcement," but that time is not quite yet.

Human beings seem to perceive unity in a collection of moral, factual, or abstract principles. On occasion they alter their choice of principles as a means toward achieving a more satisfactory sense of systematic unity, or to correct deviations of some perceived system concept from a preferred reference condition.

One result of perceiving collections of principles is a strong tendency to perceive organized entities. That is how I think of a system: as an entity having an existence that depends primarily on its organization and not on its elements. Some examples of system concepts are the United States Army, the Los Angeles Dodgers, physics, the government, a family, and The System. These are all system concepts that melt away on too close inspection.

When a fan is loyal to a baseball team, he is reacting to something that is of a most ethereal nature. In the space of twenty years, a team may change stadiums, managers, owners, coaches, and players—what is left to be loyal to? Only the system concept that made it seem that there was a "team" in the first place. Since that system concept exists in the ninth-order perceptions of the fan who is organized to perceive that way, there is no need for the team to have material existence. The fan will perceive it anyway, as long as he wishes rabidly to do so. Many are the stubborn old-timers who insist on perceiving the *Brooklyn* Dodgers, who have merely been kidnapped temporarily to a strange state.

Consider the system concept known as The System. No person can in fact interact with something outside himself known as The System. It doesn't exist anywhere in particular, save in the perceptions of a few millions of individuals. One person may interact physically with an individual bureaucrat, a judge, a policeman, a clerk, a clergyman, but never with The System. Each person with whom he interacts may have his own concept of The System and the principles on which his perception of it rests, but only that concept, not any physical System itself, determines how that bureaucrat or judge will react. Of course as a person interacts with first one official and then another he may learn the apparent principles under which they make their decisions, and after seeing many examples of these principles he may come to form a certain system concept about all officials and their structure of written or unwritten rules. That is how any person's concepts come into being. But no matter how such concepts arise, what governs a person's behavior at the ninth level of organization is *his own* structure of system-concept perceptions, and *his own* set of reference levels for those system concepts.

To sociologists ideas like this are heresy; I am saying that Society or Culture is a figment of our imaginations. Saying that, however, in no way implies that system concepts are not *real*. They are precisely as real as sensations, configurations, motions, and events. They are part of directly perceived reality, the only reality we have, to perceive *or* control. They are not even imagined—that is a technical term in this theory quite different in meaning from perception, as will be explained later. All I am doing is further identifying system concepts, as products of individual perceptual organization interacting with lower-order versions of experience. I am saying, basically, that system concepts such as Society or Culture are not to be found in the world represented by physical models of the universe; they are elements of psychological models of the universe. They are effective exactly to the degree that individuals learn to perceive them and choose goals with respect to them and develop means of maintaining their ninth-order perceptions in those goal states. To ask the *physical* significance of doing this is merely to mix one model with another. A society *is* a perception. That is its physical nature.

Still Higher Levels

I must now account for choice of particular system concepts as ninth-order reference levels, and I can't. My comprehension and my imagination fail; introspection yields nothing more. Have we in fact reached the top of the hierarchy? I can't tell—the mists are rather thick up here.

So I must say for the time being that this *is* my model of behavioral organization, as far as it concerns the ongoing performance of a competent adult human being. I must leave questions unanswered, hoping that others will find this approach interesting enough to expand upon and modify.

There are a few *guesses* I can make concerning the source of ninth-order reference levels, none very startling. Perhaps these reference levels belong to the class of motivations we term *instincts*. Instincts, after all, should occupy the top level of organization if they are not to interfere with learned behaviors. If one had an "instinctive" way of holding his right arm, he might find that learning to throw a spear is difficult. Even allowing for acquisition of some high-order reference levels, it is still possible that very generalized reference levels are inherited, serving as evolution's guide to behavioral organization. When we discuss learning, I will introduce evolution's role in a different way, but there is room for such considerations here, too.

Another possible—even probable—source of ninth-order reference levels is *memory*. The model can be made to work reasonably realistically on the basis that the most commonly perceived system concept is stored and then retrieved from memory to serve as a reference level. Indeed, we will shortly add something like this arrangement to the entire model. Unfortunately, this idea takes no account of deviant goals at ninth-order; according to this idea, everyone would converge to the same system concepts, and that is hardly true. There may be a tendency in that direction, but a tendency is not a law. In fact this idea also gives memory some false properties, for it implies that one could *remember* only the average of all perceptions of a given kind, a proposition we know is incorrect.

The solution that I prefer for this problem involves a discussion of learning of a particular type, and so will be presented later.

If I seem reluctant to postulate a tenth level of organization, that is because I *am* reluctant. At the risk of exposing a lack of spiritual development, I have to admit that I have no notion whatsoever of the possible nature of perceptions of that level. Maybe— and I say this quite sincerely—maybe our brothers from the East have something to tell us in this regard. Perhaps what some see as a universal urge toward Oneness represents the first glimmerings of a mode of perception in which all system concepts are seen as examples of higher versions of reality, so that system concepts—what we call "realities"—will some day be manipulated as casually as we now manipulate principles in service of systems. Could the human race be in the process of *evolving* the capacity to perceive and control tenth-level entities? *Inventing* it?

REFERENCES

Bruner, J. S., Goodnow, J. J., and Austin, G. A. *A Study of Thinking.* New York: John Wiley, 1956.

Miller, G. A., Galanter, E., and Pribram, K. H. *Plans and the Structure of Behavior.* New York: Holt, 1960.

Newell, A., Shaw, J., and Simon, H. "Chess-playing Programs and the Problem of Complexity." In *Computers and Thought,* edited by E. Feigenbaum and J. Feldman, New York: McGraw-Hill, 1963.

LEADING QUESTIONS: CHAPTER 13

SIXTH ORDER

1. Things in relationship to things define *space*. Changes in relationship to changes define *time*. Events in relationship to events define *process*. What would you think of calling the object of sixth-order perception *space-time processes?*

2. Pretend you are nothing but an *on* detector. How many *on* relationships can you see in your present environment? Now become an *under* detector, then an *above* detector. Can you attend to several relationships simultaneously?

3. Can you think of a way of describing or explaining behavior that relies on no perception higher than sixth order?

SEVENTH ORDER

4. The following is a flow diagram of a common program most adults have learned. What is it?

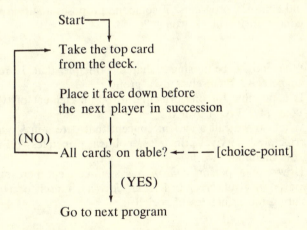

5. Can you write a program for filling a small jar with beans from a bin, one bean at a time? (Could a specific sequence of operations do the same thing?)

6. Can you explain how an *exception to a rule* involves the program level of perception?

EIGHTH ORDER

7. Aphorisms (e.g., "Honesty is the best policy") often describe principles. Can you give program examples in which some aphorism-principle can be perceived in varying degrees (for example, not leaving a tip *if* you don't expect to return to that restaurant) which may influence a perception of your honesty on the scale where honesty is the *best* policy?

8. What principle requires setting up programs for reacting to provocations?

9. General principles are kept true by selection of specific programs, and govern the kind of test involved. What general principle requires use of the following program? What aphorism describes the *program*?

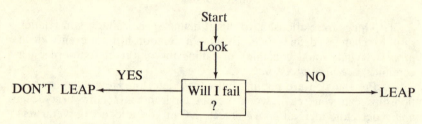

10. Principles are often perceived as *facts*. If one has an eighth-order reference level expressible as "I don't know what's wrong with me," what programs can he select to make perceived facts match the reference level?

11. Can you see a connection between a reference level for a fact and the concept of a belief? If one believes that blacks and women are stupid, what will happen if he perceives a black woman carrying out subtle and complex programs? if someone proposes a subsidy to provide higher education for black women?

NINTH ORDER

12. What might be a single shared principle that is required for people to perceive themselves as a group?

13. Is it possible for one principle to be an element of two different system concepts? Try "Loyalty."

14. What do we call a system concept that determines our choice of moral principles? survival principles? political principles? principles concerning the inanimate world?

15. How can a person *control* a system-concept perception? Hint: suppose a political observer in Russia sees (a) himself or (b) someone else violating the principles of socialism.

14

Learning

Several types of phenomena are commonly subsumed under the term *learning:* I will call them *memory, problem-solving programs,* and *reorganization.* Using a computer model as an analogy, we can distinguish these phenomena from each other. A memory type of learning corresponds to typing a sentence which is received and stored by a computer and then on some preset signal is automatically typed out again. Any time the signal is given, the sentence will be typed, proving that it has been "learned." However, the organization necessary for this operation has no relationship to what has been typed—it will work for any character string. This is rote learning and involves no modification of the system's organization.

Problem-solving programs are exemplified by the programs of Newell, Shaw, and Simon (chap. 13). Programs are fixed lists of instructions (reference levels for lower-order systems in human beings) with choice points in the lists. Both memory and present-time inputs are important elements. Problem-solving programs can be very complex, and behavior can appear adaptive because changing input information can result in switching to new subroutines that cause drastic changes in the apparent character of the program. No actual changes in organization, however, take place; the same list of operations remains in use, and even the subprograms may retain their same organization. All that changes is the path followed through the network of contingencies, all possible paths being determined when the writing of the program is finished.

A pertinent case of apparent learning of this sort occurs in many kinds of "pattern recognition" programs (Uhr, 1966). Computer inputs represent samplings of a picture of an alphabetic character. Through various means the program dissects the character into significant features, with the definition of "significance" itself sometimes being manipulated by the program. On the basis of these significant features, the program arrives at an assortment of possibilities for what the input character might be. It chooses the best possibility, and *then is told whether it was right or wrong*. The resemblance to Bruner, Goodnow, and Austin's "strategies of concept attainment" (chap. 13) is strong. Through repeatedly being shown unknown characters and then being given their correct identifications, the program alters the weights assigned to significant features or alters the definitions of significance until it minimizes its error rate.

Learning of this sort is really a form of *communication*. The teacher (who shows the computer the characters and indicates "right" or "wrong") is attempting to get the program to react to the environment in the same way that the teacher does. The teacher is already programmed to sort perceptions into categories corresponding to the characters of an alphabet; after learning, the program is able to sort perceptions in nearly the same way. What has been communicated, when learning is successful, is the means of categorizing the relevance or irrelevance of lower-order perceptions. Perhaps one reason why pattern-recognizing programs are difficult to perfect is the fact that computers share so few lower-order perceptual categories with human beings. It might be productive to consider giving computers not only intensity inputs, but sensation, configuration, motion, and event detectors as well. Various kinds of pattern-recognition strategies, indeed, can already be viewed as making use of one or another of these types of lower-order perceptions, artificially produced through program manipulations. If we see pattern recognition as a problem in communicating perceptual interpretations rather than one of discovering "real" patterns, some simplifications might be possible.

The most basic type of learning, the one on which I will concentrate here, is reorganization. The hierarchical model we already have accounts for the other types in principle if not in detail, leaving only reorganization unaccounted for. Reorganization is needed to produce *any* program, because only through reorganization can the basic set of operations and choice points be modified.

Learning as Reorganization

Reorganization is a process akin to rewiring or microprogramming a computer so that those operations it can perform are changed. Reorganization alters behavior, but does not produce *specific behaviors*. It changes the parameters of behavior, not the content. Reorganization of a perceptual function results in a perceptual signal altering its *meaning*, owing to a change in the way it is derived from lower-order signals. Reorganization of an output function results in a different choice of means, a new distribution of lower-order reference signals as a result of a given error signal. Reorganization is an operation *on* a system, not *by* a system.

Changes in organizational parameters will result in changes in behavior. These changes, however, will not resemble those resulting from altering one's goal for where he walks; they will be more like the lengthening of a child's legs during maturation, a change demanding many adjustments of behavior and permitting accomplishing old ends in new ways and accomplishing new ends that were formerly impossible.

One example of a self-reorganizing system was Ashby's (1952) *homeostat,* a collection of four simple feedback control systems which also contained a separate "uniselector" capable of altering the system's behavioral organization until a specific "survival" condition was satisfied. The homeostat could survive something that no computer program, however adaptive, could survive—an attack with a pair of wire-cutters. If one operational connection was destroyed, the uniselector could substitute another one. The uniselector itself produced no behavior; it acted to alter the physical connections in the behaving system.

Gordon Pask (1960) also built a device demonstrating physical reorganization. His device was a tray of iron-salt solution in which electrically conductive crystals could grow when direct current was applied to electrodes in the solution. These crystals would grow so as to complete connections between input and output terminals. Pask "rewarded" the tray of solution for making a desired connection by giving it some D.C. current, and "punished" it by withholding current, allowing the acid solution to dissolve the crystals. In this way he "trained" the solution tray to react in some absolutely astonishing ways. For example, he discovered that the network of crystal threads could be trained to discriminate between vibrations caused by two audible tones of different pitch!

This is what I mean by reorganization—not a change in the way existing components of a system are employed under control of recorded information, but a change in the properties or even the number of components. This category of learning is clearly the most fundamental, for it affects the kind of information that will be perceived and the kinds of computing elements available for use in programming. My objective in the remainder of this chapter is to develop a theory of reorganization: only this kind of theory can account for the existence of an adult's hierarchy of control systems. The other learning categories depend on the completion of the hierarchy and are more properly categories of behavior.

Mechanisms of Reorganization

Human reorganizing capabilities are demonstrated by the so-called plasticity of the nervous system. When brain tissue is destroyed by disease or accident, there is usually some obvious loss of function. (I suspect that there is *always* loss of function but that the loss sometimes goes undetected because function is not investigated at enough levels.) In many cases, however, some or all of the lost function can be regained through retraining. Apparently if enough computing elements remain, they can be reorganized to perform the lost function in the same way the function became organized in the first place.

This plasticity extends through the entire hierarchy, even to the level of first-order systems. Jerzy Konorski (1961) comments that the old Pavlovian idea that learning is exclusively cortical and lower behavior is inborn, "has proved with the lapse of time more and more inadequate," adding

> Therefore it seems that the time is ripe to abandon the old view and accept a new one, according to which the difference between the lower and the higher parts of the nervous system is not that the first of them control inborn activities and the second acquired activities, but that

the higher the centers, the greater is the complexity of activities controlled by them. And so those forms of plastic changes which correspond to the level of functional complexity proper to the spinal cord can occur at the spinal cord.

I am going to assume that the entire hierarchy of control systems results from a reorganizing process which begins with an unorganized nervous system, so that there can be no reliance on any function of the hierarchy we have built up thus far. If the hierarchy can form from such a start, then at least we can be sure of having handled the worst case first. Of course wittingly or unwittingly I will be assuming some preorganization; the question is really one of degree. What is innate and what is acquired? To a large extent that depends on where one decides to place "the beginning." If we say that learning begins at birth, then Konorski is probably right:

> In speaking of the innate activities of organisms, we should have clearly in mind that their occurance in the pure form is nearly nonexistent in the normal behavior of animals and man, because soon after birth the individual begins to modulate his innate responses by the feedback provided by their immediate consequences. In fact, relatively few primitive responses, mostly depending on the lower parts of the nervous axis—such as myotatic reflexes, swallowing, sneezing, and coughing—are rigid and preserve the same pattern both in various species and in various periods of life.

On the other hand, we might decide to look at birth as merely another (rather important) episode that occurs during a continuous process of growth of behavioral organization that begins with conception, changing character mainly as the structure and the environment of the growing organism change. The theory I will propose here (after this lengthy but I believe necessary preamble) seems to be the kind we need in order eventually to see the entire process of growth as one process, of such a nature that it has continuity not only over an individual's life span but on an evolutionary time scale. Robert Galambos (1961) states the essential property I would like to give this theory of reorganization:

> It could be argued, in brief, that no important gap separates the explanations for how the nervous system comes to be organized dur-

ing embryological development in the first place; for how it operates to produce the innate responses characteristic of each species in the second place; and for how it becomes reorganized finally, as a result of experiences during life.

If there is to be no gap, then we must try to discover processes of reorganization that could in principle be inherited, working through inheritable mechanisms that are not themselves shaped by reorganization but rather, in some way divorced from *what* is learned, *direct* learning. What I propose here does not go all the way, since it deals only with reorganizing processes that can be observed behaviorially. The concepts, however, can be extended beyond my application of them. Nearly everyone who has worked on self-organizing systems has used principles like mine; I am merely adapting what others have done to a specific model.

The Reorganizing System

The model I propose is based on the idea that there is a separate inherited organization responsible for changes in organization of the malleable part of the nervous system—the part that eventually becomes the hierarchy of perception and control. This *reorganizing system* may prove to be no more than a convenient fiction; its functions and properties may some day prove to be aspects of the same systems that become organized. That possibility does not reduce the value of isolating these special functions and thinking about them as if they depended on the operation of some discrete entity. One great advantage in thinking of this as a separate system is that one is guided toward physically realizable concepts; even not knowing the mechanisms involved, we can construct the theory so that *some* physical mechanisms could conceivably be involved. Thus we are not forced into implicit contradiction of our physical models of reality, the very models on which the consistency and usefulness of behavioral experiments depend.

Throughout the development of this theory, I have remained constantly aware of the "little-man-in-the-head" problem, and have tried to avoid giving the reorganizing system any property that depends on the operation of the very hierarchy that is constructed by the reorganizing system. Whatever process is involved in reorganization, it must be of such a nature that it could operate before the very first reorganization took place, before the organism could perceive anything more complex than intensities.

My model is a direct extension of Ashby's concept of "ultra-stability," the property intended to be demonstrated by his uni-selector-equipped homeostat. Ultrastability exists when a system is capable not only of feedback control of behavior-affected perceptions, but of altering the properties of the control systems, including how they perceive and act, as a means of satisfying the highest goal of all: survival.

Survival is a learned concept; the reorganizing system cannot behave on the basis of a concept, especially not a learned one. Ashby dealt with this question by defining *essential variables,* top priority variables intimately associated with the physiological state of the organism and to a sufficient degree representing the state of the organism. Each essential variable has associated with it certain physiological limits; if a variable exceeded those limits, a process of reorganization would commence until the essential variables were once again within the limits. Then, presumably, the state of the organism would also be within the limits of optimal performance. A system which reacts to the states of essential variables so as to keep them near preferred states would, in effect, guard the survival of the organism even though it would not have to know it was doing so.

That is the essential character of the reorganizing system I propose: It senses the states of physical quantities intrinsic to the organism and, by means we will discuss shortly, controls those quantities with respect to genetically given reference levels. The processes by which it controls those intrinsic quantities result in the appearance of learned behavior—in construction of the hierarchy of control systems that are the model already developed in this book. (What I call intrinsic quantities are what Ashby calls essential variables; I prefer my term for purposes of uniformity of language in other parts of the model, but will not put up objections if anyone continues to prefer Ashby's terms.)

We will therefore approach the reorganizing system as a control system. We will consider the nature of its controlled quantities, reference levels, and output function, and the route through which its output actions affect the quantities it senses so as to protect those quantities from disturbance. Since this is the most generalized control system so far considered, it will also operate on the slowest time scale of all—a point to keep in mind as we consider how this system reacts to various events. To the reorganizing system, the disturbances associated with a single trial in an experiment may be as the blink of an eye—barely noticeable.

Intrinsic State and Intrinsic Error

The controlled quantity associated with the reorganizing system consists of a set of quantities affected by the physiological state of the organism. As the state of the organism varies owing to activities, food intake, sexual excitement, illness, and other conditions, the intrinsic quantities vary, presenting a picture of the intrinsic state of the organism. The question now is, "presenting" it to what?

To the input of the reorganizing system. As we have done many times now, we will imagine a device which *senses* the set of quantities in question, and reports them in the form of one or several perceptual signals. Perception is a risky term here, however. Let us merely call such perceptual signals *intrinsic signals,* saying that they play the role of the reorganizing system's inner representation of the organism's intrinsic state. Postulating such signals is a convenient fiction, serving the same purpose as "temperature" serves in representing the kinetic state of molecules in our thinking.

To represent the fact that each intrinsic quantity has a genetically preferred state, we will provide the reorganizing system with *intrinsic reference signals.* These signals are also convenient fictions, representing the presence of stored information defining the state of the organism (as represented by intrinsic signals) that calls for *no* action on the part of the reorganizing system. This stored information may prove to be the message carried in our genes.

When there is a difference between sensed intrinsic state and the intrinsic reference signals, some device must convert this difference into action. As before, we insert a comparison function (a comparator) into the system, a device which emits an *intrinsic error signal* that drives the output of the system. The intrinsic error signal (perhaps multiple) will be zero only when intrinsic signals representing the state of the organism are all at their reference levels. Thus, the output of the system is driven by a condition of intrinsic error, ceasing only when intrinsic error falls to zero.

The Reorganizing Output

The effects of the outputs of the reorganizing system must be such as to change the properties of behavioral systems, as Ashby's uniselector switched connections around in the homeostat and Pask's solutions grew crystal threads under the influence of electric current. Several mechanisms are known to have such effects: synaptic thresholds can be altered chemically or by neural signals; new synaptic connections can grow even in the adult brain, and presumably can wither away, too. This is the sort of effect the reorganizing system's output has to have on the nervous system in which the behavioral hierarchy is, or comes to be, embodied.

The output function of the reorganizing system thus produces an effect we can define without specifying the mode of action: reorganization. This effect may occur at any rate between zero and maximum, so we can speak of rate of reorganization as a measure of the output activity of the reorganizing system. This rate would be measured behaviorally in terms of alterations in the basic parameters of observable behavior.

In order to complete the reorganizing system, we must relate rate of reorganization to the intrinsic error signal in such a way that the result will be to reduce that error signal to zero. When the intrinsic error signal is zero, reorganization must cease, and since we are making the error signal drive the system's output, that is what will happen.

In brief, *intrinsic error drives reorganization:* our model of the reorganizing system provides a handy visualization of this basic relationship, which is the model of learning I propose.

Behavior Versus Reorganization

All that remains now is to show how the output of the reorganizing system affects the quantities it senses in such a way as to reduce the intrinsic error to zero. This is the step which I think will provide a new point of view toward learning.

Clearly, the ways in which an organism behaves or fails to behave will have indirect effects on intrinsic state: the organism
will feed itself more or less well, indulge in more or less fatiguing
activities, and so on. If behavior is reorganized, the hierarchy will
carry out its control activities in different ways, having different
consequences on intrinsic state. These consequences need have
nothing to do directly with the kind of behavior involved; there
may be many hidden connections between action and physiological
result, of which the organism may never know anything. Nevertheless, changes in behavioral organization will affect the intrinsic
state of the organism: there is feedback.

And this feedback is negative. It may seem that we have not
nearly enough information to jump to such a conclusion, but in
fact negative feedback is (given one small condition) inevitable.
If there is intrinsic error, behavior will undergo continual reorganization. Control systems will alter their characteristics, controlling new perceptual variables in new ways, and this process
of reorganization will continue until intrinsic error drops to zero.
The "small condition" referred to is this: intrinsic error will drop
to zero, provided that the organism does not die before the behavioral organization occurs that restores intrinsic state to its reference level. If we ignore questions of efficiency, then even a random reorganizing process could eventually—in millions of years,
perhaps, but eventually—correct intrinsic error.

I oversimplify, of course (there is the question of orders of infinity to consider). What I am trying to illustrate is the point that
intrinsic error is self-correcting simply because reorganization is
in principle capable of altering any behavior pattern, and these
alterations are terminated by the behavior pattern (if one exists)
that succeeds in restoring intrinsic error to zero, just as, for
example, a train will keep on running until it finally finds a broken track. The behavior pattern that reduces intrinsic error to
zero stops the process of reorganization, and therefore *that behavior pattern will persist.*

Reorganization alters the properties of the control systems involved in behavior. Such changes would alter the kinds of quantities perceived, the means of correcting error through choice of
lower-order reference signals, dynamical properties of control systems, and even the state of existence of a control system. As a re-

sult, of course, visible behavior would change its character, as would experienced behavior.

The reorganizing system, however, does not sense behavior or its effects on the environment. It senses only intrinsic quantities, and its reorganizing outputs are based only on the amount of intrinsic error that exists. Therefore—and this property is exceedingly important to this theory—*the process of reorganization is independent of the kind of behavior being reorganized*. It depends only on the effects the behavior has on intrinsic state.

Once again: If intrinsic error exists, reorganization will occur at a rate depending on the amount of intrinsic error. This reorganization process will cease not when some particular behavioral organization appears, but only when a behavioral organization appears that results in restoration of the intrinsic signal to its reference level, with consequent disappearance of the intrinsic error signal that is driving reorganization. The criteria for terminating reorganizing do not depend on a control system's achieving some goal state for its perceptions, not at any level in the hierarchy including those levels associated with problem-solving behaviors. They depend only on *physiological* effects of carrying out any given behavior. Reorganization may terminate when one fails to remember or fails to solve a problem, if those failures result in restoration of intrinsic error to zero. One will then have become organized to fail in those situations. The reorganizing system has no pride.

We must therefore consider that any behavior has two major classes of effect. One kind of effect is sensory: behavior alters the state of the world that affects sensory endings, and by this means (ideally) keeps all levels of perception at their respective goal states. The other kind of effect is *physiological:* behavior alters the state of physiological intrinsic quantities through physical and biochemical processes not involving the nervous system at all. The reorganizing system alters the properties of the behavioral systems that control sensory effects, and by this indirect means controls intrinsic state with respect to intrinsic reference levels.

Thus the behavioral act of finding, picking up, and eating food involves control of perceptions of the food, including its taste, appearance, smell, position, and relationship to the organism. The same act results in biochemical changes that alter those intrinsic quantities related to the state of nutrition of the organism, and by *that* route affects intrinsic error. We can now picture the reorganizing system in relationship to the behavioral hierarchy.

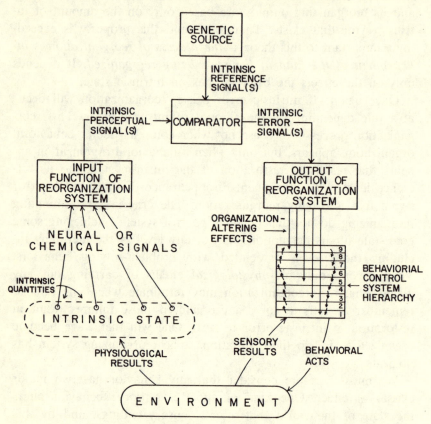

FIGURE 14.1.   *Relationship of the reorganizing system to the behavioral hierarchy and physical environment. The control loop for the reorganizing system is closed via physiological results of behavior, not through sensory effects.*

The arrangement in figure 14.1 would probably work in the sense that any reorganizing process would eventually result in correction of intrinsic error, provided that the organism did not die first. I do not assert, however, that this model is detailed enough to account for the way in which reorganization actually takes place. To make this model practicable would require knowing more about the structure of the output function, the effects of its action on the malleable part of the nervous system, and the amount and kind of preorganization of the nervous system necessary to allow this arrangement to succeed. Most of these questions can be approached experimentally.

The real intent behind this model is to establish a concept of this kind of learning process, for this concept includes the currently accepted reinforcement principle while explaining parsimoniously many observations about learning that in the older scheme are treated only as baffling empirical facts. Overly general as this model is, it nevertheless offers the hope of finding physically plausible principles underlying all the major regularities in learning of this basic kind.

Comparison with Reinforcement Theory

The ideas of reward and punishment, or *reinforcement,* are used according to a definite theoretical principle concerning how reinforcement acts. When it is stated that reinforcement acts to increase or decrease the probability that a response will follow a given stimulus, there is the implication that some direct effect occurs at the time of the reinforcing event, which alters the connection from stimulus to response. This leads to the idea that reinforcement acts specifically on the behavior being observed. Reinforcement is treated only as a sensory event, and its physiological effects are ignored except as they might become sensory events.

This leads to the peculiar result that no learning theory offers an explanation of the relationship between the type of deprivation used to motivate learning and the type of reinforcement used to shape learning. Why will a well-fed but thirsty animal *not* learn if food is used to reward behavior? Why does only water work? There are all sorts of ways to express the fact that this relationship holds true, but no ways to say *why*. Our model offers an explanation: because if physiological effects of water deprivation cause reorganization to commence, reorganization will cease only when behavior results in ingestion of water, reversing the physiological effects of the deprivation.

Reinforcement theories take into account the fact that some reinforcers are primary and some secondary (unlearned and learned), but since both types are treated as stimuli, the reason for this distinction remains unknown. Some psychologists have actually puzzled over the stimulus objects themselves, asking what gives them different "stimulus values," as if the answer were to be found in some nonphysical property of the objects. Further confusion has arisen because of the fact that formerly neutral stimuli seem to take on reinforcing value, being able to "motivate" behavior or even learning. These are the secondary reinforcers.

The model I am proposing offers a simple answer to these puzzling problems. Primary reinforcers are primary because they are capable of having direct physiological effects on intrinsic quantities. Only these effects are capable of starting or stopping reorganization. Secondary reinforcers are strictly sensory phenomena. If an organism has a reference level for one of these secondary reinforcers, the organism will appear to be motivated toward acquiring that reinforcer or toward performing some act that indirectly produces the secondary reinforcer. That kind of phenomenon is explainable as an ordinary control action that may involve no learning at all. Thus the standard concept of motivation actually encompasses two completely different phenomena: reduction of sensed errors in controlled quantities, and reduction of intrinsic error.

A primary reinforcer such as food may easily have both physiological and sensory effects. The reorganization or cessation of reorganization due to its *physiological* effects may result in appearance of a control system that controls its *sensory* effects. For example, a rat may reorganize until its behavior results in food ingestion that removes an intrinsic error caused by food deprivation; the learned behavior might consist of pressing a bar until food appears, then going to a food dish and eating the food. Involved in these control actions might well be *sensory* effects of hunger, the control systems acquired being organized to keep the sensations of hunger at zero. In the future, when hunger-associated sensations begin to appear, the control system comes into action and executes the behavior that eliminates them. If the amount of food available is sufficient to prevent the intrinsic error from becoming significant, reorganization never starts. That is why the learned control system continues to operate without change in form.

If the amount of food is restricted, reorganization will not cease when the required control system appears. The result will be random variations in the behavior—apparently senseless changes that actually interfere with acquiring food. Of course behavior will keep converging back toward the right organization since deviations increase the rate of reorganization and reduce the lifetime of ineffectual organizations. The result of using too small a reward, however, should be (and as far as I can recall, is) an increase in the "noise level" of behavior.

On the other hand, if the reward is too large, behavior will cease to alter its organization before unnecessary features have been eliminated. The result is called "superstitious" behavior (Skinner 1953). A rat or a pigeon cannot know the actually effective action—it would require too advanced a hierarchy to be able to do that. Like the witch-doctor who has found that bat's eyes, toadskins, mushrooms, urine, and the bark of a particular tree will reduce fever, the animal stops reorganizing as soon as its behavior *includes* the effective ingredient. To eliminate superstitious behavior, one must design the experimental conditions so that reward is withheld when the unwanted features of behavior appear.

The effects of intermittent reinforcements are well known: termination of the reinforcement does not result in immediate extinction of the learned pattern, but occasions a far longer persistence than is the case with reinforcements that always follow correct behavior. This fact has been a puzzle, because the "strength" of the learned behavior pattern, its resistance to extinction after reward is terminated, seems to be greater when fewer reinforcements are given. In our model fewer reinforcements should imply faster reorganization and faster extinction.

The answer lies, I believe, in the sensory aspects of the reinforcement, not the physiological effects on intrinsic state. In order to control perceptions associated with a variable that is present only statistically, an organism must acquire a perceptual function capable of detecting that variable through some averaging process. Thus the controlled quantity *as sensed* can change only slowly, for it is computed on the basis of what happens over many trials. Failure of the variable to appear on a given trial cannot possibly indicate whether the reward has ceased to appear altogether, or has simply failed to appear on *this* trial.

This means that the organism will go on executing learned behaviors related to controlling sporadic variables for long after the variable has actually ceased to appear. The lower the probability that the reward will appear on a given trial, the longer extinction must take. This significant appearing phenomenon, therefore, is merely a matter of the way a perceptual variable is defined, and has nothing fundamental to do with learning.

Extinction, by the way, could be caused in two totally different ways. It could result from reorganization that destroys a previous organization, or it could result merely from a higher-order system deciding that a formerly effective subsystem has lost its effectiveness and consequently setting the reference signal for that system to zero. Relearning a behavioral organization lost through reorganization would require the full treatment and might take almost as long as the original learning (save for useful information that has been recorded in memory). Behavior extinguished through action of a higher-order system would require *no* relearning; however, if the perceptual variables were statistical in nature and of low probability, reacquisition would be slow simply because a statistical variable detected through an averaging process cannot *appear* more suddenly than it can *disappear*.

One last topic from the bin of puzzling learning phenomena. So-called *one-trial learning* is not, in my model, learning at all but a memory phenomenon. One sees how to solve the puzzle while watching another person do it, and then reproduces the remembered moves using his own already learned behavioral system. Our model has no memory in it yet, so that subject will be put aside until the next chapter.

The Nature of Learning

The greatest contrast between my learning theory and reinforcement theory is in the concept of the learning process itself. Reinforcement theory implies that a reward acts on the specific behavior being learned. If a rat is to be taught to press a lever when a light comes on, the food-pellet reward is thought of as acting to strengthen the neural connection between the light stimulus and the lever-pressing muscles. Thus, what is learned is a specific act in response to a specific event. The learning—the change in probability—occurs in little increments each time the reinforcement is given.

In contrast, my learning model represents changes in behavior as reflecting a continual process of reorganization which persists as long as there is intrinsic error. Giving a reward *slows* this process through physiological, not sensory, effects. As behavioral organization approaches the state where it produces the reward more and more often, reorganization proceeds at a slower and slower rate. In effect, the lifetime of behavioral organizations near the required form is longer than the lifetime of irrelevant organizations; hence there is a bias toward retaining patterns closest to the correct ones. A steady-state condition is reached when (1) the behavior pattern produces enough reward to terminate reorganization altogether, or (2) the best available behavior pattern produces some limiting amount of reward with some level of reorganization remaining. Case (1) results in regular, noise-free behavior; case (2) results in behavior that repeatedly drifts away from the optimum pattern, but stays close to that pattern. The final product of this process is not a specific behavior, but a *control system*. This control system is, of course, capable of controlling those sensed variables that must be controlled in order to keep the reward coming. If it were not, it would be altered further by reorganization. But being an organization and not an act, the system is capable of controlling the quantity with respect to a variety of reference levels in a variety of situations involving different sources of disturbance. There is "transfer" from one situation to another (also an unexplained phenomenon under reinforcement theory).

It is hard to accept the idea that reward *stops* the process responsible for changes in behavioral organization; reinforcement theory leads one to think of reward as *causing* those changes. By this time, however, the reader must be getting at least a little immune to the shocks that feedback theory produces as it makes us switch our ideas of cause and effect around. These ideas are much like older ideas—Thorndyke's "law of effect" in particular—but are different enough to require rethinking.

It is even harder to accept the idea that the fundamental process behind learning does not depend on what is being learned. The reorganizing system cares only about intrinsic error, which is the same regardless of what caused it. It does not care whether the behavioral organization that eliminates intrinsic error is elegant or crude, efficient or wasteful, logical or illogical, systematic or messy, prudent or foolish, realistic or superstitious. The "value system" of the reorganizing system is simple: intrinsic error is bad, and lack of intrinsic error is good. The reorganizing system is totally pragmatic: if it feels good, do it; if it feels bad, change. If change involves changing system concepts, principles, programs, relationships, events, motion, configurations, sensations, or intensitives, it's all the same. Push the *change*-button—it's the only one there is. If the result isn't "good," push it again.

Punishment

Before going on to consider possible complications of this simple picture of learning, we must consider aversive reinforcement, which I have left out of the discussion to prevent confusion. Aversive reinforcement, or punishment, is anything that causes or increases intrinsic error. If a behavior pattern regularly causes intrinsic error, the reorganizing system will be driven into activity by that behavior, and that behavior will be reorganized out of existence. (I trust that the reader can supply his own reminders that avoidance behavior can be a learned control phenomenon, too: reference level of zero.)

As B. F. Skinner (1968) has proven beyond doubt, punishment is a poor way to teach anything. All that punishment can do is cause behavior to reorganize; it cannot produce any specific behavior, because reorganization can be terminated by *any* change that destroys the feature of behavioral organization causing the intrinsic error. Using aversive reinforcement, one can be sure of eliminating some aspect of behavior, but can have no way of predicting what the resulting new organization will do. Behavior is capable of change in too many dimensions to permit a person to think of controlling it by hemming it in with punishing consequences that leave only the desired behavior unpunished. Unfortunately, it is easier to invent punishments than rewards, and people have a way of trying to provide themselves with their intrinsic needs, thus making themselves unrewardable. More on this subject of controlling behavior in a later chapter.

Complications

The reorganizing system is certainly not as simple as I have made it so far. For one thing, the distinction I make between sensory and physiological effects of reinforcements is not as sharp as it seems at first; even a neural signal carrying sensory information involves physiological effects which potentially would have an effect on intrinsic state. It is well to remember that the reorganizing system has been quite arbitrarily separated out from the whole organism, and that it might be an aspect of every subsystem, an aspect which is simply not taken into account by the control-hierarchy analysis of the whole system. There is no reason to think that nature has tried to make it easy for us to understand ourselves by separating our major functions into neat packages that we can open one at a time. The *only* reason I have performed this separation is that not doing so makes the picture too complicated for me to think about. Some day, when we have come to understand the separate packages better, we may be able to dump their contents into one big package and see the system as it really is—as one elegant organization.

Even in thinking about separate systems there is room for much improvement. I have spoken about intrinsic reference levels as if they specify nothing more than the operating points of vegetative functions. That is almost certainly too limiting. As long as we do not try to invent reference levels having to do with aspects of behavior that could not be inherited (such as a reference level for car driving), we are free to try out any proposal. For example, it is feasible to think that the reorganizing system senses certain types of signals in the learned hierarchy, signals from which can be obtained information about the general state of organizations of the hierarchy, independent of specific perceptions of behaviors. *Total error signal* would be such a piece of information. A hierarchy in which there was a generally high level of error would be a poorly organized hierarchy, needing reorganization simply to make its control actions more effective. The reorganizing system does not have to know what the error signals mean in terms of the external world. It can optimize the system just by reorganizing it until errors are minimized. As we will see in the chapter on memory, this accounts nicely for dreaming as a means of improving control systems during sleep. "Nicely" isn't the same as "correctly," of course, but we can't have everything.

Built-in intrinsic reference levels may pertain to aspects of intrinsic state that are apparently abstract. For example, part of the genetic blueprint may be reference levels that contain the "general idea" of perceptions of all the various levels considered in this book, together with specifications for the general control type of organization (which is the same at all levels). There may be intrinsic reference levels pertaining to rather abstract needs, such as a need for some degree of harmony or beauty in our perceptions, necessarily vague and general attributes.

Jerome Bruner (1968) has considered the possibility of complex intrinsic reference levels under the heading, "The Will to Learn." He says,

> Almost all children possess what have come to be called "intrinsic" motives for learning. An intrinsic motive is one that does not depend upon reward that lies outside the activity it impels. Reward inheres in the activity itself.
>
> Curiosity is almost a prototype of the intrinsic motive. Our attention is attracted to something that is unclear, unfinished, uncertain. We sustain our attention until the matter in hand becomes clear, finished, certain.

Aside from the question as to whether, say, "unclearness" *inheres* in the subject matter being made clear, Bruner's concept is completely compatible with mine. The intrinsic reference level (or class of reference levels) specifies a desired consequence of learned behavior that is independent of what is being learned; hence it can be inherited as a useful guide to reorganization regardless of the environment into which the organism chances to be born.

As another intrinsic motive, Bruner suggests the "drive to competence," which translates easily into intrinsic reference levels relating to the quality of control systems. Still another intrinsic motive proposed is "a deep human need to respond to others and to operate jointly with them toward an objective." This concept is less convincing. It may merely express a consequence of the fact that human beings *must* form societies (ninth-order system concepts) both to minimize their intrinsic errors due to the difficulties of surviving alone, and to protect themselves against the intrinsic errors that noncooperating human beings can induce in one another. But that old controversy need not concern us here.

Another place where there is room for improvement in our model is in the concept of *how* reorganization is directed. I have been assuming that reorganization is essentially random. It may well be random with respect to any learned scheme, of course, but that does not mean it has to be random with respect to all criteria. There is no reason why the reorganizing system could not act on the learned hierarchy in maximally efficient ways so that in-effective behaviors are quickly eliminated and effective ones quickly found. In the final section of this chapter, I will offer some speculative proposals about ways in which reorganization might be more efficient than a purely random process, proposals for which there is at least a little evidence of practicality.

Awareness, Consciousness, and Volition

It would be greatly to an organism's advantage if the reorganizing system could somehow avoid constructing positive feedback systems or unstable negative feedback systems. The problem of assuring stable negative feedback by means of automatic self-organizing features of a system comes under the heading of *adaptive control*. Norbert Wiener, in his *Cybernetics* (1948), presents a general conceptual scheme by which such adaptations could be produced (see figure 14.2).

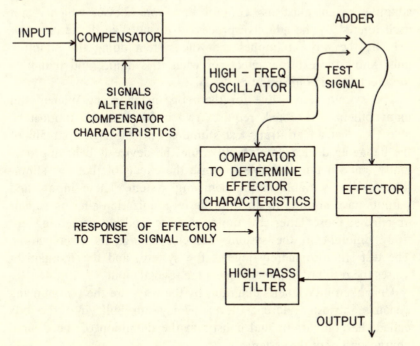

FIGURE 14.2. *Wiener's diagram (adapted).*

The main path in Wiener's diagram (adapted) goes through the compensator, the adder, and the effector; this would represent a portion of a control system, the portion that can be modified to assure stable negative feedback. A high-frequency oscillator inserts (via the adder) an arbitrary test stimulus that adds to the excitation of the effector. The high-pass filter removes the arbitrary variations and ignores the slower variations caused by signals originating in the compensator. Thus the comparator receives only a signal representing the response of the effector to a known disturbance, a test simulus. Inside the comparator is a computer that determines the desired characteristics of the effector and, on the basis of the discrepancy, generates signals. These signals (in Wiener's diagram) enter the compensator which is built so that they can change its characteristics in known ways. The result is to give the overall combination some desired characteristic.

This arrangement, while not the most effective (why not alter the effector's characteristics, to complete a feedback loop?), illustrates two facts: one, Wiener got almost everywhere before anyone else did, even if he overlooked some details, and two, an adaptive system must also contain an *adaptor* device which is not itself altered by the adaptive process. I do not like the term *adaptive,* by the way: it implies that the system doing the adapting must know the external effects of what it is doing, and that puts too great a strain on heredity.

The system responsible for the reorganization, as Wiener and many others have noted, requires two major features. It must be able to inject an arbitrary test stimulus into the signal stream of the behaving device (preferably while the device is behaving normally), and it must be able to sense the effects of that test stimulus on some variable in the behaving system. These inputs and outputs have nothing to do with the reorganization-altering signals or effects; those latter are quite separate and do something entirely different to the system, namely, change its organization. The test stimulus merely joggles the system, and the reorganizer senses the result of that joggling via the special input.

Unspoken in Wiener's diagram, by the way, are the reorganizing system's intrinsic reference levels. They are built into the box called the comparator and constitute the definition of the desired characteristics of the system.

This is the kind of organization needed by the reorganizing system to make its reorganizing effects on the learned hierarchy more effective than a random strategy. If the reorganizing system could send a test stimulus into the hierarchy superimposed on some reference signal, and if it could sense the resulting change in the perceptual signal of the same system, then it would be able to avoid setting up positive feedback systems and unstable negative feedback systems during reorganization.

Furthermore, if the reorganizing system could sample perceptual signals from, and send test stimuli to, *any* part of the hierarchy, selectively, reorganization could be limited to those systems in active use. This also seems like a necessary feature, for without it any intrinsic error could result in modification of any control system whether or not that control system had anything to do with the cause of the intrinsic error. That could prove disastrous.

Giving the reorganizing system access to hierarchical perceptual signals, and giving it a means for causing arbitrary behavioral acts, in no way makes the reorganizing system into a smart little man in the head. Received information is used for purposes irrelevant to what the learned hierarchy is doing and irrelevant to the meaning (external counterpart, that is) of the perceptual signals. Test stimuli are arbitrary, not being based on any learned considerations. They may produce organized behavior, but only what the learned hierarchy is already organized to produce when a reference signal is injected into it in the appropriate place. It may be feasible to allow the test stimulus signals to be injected *anywhere,* although I do not consider that possibility here.

To the reorganizing system, under these new hypotheses, the hierarchy of perceptual signals is itself the object of perception, and the recipient of arbitrary actions. This new arrangement, originally intended only as a means of keeping reorganization closer to the point, gives the model as a whole two completely different types of perceptions: one which is a representation of the external world, and the other which is a perception *of perceiving.* And we have given the system as a whole the ability to produce spontaneous acts apparently unrelated to external events or control considerations: truly *arbitrary* but still organized acts.

As nearly as I can tell short of *satori,* we are now talking about *awareness* and *volition.*

Awareness seems to have the same character whether one is being aware of his finger or of his faults, his present automobile or the one he wishes Detroit would build, the automobile's hubcap or its environmental impact. Perception changes like a kaleidoscope, while that sense of being aware remains quite unchanged. Similarly, crooking a finger requires the same act of will as varying one's bowling delivery "to see what will happen." Volition has the arbitrary nature required of a test stimulus (or seems to) and seems the same whatever is being willed. But awareness is more interesting, somehow.

The *mobility* of awareness is striking. While one is carrying out a complex behavior like driving a car through to work, one's awareness can focus on efforts or sensations or configurations of all sorts, the ones being controlled or the ones passing by in short skirts, or even turn to some system idling in the background, working over some other problem or musing over some past event or future plan. It seems that the behavioral hierarchy can proceed quite automatically, controlling its own perceptual signals at many orders, while awareness moves here and there inspecting the machinery but making no comments of its own. It merely *experiences* in a mute and contentless way, judging everything with respect to intrinsic reference levels, not learned goals.

This leads to a working definition of *consciousness*. Consciousness consists of perception (presence of neural currents in a perceptual pathway) *and* awareness (reception by the reorganizing system of duplicates of those signals, which are all alike wherever they come from). In effect, conscious experience always has a point of view which is determined partly by the nature of the learned perceptual functions involved, and partly by built-in, experience-independent criteria. Those systems whose perceptual signals are being monitored by the reorganizing system are operating in the *conscious* mode. Those which are operating without their perceptual signals being monitored are in the *unconscious* mode (or preconscious, a fine distinction of Freud's which I think unnecessary).

This speculative picture has, I believe, some logical implications that are borne out by experience. One implication is that only systems in the conscious mode are subject either to volitional disturbance or reorganization. The first condition seems experientially self-evident: can you imagine willing an arbitrary act unconsciously? The second is less self-evident, but still intuitively right. Learning seems to require consciousness (at least learning anything of much consequence). Therapy almost certainly does. If there is anything on which most psychotherapists would agree, I think it would be the principle that change demands consciousness *from the point of view that needs changing*. Furthermore, I think that anyone who has acquired a skill to the point of automaticity would agree that being conscious of the details tends to *disrupt* (that, is, begin reorganization of) the behavior. In how many applications have we heard that the way to interrupt a habit like a typing error is to execute the behavior "on purpose"—that is, consciously identifying with the behaving system instead of sitting off in another system worrying about the terrible *effects* of having the habit? And does not "on purpose" mean in this case *arbitrarily*, not for some higher goals but just to inspect the act itself?

There is enough informal evidence, I believe, to let us take this hypothesis about consciousness seriously. Associating awareness and volition with the reorganizing system gives us somewhere to start asking more detailed questions. At least we can begin looking for obvious counterexamples. And do you know of any other behavioral theory that has hazarded a guess as to what awareness and volition might be *for*?

A Final Note

John Platt, most of whose ideas concerning perception are pleasantly compatible with mine, has proposed an idea that has promise for adding to the "fine structure" of the reorganizing system. In general, the properties of this system can be as complex as we like, provided only that they be independent of the organism's experiences. We cannot have nature anticipating the happenstance world of a single lifetime. The only influence we can allow the environment to have in directing the details of the reorganizing process is on an evolutionary time scale. Platt's proposal meets this criterion.

Platt (1970) proposes "that the dynamic search for invariances may . . . be a general principle of organization in the higher-order processes in the brain." An example is the establishment of *straightness* as a perceptual category. Platt points out that straightness of a line can be detected strictly on the basis that scanning the point of focus of the eye along the line (the "dynamic" aspect) *fails* to change the perceptual appearance of the line. This remains true no matter what optical distortions are involved.

This principle can be generalized in such a way that invariances can be discovered without relying on any a priori geometric concepts, or indeed on any a priori concept at all except the principle itself. If a perception or group of perceptions can be found that is invariant with respect to some behavioral (control) action, that perception or set of perceptions can form the basis for a new perceptual category. We do not know if straight lines are "really" straight, but we can discover that the act of scanning the eye along them leaves them unchanged, and that can *be* our fundamental definition of straightness.

The reorganizing system as I have proposed it is equipped to inject the required disturbances and detect the results—in this case, *lack* of correlation. We must make the reorganizing system smarter, now, in order for it to act appropriately on the basis of this information, but it still needs to know nothing about the significance of these invariables in external reality. Speculations about that significance can still be left to our learned logical seventh-order systems.

If we suppose that the brain is initially structured to favor nine types of perceptual transformation (which defines nine classes of invariance), the search for invariances is less taxing than it would be if perceptual levels were formed from a random network. The search would be narrowed to a search for specific examples of a given class. Platt's idea suggests a new class of experiments which might "catch the reorganizing system in the act," and reveal whether perceptual categories are partly built-in or totally acquired. We might even find whether the nine levels of perception are totally arbitrary or are perhaps based on some real levels of organization of the outside universe.

REFERENCES

Ashby, W. R., *Design for a Brain*. New York: John Wiley 1952.
Bruner, J. *Toward a Theory of Instruction*. New York: W. W. Norton, 1968 (pp. 114–15).

Galambos, R. "Changing Concepts of the Learning Process." In *Brain Mechanisms and Learning,* edited by J. F. Delefresnaye. Springfield, Ill.: Charles C Thomas, 1961.

Konorski, J. Comments in *Brain Mechanisms and Learning.* p. 641.

_____. *Integrative Activity of the Brain.* Chicago: University of Chicago Press, 1967.

Pask, G. "The Natural History of Networks." In *Self-Organizing Systems,* edited by M. Yovits and S. Cameron. New York: Pergamon Press, 1960.

⨯ Platt, J. "The Two Faces of Perception." In *Perception and Change.* Ann Arbor: University of Michigan Press, 1970.

⟨ Skinner, B. F. *Science and Human Behavior.* New York: Macmillan, 1953.

_____. *The Technology of Teaching.* New York: Appleton-Century-Crofts, 1968.

Uhr, L., ed. *Pattern Recognition.* New York: John Wiley, 1966.

Wiener, N. *Cybernetics.* New York: John Wiley, 1948.

LEADING QUESTONS: CHAPTER 14

1. If a tablespoon of sugar makes a glass of lemon juice in water more rewarding, would ten tablespoons make it still more rewarding?

2. Rewards, it has long been recognized, cease to be effective when the organism becomes satiated. Can satiation be explained without the concept of a reference level? If you know Hullian theory, can you see the concept of a reference level as a simplification of the idea of *reactive inhibition?*

3. You are trying to solve algebraic problems and are being told after each attempt either "right" or "wrong." From your own experience would you say that getting the right answer becomes rewarding because the word *right* is rewarding, or that the word *right* becomes rewarding because it follows a successful attempt? Suppose the observer says "right" when you know the answer is wrong, or "wrong" when you know the answer is right: Would the reinforcement value change?

4. It has been found that rewards must follow execution of the desired behavior as soon as possible for maximum effectiveness. Suppose you have an assortment of buttons to push to get a symbolic token. After you happen to push the right button, there is a delay of ten seconds before delivery of the token, during which delay you go on pushing buttons. What would you conclude about which button makes the token appear? Subjectively, is there any mystery here?

5. Whom would you rather have as a teacher: a person who showed no friendliness except when you performed as expected, or a person who was always friendly even when you were slow to understand? For which teacher would you work the hardest? Are all students alike in this

respect? If a person will work hardest in order to get friendliness, what does this tell you about the friendliness he perceives and wants in general?

6. When you are trying to learn something, do you ever get into an uncomfortable position?

7. What difference do you see between learning to aim a bowling ball and learning to bowl opposite handed? Which requires reorganization, and which the selection of a different reference level for a familiar perception without reorganization?

8. Which of the following accomplishments require reorganization (of perception, comparison, or output means), which depend only on memory, and which require only control systems that could have been previously learned?

    a. Steering a straight course with one front tire quite soft.

    b. Learning the English equivalent of the word *pferd*.

    c. Seeing a pferd grazing in a pasture.

    d. Tracing a line with a pencil while watching your hand in a mirror.

    e. Learning what time the next show starts.

    f. Learning to reverse (subjectively) a line drawing of a cube at will.

    g. Detecting that one's chess opponent is using the Luzhin Defense.

Memory

From the standpoint of a behavioral experimenter, memory is an exceedingly complex phenomenon with no certain physical basis. Not only can human beings repeat sounds they have just heard, but they can pronounce sounds on the basis of what they have just read, and repeat acts that they have seen others perform. Practically every regularity in behavior can be interpreted in some way as a memory phenomenon. Even the physical state of the organism can be seen to fit the most generalized definition of memory: present traces of past experience. Big muscles are memories of exercise.

Too generalized a definition of memory, however, is of little use because such definitions melt indistinguishably into concepts like growth or performance. I think that we should deliberately forego the maximum possible generality, if only to give us something specific to talk about. Memory can be treated as a reasonably well-defined phenomenon, *the storage and retrieval of information carried by neural signals*. Under this definition, the structure of the learned hierarchy of control systems, although constituting a trace of past experience, would not be called "memory," because that structure itself is never represented in the form of neural signals. It carries neural signals, but is invisible to them.

The previous chapter on learning dealt with long-term changes in behavioral organization resulting from changes in the effective structure of the brain. We have, therefore, already dealt with a large class of phenomena that is commonly studied under the label of memory, without once depending on the storage of information carried by neural signals. In this chapter we will investigate only the significance of stored information, and I will stubbornly insist on meaning *only* that by the term *memory*.

Knowing the physical mechanism of memory is not essential to the development here, but the conceptual model of memory one adopts cannot help conditioning his concepts of the function of memory. I am going to adopt here the RNA theory of memory storage, and specifically reject the older idea that memory exists as closed circuits of neural connections (for example, Young 1964; Ranson and Clark 1947). We have, after all, found a different use for closed circuits, as time integrators (chap. 3). Time integration can be interpreted as a limited sort of short-term amplitude memory, but will not be dealt with that way here. I will assume only long-term memory in this model.

In the RNA theory (Hydén 1969), there is evidence that neurones synthesize proteins at a substantial rate when they are firing; these proteins may be involved with the chemistry of glial cells, which are densely packed among the brain's neurones, outnumbering the neurones ten to one. Whether or not there is involvement of the glial cells, there is a good possibility that RNA molecules, modified by neural signals, are part of the storage process. Hydén says,

> The modulated frequency generated in a neuron by a specific stimulation is supposed to affect the RNA molecule, and to induce a new sequence of nucleotide residues along the backbone of the molecule. This new distribution of components will then remain; the RNA has been specified. . . . This leads also to the specification of the protein being formed through the mediation of the RNA.

In effect, this theory may lead us to discovery of the "magnetic tape" on which memory is impressed before we have found the tape recorder to use it in. Even if this proves to be the physical form of memory storage, we are far from knowing what is stored, what determines the recording or nonrecording of information, and especially how memory information is accessed and retrieved. Here behavioral experiments and direct experience may be as valuable as biochemical investigations in telling us what capabilities to look for.

We have, fortunately, some memory devices to study that are fully understood in terms of physical models. While there is no guarantee that organic memory will have exactly and only the features of computer memories, there seem to be some general principles that would be difficult to imagine violating. These can serve as a guide to our thinking until we know better.

The Principle of Interpretation

We are assuming that memory is recorded in the form of a physical change in a molecule. That physical change must depend, according to some regular physical law, on the neural signals carrying the information to be recorded.

The principle I propose here concerns the retrieval of the stored information. Whatever the retrieval mechanism, it must in effect perform the inverse of the recording operation and must perform that in just as regular form. For a tape recorder, that means that a tape recorded with a two-track head and low-frequency compression must be replayed at the same speed at which it was recorded, on a machine having a two-track head and low-frequency *expansion*, if the object is to recreate the original information. The information stored in physical form is not independent of the recording and retrieval apparatus. Quite the opposite: an essential part of the stored information is contained in the mechanisms involved. If a magnetic videotape is replayed on an audio machine, gibberish—neither picture nor recognizable sound —will result.

This principle can be carried even farther. Not only must the retrieval be the inverse of the storage operation, but the result of the retrieval must be handled appropriately. A videotape recording is impressed on the tape magnetically; playing the tape back on an audio machine having a magnetic pickup *is* in a sense applying an inverse operation. But the result is gibberish because the recovered signal is processed by a sound-reproducing device and not a picture-reproducing device. What is done with the information after retrieval is just as important as the retrieval process itself. Information theory notwithstanding, the information in a signal cannot be defined without also defining the nature of the receiver. That holds true for memory devices just as much as for any other information-transmitting device.

The significance of this principle for a model of organismic memory is that memory has to be a *local* phenomenon. We cannot have memories simply being dumped into some community hopper for indiscriminate use by any chance subsystem. Instead, every subsystem must have its own unique memory apparatus, complete with storage and retrieval mechanisms, and information recorded from signals in that subsystem must remain associated with that subsystem.

This principle can be summed up rather simply. In order for neural signals to be recorded and replayed with their original significance, the effect of the storage must be that of a time delay in the signal-carrying path. The replayed information must reach the same destination that is reached by the signals being sampled for recording, and must be of the same physical form as the original information. To assume otherwise entails gross violations of parsimony.

The distribution of memory among all subsystems is accomplished with a vengeance by the RNA hypothesis: memory is associated with *every synapse!* The principle of interpretation implies that information is not only recorded at every synapse, but is replayed at the site of recording to create a new neural signal that is a delayed version of the original.

We do not have to apply the principle at that refined a level. For our purposes it is sufficient to associate memory with the functions in our model. I will draw the memory feature as if it were separate from the function—another convenient fiction, I am afraid. I will also forego the application of this principle to *all* functions, restricting this discussion to the perceptual function. There are applications to the comparison and output functions as well, but I have not developed them at this time.

Figure 15.1 shows how perceptual memory is to be added to *every* subsystem in the model. This is a first approximation to be developed further in later parts of this chapter. This arrangement satisfies the principle of interpretation of memory. Perceptual signals are recorded off the channel leaving the perceptual function and, upon retrieval, appear in the same channel. Thus, replayed perceptual signals are subject to the same interpreta-

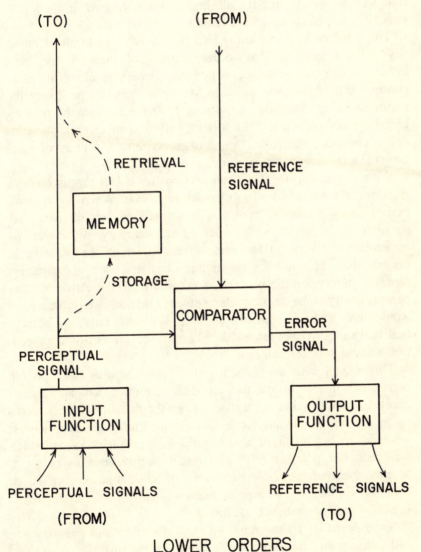

HIGHER ORDERS

(TO)   (FROM)

RETRIEVAL   REFERENCE
                    SIGNAL

MEMORY

STORAGE

COMPARATOR   ERROR
              SIGNAL

PERCEPTUAL
SIGNAL

INPUT
FUNCTION

OUTPUT
FUNCTION

PERCEPTUAL SIGNALS   REFERENCE SIGNALS

(FROM)   (TO)

LOWER ORDERS

FIGURE 15.1.

209

tions given to the original signals or present-time signals. When a memory appears in the perceptual pathway, it is just as though lower-order signals had arrived to stimulate the perceptual function, the main differences being those imposed by limitations of the recording, storage, and retrieval processes. Subject only to the mentioned limitations, the replay of a remembered perception will be dealt with by all higher-order systems just as if a present-time perception had occurred.

This concept leads naturally to a picture of eight levels of memory. (There are no lower-order sources of memory for first-order systems to perceive; hence the lowest level of memory content should be *sensations*.) Memories can range from the vividness of second-order sensations to the ectoplasm of remembered system concepts. This sort of variation in quality of memory is commonplace, but I know of no systematic studies of hierarchical relationships among kinds of memory.

With this arrangement we can account for a fact that is obvious in retrospect but almost too obvious to notice. When we remember, we may remember erroneously sometimes, but we never remember in terms of a new perceptual category. Whatever we remember is always in the same terms in which we perceive in present time. It would be unparsimonious to create a completely separate perceptionlike process to take care of subjective remembering; every time a new perceptual function was formed, it would have to be formed in duplicate. We need only *one* perceptual hierarchy in this model to take care of present-time perception and memory phenomena.

This model also accounts for the fact that one can apply a perceptual interpretation to recorded memories which was not applied to the original perceptions when they occurred. This shows up in the way we as adults remember our childhood experiences; we tend to apply adult interpretations to experiences to which we could not possibly have given such significance as children. Many psychoanalytic interpretations of childhood memories, at least as applied by amateurs, seem to show this characteristic. Is a baby really capable of jealousy?

Stromeyer (1970) has removed all doubt about this phenomenon with an astonishing experiment done in the manner of Julesz' elegant investigations of binocular vision. These experiments involve the use of computer-generated dot patterns in 100 x 100 arrays. The patterns are random; however, a stereo pair is formed by shifting a portion of one copy of the random pattern by several units to the left or right. The shifted area is totally undetectable in either pattern alone, but viewed stereoscopically results in a "floating" area in the pattern, raised or depressed relative to the remainder of the dot pattern by an easily visible amount.

One woman who had eidetic recall was tested by Stromeyer in an experiment involving memory—it took a daring mind to think of doing this. Stromeyer presented the stereo patterns to the woman, one pattern to each eye, but with a delay of 24 hours between the two presentations! In terms of our model, each pattern contained second-order information only; the third-order depth information was simply not obtainable from either pattern alone. Nevertheless, the woman was able to combine the two images in her memory and correctly identify the floating pattern. She also was able to perform similarly to combine images in different *colors.*

This experiment fully supports the present theory of memory; we would interpret it by saying that the second-order perceptions were stored (with incredible fidelity and detail), and were later replayed into the normal visual channels that reach third-order depth-detecting perceptual functions, just as would be done with present-time stereo pairs.

Whether or not every perception is recorded, we can be sure that not every recording is constantly being replayed, nor upon replay is all recorded information simultaneously retrieved. Retrieval is an ordered and controlled process. We now turn attention to a principle relating to this ordering and control, which will lead to a further modification of our model.

The Principle of Addressing

Every memory device of which we know has in addition to the storage and retrieval apparatus a third feature, *a way of selecting particular recordings for replay.* The natural question is, on what basis could such selection take place? If one knew what the recording was going to be, he would already have the information in the recording and would not need to retrieve it; if he did not know what was recorded, he would not know which recording to select.

In computer memories this question is only partly answered. Most current computer memories are divided into storage *locations,* sets of magnetic cores, for example. Each location can contain a certain number of bits of information, in any of the possible combinations of 1 and 0. Associated with every location is an *address,* a number which refers to one and only one location. When a set of signals is sent to the address input of the memory device, carrying a bit pattern corresponding to some particular address number, the contents of the memory location having that address are extracted from memory and replayed in the output channel.

The address signals are used as follows. Suppose a computation has just been completed, with a certain number resulting, R. For future purposes, it is desired to store that number. The program is written *by the programmer* (who knows that R is to be used later) so that this number R is stored at a known address in memory. Later, then, when R is needed again, the program is written so it sends the code for that address to the memory device, and R is retrieved. The programmer does not have to know what bit pattern will result from the computation, representing the number R, but whatever it is, he knows where it will be stored and how to get it back.

Implicit in the way computer memories are used, therefore, are properties of the programmer's *human* memory. It is human memory that recalls the name of the result that is wanted later on and the address (or address-generating program in more sophisticated programs) that goes with that result. A programmer who loses track of the association of addresses with the kind of information stored in those addresses simply cannot write programs. No matter how sophisticated the program, or what level of language it employs, behind it there is a human being using a *different* sort of addressing scheme.

The human type of addressing being discussed is called *associative addressing,* or *content addressing;* computer memories that work this way are just coming into regular use. In associative addressing, the information sent to the computing device's address input is not a location number, but a fragment of what is recorded in one or more locations in memory. Memory is still divided into storage units, each unit containing many bits of information, but these units have no specifically addressable locations. Furthermore, when an associative address is sent to such a memory device, information may be retrieved from many locations, not just one.

Whether or not the contents of a given memory unit are retrieved depends on whether or not the address fragment matches part of the stored information. Any part of the stored information can be used as an address, a match resulting in replay of the rest of the information in that memory unit.

Associative addressing is, I believe, the most generalized form of addressing we know about, including all other kinds. Even addressing by location can be seen as a special case of associative addressing, as it is used by programs and programmers (but not as that kind of memory device is designed). An address and the contents of the location addressed, *taken together,* form an associative pair. A programmer may ask himself, "Let's see; where did I store the value of Pi? Oh, yes, in location 10." Later on, he may ask himself, "What is in location 10? Oh, yes, the value of Pi." Thus, addressing by location consists of forming a set of associative memory units, each one of which contains a unique address and some data. If the data never change, the association can be used in either direction; either part of the memory unit can be employed as the address of the other part. When the data can vary, the process may work successfully only in one direction, since one does not know the data part of the address.

Associative addressing even includes addressing by time or sequence, as on a tape recording. In order for an associative address to have temporal characteristics, all that is required is that information from some kind of clock be recorded along with whatever else is recorded. Generating clock times as associative addresses then evokes from memory a sequence of recordings. In human memory we would seldom literally find clock-times recorded, but in our memory are time-dependent experiences of many kinds that can serve as temporal sequencing information. If one could generate an associative address consisting of just the temporally sequenced information, he would remember the associated information in temporal sequence. An example is one's body size; one can search his memory using body size as an address and recapture a sequence called "growing up."

In the most generalized form of associative addressing imaginable, memory would not be divided into discrete units. Instead, the units would be formed by regions of recordings containing a common element. Because of the many dimensions of experience, common elements might overlap the areas to which they pertain or be common to segments of different kinds of experience.

The associative memories now being constructed as integrated circuits are simultaneous-access devices; that is, an address signal sent to the memory's address input reaches all memory units at once, and every unit in which there is a match with the associative address responds by outputting its contents. If human memory worked that way, remembering would result in pandemonium, and if that were the total process in the machine memory, the same problem would arise. In the machine memory, the problem is solved by an external circuit that *scans* the responding locations one at a time, generating a list of all the associated information evoked by the address, with the various memory-unit contents separated neatly.

Human memory does not have quite the same problem because it is distributed among thousands of subsystems that can all operate at the same time; hence we can have an equal number of memory units responding at once without creating confusion. Rather the opposite effect results; the simultaneous replay of recordings in many separate subsystems can lead to rich and complex experiences. But within the set of recordings pertaining to a given subsystem, a problem of pandemonium does still exist. In human memory this problem seems subjectively to be solved by graded responses that mutually inhibit one another so that the strongest response wins, or alternatively by a threshold of response so that the associative address must attain a minimum degree of match with a recorded unit in order to trigger replay of the whole unit.

The property of graded response depending on the completeness of the address information seems to be evident in human memory. If one uses, say, the image of "red" as an address, this scrap is too small to evoke anything but the image of red; it pertains to *too many* incidents, and hence uniquely addresses none of them. In that case one does not receive a unique memory impression but rather an average impression, one that can be totally unintelligible.

Selecting a unique experience from memory thus becomes a question of constructing an associative address that evokes the strongest response from just one recorded unit, and very few (or else mutually contradictory and hence blurred-out) responses from other units. Mismatches may well act to reduce the response from a given unit, further improving discrimination. I am not familiar enough with the literature on memory to know whether experiments bear out these suppositions.

Much information, however, is available concerning the effects of employing good schemes for generating associative addresses for human memory. The Russian psychologist Luria, for example, followed the career of S., a man who, according to Luria, apparently never forgot *anything* during the 20 years during which Luria studied his memory feats (1968). Among the astonishing feats of memory performed by this mnemonist was to memorize a list of nonsense syllables constructed by randomly cycling *ma, va, sa,* and *na.* The mnemonist showed perfect recall of this list after it was presented *once* and demonstrated perfect recall, reading the list forward or backward, up columns or across rows, four years later, and again *eight* years later.

S. was undoubtedly possessed of (or by) memory apparatus of unusual properties, his abilities perhaps being connected with some of his mental difficulties such as an inability to generalize in a normal way. Part of his great skill, however, lay in methods he claimed to have worked out himself for forming clear and unique associative addresses. For example, when a list of words or even syllables or numbers was being read, S. would imagine himself in some familiar place, taking an orderly walking tour of a building or garden. As he walked, he would form visual images incorporating the material to be remembered, and stand, hang, lay, stuff, or otherwise conspicuously deposit the items around the imagined place. In terms of our model, he was calling information up from memory, and re-recording it along with the items to be recalled in such a way that unique associative addresses could easily be generated. When S. wanted to recall the list, he had only to remember the walking tour; as he strolled, he had only to notice the items as he came across them.

This method is in fact the oldest recorded mnemonic aid, dating back to at least the first century B.C. It was known then as "the method of loci," and was widely practiced. In *The Art of Memory*

(1966), F. Yates describes a typical scene: ". . . the rules summon up a vision of a forgotten social habit. Who is that man moving slowly in the lonely building, stopping at intervals with an intent face? He is a rhetoric student forming a set of memory loci."

Incidentally, in *Plans and the Structure of Behavior*, Miller, Galanter, and Pribram discuss plans for remembering, which involve the same principle, or rather another version of it which is also very old: forming bizarre images which are then placed in imagined relationships to form unique associative addresses for numbers and other kinds of items. A few years ago I used the method of loci (after reading *The Art of Memory*) to teach my youngest daughter her multiplication tables, through which she was struggling in the haphazard fashion that is popular in our school systems. In five daily sessions of about ten minutes each, she memorized (apparently permanently) the whole table through 12 x 12. I cannot imagine why rote learning is not *always* taught in this way; there's nothing to it. Try it yourself, with a list of say thirty randomly-selected verbal items. If you are careful to form clear and well-lit images as you tour some familiar room in imagination, you should be able to repeat the list perfectly in one try. The effects are particularly startling if you think you have a "poor memory." Most mail-order "memory courses" use this approach or a similar one; apparently this method is unknown (or at least rarely discussed) mainly among professionals who study memory scientifically.

Having gone this far, let us now deliberately back off a bit and settle on a more general idea than any of those presented. The main intent of the preceding discussion was to get across the concept of addressing and suggest a few relatively solid approaches, none of my own invention. For our model we do not need to be so specific. All we need to postulate is *some* addressing scheme, some way in which information can be sent to memory devices not to be recorded but in order to pick out specific recordings for replay. *Memory, in order to be useful, must be under control of some orderly addressing mechanism.* That is the principle I wish to communicate, and now I trust that its meaning has been somewhat clarified.

I will employ this principle to give the hierarchy of control systems a new property which accounts not only for perceptal remembering, but for the ability of organisms to reproduce past perceptual situations through actions. Once it is noticed that the model lacks this ability, one sees how essential it is.

As it stands now, the model contains nothing to evoke memories; no source of addresses for the memory box of figure 16.1. Furthermore, there is not even a way for the system to re-create a specific past perceptual signal, for reference signals are generated independently of perceptual signals and only by chance would demand recreation of a perceptual situation that had actually occurred before. There are many situations in which past perceptual situations *are* re-created, quite specifically and precisely. A choir director blows a note on his pitch pipe and one second later, fifty voices recreate the same pitch in 102 ears. A man shows a boy how to make a multiple jump in checkers and half an hour later the boy does it to the man. A person memorizes a street address and six months later drives slowly along a street until he perceives a matching house number.

We do not need to create a special apparatus to take care of these special reference signals. They are taken care of adequately by a single postulate: *all* behavior consists of reproducing past perceptions. One change in the model covers all cases, including many we have not yet considered. The change is this: We will assume from now on that *all reference signals are retrieved recordings of past perceptual signals*. This requires giving the outputs from higher-order systems the function of address signals, whereas formerly they were reference signals. The address signals select from lower-order memory those past values of perceptual signals that are to be recreated in present time. Thus the higher-order output function still acts to select reference signals for lower-order systems, but now it does so by way of addressing the memories of those lower-order systems. This, incidentally, solves the problem of translating an error in a higher-order variable into a specific value of a lower-order perception, a problem that has quietly been lurking in the background.

We are thus led to a new diagram of the control-system unit of behavioral organization. Figure 15.2 shows two routes that could be taken by retrieved memory information. One produces perceptual memory, entering the perceptual-signal path. The other produces reference signals that enter the comparator. Since

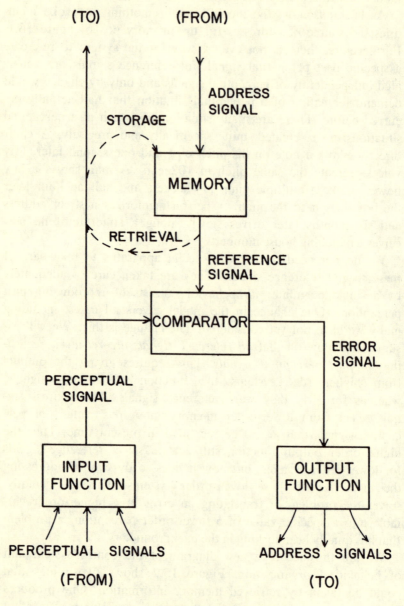

HIGHER ORDERS

(TO)   (FROM)

ADDRESS
SIGNAL

STORAGE

MEMORY

RETRIEVAL

REFERENCE
SIGNAL

COMPARATOR

ERROR
SIGNAL

PERCEPTUAL
SIGNAL

INPUT
FUNCTION

OUTPUT
FUNCTION

PERCEPTUAL SIGNALS

(FROM)

ADDRESS SIGNALS

(TO)

LOWER ORDERS

FIGURE 15.2.   *Control via memory addresses.*

there is only one address signal, these two routes must carry the same information. Let us consider what each route implies, for we can still make one last addition to the model with profit.

Take an example of remembering. One muses, "Who *was* that girl at Aunt Mabel's house in the red dress?" The address signals *girl*, *Aunt Mabel's house*, *red*, and *dress* are sent (as sketchy images) to lower-order memory address inputs. Since neither Aunt Mabel nor her house appears in memory wearing a red dress, the only response is an image of the girl who wore the dress. The full recording (or set of them) replays into the perceptual-signal channel, and one experiences the memory.

But according to figure 15.2, this recorded information gets superimposed on present-time perceptions, which is a wrong prediction, and it also initiates control actions by demanding perception of the girl in present time. While that might occur, it need not; our model so far *forces* action to occur every time a person remembers, another wrong prediction. What really happens is that we experience a visual memory of the girl in the red dress *at the expense of present-time perception*. The more vivid the memory, the more it replaces present-time perception; the more vivid we want the memory to be, the more we must ignore present-time visual images. (Stromeyer's experiments clearly showed this effect). And we certainly do not start running around looking for the girl in the red dress, who is now forty years old and wouldn't be caught dead in red. We remember *instead* of perceiving and *instead* of acting, or at least we may consider those as limiting cases.

Keeping that problem in mind, let us consider another. If every behavior is directed by reference signals from memory, why do we not perceive memories every time we act? We can surely tell (normally) whether we are experiencing present-time perceptions or memories. When we act, it seems that we perceive the present-time perceptual consequences, not the reference signals. Sometimes, of course, as when one attempts to signal a turn from a car window that isn't open, one catches a glimpse of the reference signal, the reference arm that is sticking out while the perceived arm crumples against the glass. But normally it seems that we have a choice between using memory as a source of actions or as a source of perceived memories, with some degree of mutual exclusivity between these states.

Apparently we can perceive *either* perceptual signals *or* memory signals and we can *either* remember *or* act on the basis of memory signals. There is some kind of switching or mixing function at work, and we must try to get it into the diagram. (See fig. 15.3). Two switches, unfortunately, are required. Fortunately, we can read meaning into all four of the possible switch combinations. These four correspond to what I call the *control mode*, the *passive observation mode*, the *automatic mode*, and the *imagination mode* (shown in the diagram).

The Control Mode

Both switches are vertical; I believe we have adequately covered this case.

Passive Observation Mode

Perceptual switch only vertical; memory output goes nowhere, leaving a reference signal of zero—this is the configuration if the system is to acquire a new reference level for a controlled quantity it can already control, without acting. Consider a person being taught how to draw the Greek letter *lambda*. He knows how to draw simple figures already; he observes the figure as someone else draws it, recording the perceptual result in the local memory of all systems involved (each in the passive observation mode). To reproduce the figure, he then addresses the new memory, with the switches in the control mode.

A large fraction of formal education requires that students be in the passive observation mode for long periods of time and seems to produce numbers of people who have trouble getting out of it again. It might be nice to know what changes the position of the perceptual switch—I have no idea at present.

Automatic Mode

Memory switch only vertical; perceptual switch connected to no signal source—the control system operates normally, but no copy of the controlled perceptual signal goes to higher-order systems. Neither does any recording take place.

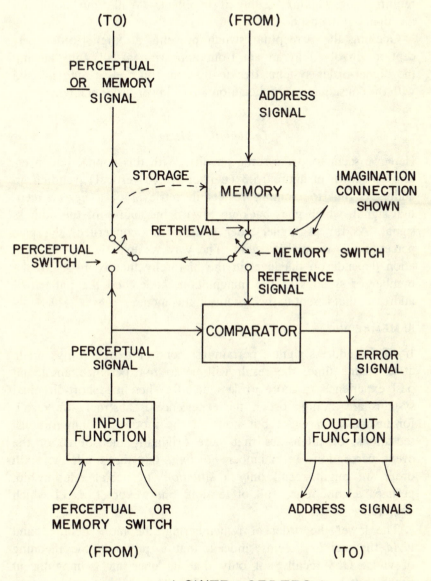

HIGHER ORDERS

FIGURE 15.3. *Final form of the unit of behavioral organization.*

We operate with subsystems in this mode constantly. When we are walking, for example, we do not want to be bothered by perceptions of all the implications of the fact that we are walking; we send the order to the highest-level control system actually required for walking, telling it in effect, "Walk, but don't tell me all about it. Just do it."

Opening the perceptual switch prevents all higher-order perceptions involved in an act from appearing at all, thus leaving the higher-order systems free to do something else, such as deal with the consequences of the automatized lower-order behavior.

Imagination Mode

Here we seem to strike some paydirt. With this connection in effect, as shown in figure 15.3 (neither switch vertical), sending an address signal to memory results in retrieval of a past perceptual signal, which goes back up toward the source of the address signal. As far as higher-order systems are concerned, the past perception is occurring again. The way we experience this situation depends on the level in the hierarchy that is involved, the number of systems in the imagination mode, and the pattern of addresses that is sent to the systems in this mode.

REMEMBERING

If all the address signals pertain (somehow) to recordings made at the same time, the result will be to re-experience an actual past experience in more or less detail. When the short-circuited systems are of high order, the experience is abstract: we recall, for instance, an event but none of the motions, configurations, sensations, or intensities that were originally the source of the event perception. I remember *bowling*, but that's all. At sixth order we might recall only a *situation*, a special relationship, perhaps a conference full of tension, but we don't recall which conference.

The lower the order of remembering, the more detailed and *vivid* the memory seems; indeed, that is probably the meaning of *vivid*. One recalls not only that he once ate a magnificent peach, but remembers the sweet juices and the just-right texture and the gray hair of the lady who offered it and a hundred other details. And he remembers how he *felt*; the emotion, too, the sensed state of himself, is recalled. That, I imagine, is why so many of us find it difficult to close the imagination connection at low orders. Not a lot of life has been like a magnificent peach handed us by a kindly old lady. If one must remember Grandma, it is easier to remember *that* she died, as an event devoid of supporting details.

Something special must be required to result in generation of temporally connected address signals. Nothing in the model *requires* this to happen. We will have to consider this question longer, either until we find the prerequisite experimentally or until the model goes away. Address signals do not *have* to be temporally associated; that is the next case to be considered, where they are not.

IMAGINING

If we place no restrictions on the temporal relationships among address signals sent to systems in the imagination mode, remembered perceptions can be recreated in any combinations, resemblance to past experience being lost at higher levels. Again depending on the order at which the imagination connection is made and on the number of systems involved, the consequences are known under a variety of labels.

Suppose one is trying to find a good program—say a program for dealing with the next few moves in a chess game. "If he moves his knight *there,* I'll move my rook *here,* but if he moves his knight the other way, I'll take it with the pawn." Of course in chess one is not permitted to move the pieces freely, nor would a good chess player (as I imagine him) babble to himself like this. Instead, he would simply *imagine* the relationships, not actually making the memory-derived images into active reference signals, but looking at them as if they had been accomplished. That is how a reference signal would look via the imagination connection—as if the lower-order systems had acted instantly and perfectly to make perception match the reference image.

Only when a program is found which when run to manipulate imagined perceptions satisfies one's heuristic principles does one flip the memory switch to the reference position and the perceptual switch to the present-time position, putting the program into operation and initiating the lower-order behaviors that execute the first move in the program.

Language is marvelous in the way it permits us to pass over difficulties without a ripple. Note how skilfully I bypassed the question of *what* flips the memory switch. "One" flips it! I plead guilty to obfuscation—the model obviously lacks some details which I am not now prepared to supply. I will continue to obfuscate, having no present alternative.

I have just described the role of the imagination connection in the activity known as *planning;* with nothing but a change in content, this is a general description of *thinking.* Some people imagine words when they think; some imagine other perceptions. "Abstract" thinkers manipulate imagined programs or principles (not actually working out the "details"—lower-order perceptions). "Concrete" thinkers manipulate specific events, movements, configurations, or sensations.

As far as systems above the imagination connection are concerned, imagining or thinking is the same as behaving. The only difference is in the ease with which perceptions can be manipulated. Behaving requires that all lower-order systems be actively operating to control perceptions via the environment, whereas thinking requires only that one be able to select reference levels such that if they were instantly accomplished, the higher-order error would remain small. In the imagination mode, of course, they *are* instantly accomplished.

One does not generally operate with *all* systems at a given order in the imagination mode. To do that would shut off all overt behavior and all present-time perception, substituting an internally generated experiential world for the one based on external events. But a condition like this does occur—once a day for about eight hours, for every normal person. I mean, of course, *sleeping.*

Sleep rests the body; in some stages of sleep that is the main effect. *Dreaming,* however, rests the mind, as William Dement and his co-workers discovered in their investigations of REM sleep (1969). Dreaming involves a loosening of all the normal connections from level to level, those that constrain our behavior to be consistent with the apparent properties of reality. Principles apply differently or not at all; programs run wild; impossible relationships occur; events occur together even if they are mutually exclusive; motion is unlimited and configurations strange. It is exactly as if most of the control systems at most of the orders were in the imagination mode.

Awareness is part of dreaming; it moves here and there to encompass many levels or concentrating obsessively on a single perception. Volition is unhindered—everything attempted produces an effect. I am far from the first to suggest that dreaming involves a process of reorganization, that it is a problem-solving period. What I have to add is only a slightly different conception of the nature of the problems that are worked on during dreaming.

I think dreaming can be thought of, at least in part, as *feasibility testing,* a process analogous to Freud's *reality testing* but accomplishing something basically different. Whereas in reality testing one is concerned with seeing whether a given control system is suitable for the actual environment one finds himself in, feasibility testing is concerned with discovering and repairing basic design defects in the control systems themselves: "down time," my wife says.

In the imagination mode a single control system or isolated group of systems will instantly "accomplish" any goal set, for it can manipulate its perceptions in ways unfettered by the rules embodied in lower-order systems. But if there is a design defect, it may be that no matter how the imagined perceptions are manipulated, the reference level being specified cannot be matched by perceptions. Hence those awful dreams in which everything one tries fails. The trouble is not in the intransigence of the environment, but in the structure of the control organization itself. Only by totally isolating a subsection of the hierarchy in the imagination mode can failure of control be traced uniquely to the control systems' basic unfeasibility. If the hierarchy cannot correct its errors even in imagination, how much less successful will be its operation in an unpredictable and poorly known environment? If I drive away my loved ones in my dreams, how well am I really organized to keep them close to me when I am awake? My program isn't even *internally* feasible.

An example of a basically unfeasible organization is *conflict:* two systems so designed that if one corrects its own errors, the other cannot, even in principle, even in an ideally manipulable environment. This particular defect is important enough to merit a chapter of its own, later on.

Imagination has another function: to supply missing but not crucial perceptions. If one is running through a program, for example, there could come a time when an event has to occur before the program can proceed: the checker on the rallye run must wave a go-ahead. The event occurs—or was he scratching his head? The signal was equivocal. So one *imagines* it (arbitrarily— does volition operate the switches?), allowing the program and the rallye to proceed.

This phenomenon has long been known as *closure*. What present-time perception fails to supply is filled in by the unsuccessful reference signal itself instead of the perception it was supposed to produce. The perceptual switch is not even perceived as having switched; perhaps the switch has taken place only in a few insignificant subsystems. One thinks he experienced the entire perception, which of course he *did,* at a higher order. There *is* no perceptual gap, because it was filled in from memory.

When something happens to close the lowest-order imagination connections, a person *hallucinates*. Someone's voice speaks startlingly out of nowhere; a person or an animal suddenly appears; one is transported to a different place with complete realism. If the lowest-order connections are made at random, one experiences weird distortions and juxtapositions: a man with a bird's head, a crooked wall waving like a flag, a sense of elongation, or tremendous distance, or distorted size, or impossible colors or smells. So I am told by people who have confided in me.

Experiences like these, which come from illness or drugs, are vivid because they are of low order, bizarre because they are random and cut off from the usual relationship with sensory stimulation. They are also fascinating and entertaining and fraught with new experiences. But they are false, they are not "alternate realities." They are nothing but the brain talking to itself, isolated from the real object of its perceptual functions. It is sad that so many people mistake this short circuit for enlightenment—especially sad if enlightenment is another real phenomenon, as I believe it is.

A Modicum of Evidence

Aside from the facts that the brain contains almost any imaginable signal connection and shows a great deal of spontaneous activity, the evidence concerning the imagination connection is indirect. The most suggestive and recent I have found is work reported by E. Roy John of New York Medical Center (1972).

Measuring external electrical fields caused by activities in a cat's brain, John investigated the appearance of wave shapes characteristic of responses to visual and other stimuli. Electrical variations could sometimes be as distinctive as oscilloscope presentations of vowel sounds. One experiment involved training cats to respond differently to two different stimuli; each stimulus produced a characteristic and easily identified wave shape. When a cat made a wrong response, the wave shape was often that corresponding to the wrong stimulus and not to the one actually presented, as if the cat had responded to a memory of the wrong stimulus. John himself identifies this phenomenon with memory and imagination, specifically relating it to similar experiments in man:

> A substantial body of data from human beings not only supports the contention that these released patterns of electrical activity actually correspond to the activation of specific memories, but establishes unequivocally that there is a subjective correlate to the appearance of these released potentials. When an event expected by a man does not occur, a cerebral potential appears at a latency [delay] similar to that of potentials usually evoked by the expected stimulus [see section above on closure]. Evoked potentials elicited in man by absent but expected events have been reported by numerous workers, including most recently Weinberg et al. We earlier reported similar findings in the cat. These cerebral events have been interpreted by Weinberg et al. to reflect the generation of processes corresponding to the memory of past or imaginary stimuli. Working in our laboratory, Herrington and Schneidau demonstrated that in some subjects the shape of the waveshape released when a particular geometric form was imagined closely resembled the waveshape evoked by the actual presentation of that visual stimulus.

Released potentials are not neural signals in specific pathways. They are more like what one would see of the operations of a computer by holding a high-impedance oscilloscope probe near the backplane wiring of the computer while the program was running. But in brain experiments correlations even of a general nature are valuable. They are among our best tools for observing the operation of the intact brain, second only in precision to subjective experience.

If, as Pribram suggests (1969), memory involves a distributed process akin to holography, and if perceptual functions are of similar nature, being distributed throughout limited volumes of the brain, these evoked-potential experiments may prove to provide more precise information about brain activities than now seems possible under my one-signal-per-channel hypothesis. Our model would not be altered by such a discovery, and its direct investigation would even be simplified, although we would lose the ability to perform very specific localization experiments to determine how the various functions are internally organized.

Conclusion

With the inclusion of memory, this model has come as close to being human as I can make it. Loose ends will just have to dangle for a while. Most of the model is testable, one way or another; I will suggest some methods in the next chapter.

We now have a sketch of a nine-level hierarchy of acquired control systems capable of reproducing past experiences at many levels, thinking and otherwise imagining, and reorganizing its own basic properties so as to maintain itself close to its genetically-defined optimum. Is the model correct? I do not know. It is complete, however, and that means that every experiment we try will almost surely prove critical. At least that is my hope and was my original reason for insisting on completion, even at the obvious risk of going beyond the evidence.

REFERENCES

Dement, W. C., Henry, P., Cohen, H., and Ferguson, J. "Studies on the Effect of REM Deprivation in Humans and Animals. In *Mood, States, and Mind,* edited by K. H. Pribram. Baltimore: Penguin Books, 1969.
Hydén, H. "Biochemical Aspects of Brain Activity." In *Memory Mechanisms,* edited by K. H. Pribram. Baltimore: Penguin Books, 1969.
John, E. R. "Switchboard Versus Statistical Theories of Learning and Memory." *Science* 177 (1972): 850–64.
Luria, A. R. *The Mind of a Mnemonist.* New York: Basic Books, 1968.
Miller, G. A., Galanter, E., and Pribam, K. H. *Plans and the Structure of Behavior.* New York: Holt, 1960.
Pribram, K. H. "The Four R's of Remembering." In *On the Biology of Learning,* edited by K. H. Pribram, New York: Harcourt, Brace, & World, 1969.

Ranson, S. W., and Clark, S. L. *The Anatomy of the Nervous System.* 8th ed. Philadelphia: W. B. Saunders, 1947.

Stromeyer, C. "Eidetikers," *Psychology Today* 4 (1970): 77–80.

Yates, F. A. *The Art of Memory.* University of Chicago Press, 1966.

Young, J. Z. *A Model of the Brain.* London: Oxford University Press, 1964.

Leading Questions: Chapter 15

1. Without actually doing it, imagine placing your right forefinger over the word *the,* preceding. Now actually do it. Does this make the relationship between imagination and reference levels clearer?

2. Try the same thing, but this time imagine pressing with a certain amount of force, to create some specific amount of pressure sensation from the forefinger. Is this a different *level* of imagination?

3. Can you repeat the above, paying attention to a specific fourth-order perception (motion)? a sixth-order perception (try "above")?

4. Imagine this page on fire. What happens to perception of the actual page when you do that? Does it seem that imagination and perception in the same channel are mutually exclusive?

5. Suppose a person had a memory of his mother buying a new red dress on the day before she died. If the memory of the red dress were transplanted into another person's brain (assuming it could be), would the recipient experience that memory as the donor does?

6. Think of the concept of "spinning" without imagining any object. Can you still detect that same impression when you imagine a roulette wheel spinning? What orders of perception are involved?

7. Look around the room. How many aspects of the room as you experience it are actually imagined rather than perceived? For example, do you imagine that the floor extends underneath objects resting on it and hiding parts of it? Do you imagine hidden parts of objects? Do you imagine the part of the room behind you?

8. Where are the car keys?

9. Why is it hard to recall a specific instance of getting dressed? What would you do tomorrow morning to give *that* example of getting dressed a unique memory address?

10. The oldest known memory technique is the "method of loci." This involves memorizing a list of objects, e.g., by placing them conspicuously (in imagination) in a familiar room one at a time, as if one is making an orderly tour of the room. To recall the list, one simply recalls the tour. Try it in the following list (go over it *just once*). *Don't* put the objects where a similar object actually might be.

an apple	a dozen eggs
the Mississippi River	a fishing pole
Calvin Coolidge	six inches of black thread

an atomic power plant

a ball-point pen

a burnt match

the symbol, π

a ringing telephone

bright purple socks

fourteen navy beans

a tiny dog

one pound of mercury

a one hundred watt light bulb

a new box of staples

the Empire State Building

a dirty cup

lemonade

an easy chair

homework

another burnt match

false teeth

How many of the twenty-four items did you miss? What was wrong with the addresses of missed items (out of sequence, too dim, confused with object already there, not imagined in a conspicuous place, etc.)? How is this different from simply "memorizing a list" such as a vocabulary list for a foreign language, or a list of nonsense syllables?

16

Experimental Methods

The theory in this book is based not on extrapolation or generalization but on model building as discussed in chapter 2. The experiments which will test and improve the theory will therefore not rely heavily on statistics, but far more on determination of the properties of a system as measured in its behavior.

The concept of measurement of properties is not entirely alien to psychology. In psychology there have been extensive studies of the physical correlates of vision, hearing, taste, and other sensations (order 2), the properties of neuromuscular behavior (including feedback-oriented studies of tracking) and other lower-order properties of behavioral systems in general. The lack of a coherent model of multiordinate behavioral organization, however, has prevented any of these approaches from coalescing into a study of the whole human system and has forced most psychological research into an addictive dependence on statistics.

My objections to the statistical approach to behavioral research, exposed here and there in previous chapters, are not based on a dislike of statistics per se. Rather they reflect my dislike of the blindness of statistical manipulations to organizing principles, and of the way statistical facts entice us to overlook the individual organismic properties that must underlie all statistical facts. There is a magical aura about statistical relationships. Certain events manipulated by an experimenter correlate with subsequent changes in behavior, with no causative links at all being visible: the relationship, for all anyone can tell, may in fact be magical.

Of course the hope is that a statistically significant relationship will provide a hint as to underlying causes, and I suppose things must work out that way sometimes. The hope, in any case, is probably vain for all practical purposes because when one is studying a complex system, he is likely to find that any event will be followed by alterations of many aspects of behavior to at least some degree. Given sharp enough statistical tools and un-limited freedom to repeat experiments, one could probably detect a significant correlation between any variable and any other vari-able involved in behavior.

Without an organizing model, there is no way to tell whether a significant correlation has any importance. For example, it is certainly true that running some programs in a computer will cause the magnetic cores in the memory to heat up more than they would with other programs in effect. Without an organiza-tional model of the computer at hand, one might be able to pick this relationship out of the random noise, and it would prove to be highly significant—statistically. Organizationally it would be of only minor interest, if any. Most important, when one *has* an organizational model he simply stops using statistics as a means for discovering things. It just isn't needed any more, except to eliminate residual uncertainties in measurements or to average out variations one doesn't wish to consider for the moment.

The experimental methods we will look at in this chapter are largely nonstatistical. They do not concern the behavior of masses of subjects, but of single individuals considered one at a time. They are all aimed at testing or elaborating on one organizational model; that model, not random guessing, is the source of hypo-theses to be tested, and the tests, not being statistical, make room for no counterexamples. All counterexamples are critical and re-quire revision of the theory.

The Basic Experimental Paradigm

In chapter 4, a method for identifying control organizations was sketched in. This method, formalized as "The Test for the Con-trolled Quantity" (or just "The Test"), is an adaptation of a technique used by servomechanism engineers to measure the prop-erties of control systems. It consists of applying a known disturbance to the quantity thought (or known) to be controlled and observing in detail the subsequent behavior of that quantity under the influence of the continuing steady disturbance and the behaving system's output.

Our problem is different from that of the servomechanism engineer. He knows that there is a control system and he knows what it controls; he is interested mainly in the details of *how* control is effected. We, on the other hand, are trying to establish whether or not a control system exists, and need only the most rudimentary knowledge of its detailed properties. We will therefore use disturbances differently and look for different aspects of the results. First, however, let us review some fundamentals.

Consider once again the meaning of the term *controlled quantity*. A controlled quantity is controlled only because it is detected by a control system, compared with a reference, and affected by outputs based on the error thus detected. The controlled quantity is defined strictly by the behaving system's perceptual computers; it may or may not be identifiable as an objective (need I put that in quotes?) property of, or entity in, the physical environment.

In general an observer will *not,* therefore, be able to see what a control system is controlling. Rather, he will see an environment composed of various levels of perceptual objects reflecting his own perceptual organization and his own vantage point. He will see events taking place, including those he causes, and he will see the behaving organism acting to cause changes in the environment and the organism's relationship to the environment. The organism's activities will cause many changes the observer can notice, but what is controlled will only occasionally prove to be identical with any of those effects. Instead, it will normally be some *function* of the effects, and the observer's task is to discover the nature of that function.

Since the observer cannot simply observe a controlled quantity, he must test hypotheses. He is looking for a definition expressing the quantity as some function of observables, such that a disturbance applied to the environment that tends to alter the quantity is opposed by the behavior of the organism. If every disturbance acting on the quantity is nearly canceled by an equal and opposite effect of the organism's actions on the same quantity, that quantity is a controlled quantity by definition, and the organism is organized as a control system relative to that quantity, also by definition.

The purpose of The Test is to reveal what is wrong with definitions of controlled quantities. Generally a controlled quantity will be defined as a function of several observable variables—the distance between the positions of an organism and an object, the three-dimensional orientation of something, and so on. If an irrelevant variable is made part of the definition, The Test will expose it in a very simple way: disturbances tending to alter that variable alone will not be opposed.

That is the crucial factor in applying The Test. When a potential controlled quantity is defined, that definition implies some assortment of events that (acting alone) would cause a predictable change in the defined quantity. *If the change occurs as predicted, there is no control system controlling that quantity.* If the predicted change fails to occur, or is much smaller than predicted, and if the reason for failure can be traced to the organism's behavior and nothing else, then the organism contains a control system controlling that quantity.

There will be ambiguous cases: the disturbance may be only weakly opposed. That effect could be due not to a poor control system but to a definition that is only remotely linked to the actual controlled quantity. For example, if when you open a window I *sometimes* get up and close it, you might conclude that I am half-heartedly controlling the position of the window when in fact I only shut it if the room gets too chilly to suit me. I could be controlling sensed temperature very precisely, when necessary, but by a variety of means: shutting the window, turning up the thermostat, putting on a sweater, or exercising. You are on the track of the right controlled quantity, but haven't got the right definition yet. It is safest to assume that an ambiguous result from The Test is the fault of the hypothesis and to continue looking for a better definition of the controlled quantity.

As described so far, The Test may seem to be an artificial and awkward procedure, subject to uncertainties and complicated to apply. In fact, it is a simple and intuitively satisfying technique that seems perfectly natural once it is tried. The best way I have found to become familiar with it is through a game which requires its use.

The Coin Game

Let S, the Subject, arrange four coins on a table so they satisfy some specific condition or exemplify some specific pattern (e.g., any isosceles triangle). E, the Experimenter, is to discover what S has in mind, without any verbal communication. S should write down his definition of the pattern or condition. E disturbs the coins in some way—any way. If the result is a change in the pattern or condition away from S's reference level, S must correct the error. If no change results, S merely waits (or to speed the game, says "no error"). This process continues until E is certain he can demonstrate three disturbances that *will* cause corrective moves and three that will result in a "no error" response. E and S then compare their definitions of the controlled quantity.

I recommend playing this game with someone because there is no better way to see how The Test works. One of the first natural predictions to fail is the feeling that practically any disturbance will be resisted. As E gets one "no error" response after another he will realize how easily his own perceptions can miss what the subject is perceiving and controlling. Another early (and to some, shocking) realization is that one normally cannot say what the subject "is doing" even though the error-correcting actions are completely visible and obvious. The experimenter's perception of what the subject is doing is completely irrelevant unless E has some reason to think he knows what S is perceiving. It is all too easy, as E will soon discover, to "make sense" of S's behavior: E will come up with many hypotheses that fit the coin patterns but fail The Test. It will become all too clear that an ability to see patterns in behavior, an ability that some might feel proud of, can lead more easily to a wrong description than a right one. What matters is not E's pattern-perceiving skills, but S's. The Test is unforgiving of mere cleverness: it demands correctness.

Another educational feature of the game is the way it puts verbal analysis aside. I know of no clearer demonstration of the difference between perceiving and talking about perceptions. When E and S compare written definitions at the end of the game, they may often find that they have used quite different language, different verbal analogues of the controlled quantity. S may have been preserving a "zig-zag" pattern, and E may conclude it is the letter N or Z. If they are both word-oriented types, E and S may argue about whose definition is the "right" one, forgetting that E has discovered what S was in fact controlling, whatever either of them likes to call it. Even S can be mistaken in this argument, because he may verbally define the controlled quantity to himself in a way that suggests many aspects of it that he does not actually control—a complex definition may boil down to a trivially simple perception.

Because The Test can reveal even abstract seeming controlled quantities without the need for verbal communication, it is applicable to the behavior of any organism, from the amoeba up, or, for that matter, to any control organization, living or not. It is a completely general method for discovery of control phenomena.

So far we have seen The Test applied in a piecemeal way to pick out single controlled quantities without concern for hierarchical relationships. We will shortly consider the use of The Test for exploring a hierarchy of control systems and for studying learning, but before that I want to present an example of moderate sophistication in which The Test was used implicitly to create an analysis of a rat experiment. The following has been published in more detail elsewhere (Powers 1971) and illustrates one way in which this new approach offers an alternative to customary explanations of experimental results.

Analysis of a Rat Experiment

The experiment in question was done by someone else (Verhave 1959); I have merely reinterpreted the data. Rats were trained to press a bar to avoid a shock given through a grid on the floor of a cage. Then the following experimental conditions were established: an interval timer was connected so that it would reset and start timing when the rat pressed the bar some preset number of times or when the timer reached some preset time limit. If the rat did not press the bar enough times, allowing the timer to reach its limit, a shock would be delivered to the rat as the timer began a new cycle. If the number of presses required were 8, as in one experiment, the rat would *never* receive a shock if it pressed the bar so rapidly that 8 presses always occurred before the timer ran out. If the rat *never* pressed the bar, it would receive a shock each I seconds, where I is the time limit set on the interval timer.

In each experimental run, the time limit I was set to values ranging from 15 seconds to 5 minutes. After each change of I, the rats were allowed to experience the experimental conditions for 4 hours, and the final average rate of bar-pressing was recorded. One experimental run done three times occupied several weeks of laboratory time.

The results were to be expected. The less time the rats had in which to execute 8 presses, the faster their average rate of pressing. With I set to only 15 seconds, the average rate for one rat was 70 presses per minute; with I at 300 seconds, the rate of pressing was only 5 per minute. Notice that these rates of pressing are too high: 8 presses every 15 seconds is only 32 per minute (vs. 70); 8 presses in 300 seconds is 1.6 presses per minute (vs. 5). Why did the rats work harder than they had to?

The answer, in a subtle way, involves The Test. What controlled quantity is kept from being disturbed (almost) by the rat's behavior? Anthropomorphizing, we would surely look first at the shocks, for which rats, like ourselves, probably have a reference level of zero. But how can shock be controlled? Once given, there can be no preventing the shock; not given, there is nothing to oppose. This challenge to the feedback theory is exactly why I chose this experiment to analyze.

In the coin game, the individual coins are not controlled—something about the coins, as perceived by S, is the controlled quantity. In the shock-avoidance experiments something about the shocks, and not each individual shock, must be the controlled quantity. The simplest first guess is that the something is the average rate of occurrence of the shocks. It is certainly possible for even a simple nervous system to construct that perception from raw sensory data. There may be physiological averaging of shock effects, leading to a perceivable internal state representing the average rate.

Verhave told me that the average rate of occurrence of shocks never rose above one or two per hour, after a final rate of pressing had been reached for each adjustment of I. If the rats had not done anything, the lowest shock rate would have been 12 per hour; the highest, 240. That is the natural range of values for the controlled quantity. ("Disturbances" can often occur in the form of physical properties of the environment that affect a quantity—here, properties of the experimental apparatus.) With the rats responding, the rate fell to essentially zero. The controlled quantity, obviously, is closely akin to the average rate of occurrence of the shocks.

The rats worked harder than is ideally necessary for one simple reason: they were unable to press the bar for hours on end at a perfectly regular rate, nor did they invent the strategy of making all the presses in one burst (they could not have known when to do that except after a shock). Instead, they pressed more or less irregularly, at some average rate, but with considerable variation in the rate. As a result, even though they pressed rapidly enough on the average, they would slip every now and then to too slow a rate, and get shocked. In order to keep the shock rate low, therefore, they *had* to press at a rate faster than necessary, to reduce the number of too-slow groups of 8 presses.

I assumed that the reference level of the controlled quantity would be zero: rats avoid shocks. Thus any residual shock rate was an error, and to complete a model of the rat (for this one behavior) all that was left was to define the output function that converts the average error (in shocks per minute) into an output behavior (in bar-presses per minute). Naturally, I picked a linear model as a first guess. The variations in rate of pressing were added to this model as if there were a noise source causing a distribution of rates of pressing about the average rate.

The setting of the interval timer was a property of the environment, in the feedback path connecting output back to input—bar-pressing rate to shock rate. For any setting of the timer and any average rate of pressing, the rate of shocking could then be computed from the assumed distribution of rates of pressing. That took care of the rest of the feedback loop.

Only two unknowns enter this model: one is the rat's sensitivity to an error measured in presses-per-minute per shock-per-minute. The other is the range of variation in the bar-pressing rate, also a property of the rat. Both parameters were adjusted to fit the theoretical curve to the data; the average (RMS) error in this fit was about three presses per minute.

I then tried a different definition of the controlled quantity— *the probability of a shock per interval I*—and went through the fitting again. Now the error was about one press per minute, which was within the scatter of the data. (This fit is shown in fig. 16.1.) Clearly the second definition of the controlled quantity is the better one.

Both parameters have specific predetermined physical meaning—that alone is enough to differentiate this kind of curve fitting
from that normally done in such experiments where the parameters are given ad hoc meaning or none at all. But one would
like to do more than fit curves to data points. Predicting data
would be even more satisfying. That was done next.

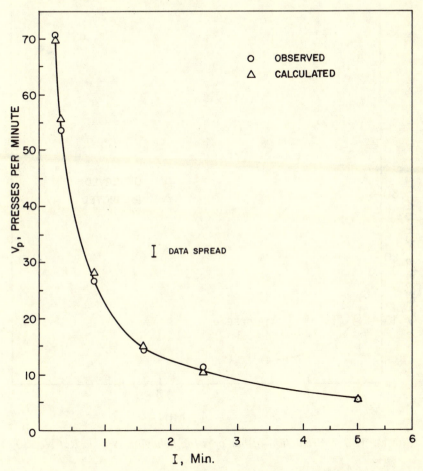

FIGURE 16.1. *Fit of theoretical curve to data; N = 8, Rat No. 17.*

Data was obtained for a second experiment using a different
rat. This experiment differed in another way—the rat had to press
the bar only *once* instead of 8 times during the interval I in order
to postpone the shock. The number of presses required appeared
explicitly in the system equation, so it was merely changed from

an 8 to a 1, and the curve was recomputed using the parameters determined from the behavior of the other rat in the other experiment. The theoretical curve fit the new data within *less* than 1 press per minute (see fig. 16.2).

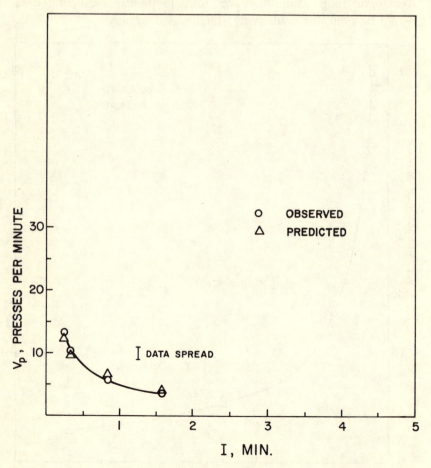

FIGURE 16.2.   *Prediction of bar-pressing behavior. N = 1, Rat No. 20.*

The point of this example is to show how isolated instances of behavior can be analyzed in control-system terms, and how The Test shows up quite naturally as one tries various hypotheses about the controlled quantity. This kind of analysis—especially when applied to rats—is not everyone's dish, but is useful to think about to widen one's view of how The Test can be applied. I picked an experiment that was not carried out with feedback theory in mind, in which the variables did not at first seem amenable to continuous-variable treatment, and that allowed no verbal communication, primarily to show that many apparent limits to the applicability of this theory are not really limits.

I would not, however, deliberately design an experiment that requires such complicated treatment. The information obtained about the rats' inner organization was almost nil; there was too much random variation, probably caused by using shocks as a controlled quantity and thus most probably triggering off *reorganization* due to intrinsic error. The feedback loop was prone to instability due to the either-or nature of the criterion for giving or not giving a shock. The experiment was far from ideal as a tool for investigating control organization.

Experiments with rats might be devised involving continuous control (not on-off bar pressing) and designed specifically to give the animals direct control over whatever controlled quantity is being tested. Then one could approach directly the crucial questions: can this rat control this sort of quantity, and if so, how well? If the rat appears to be controlling some quantity, is it the one originally intended, or something else? Many current approaches to animal behavior research could easily be adapted along these lines.

The Parable of the Rubber Bands

There is another demonstration/game/experiment that seems to help understand The Test and its application to experiments. It has the same main advantage as the Coin Game—it is highly portable. This demonstration also involves two players, Subject and Experimenter, and the equipment is even cheaper: two rubber bands, knotted together, as in figure 16.3.

FIGURE 16.3.

S and E each put a forefinger in a loop at an end of the rubber band pair, and they hold the rubber bands slightly stretched just over a table top. S now determines to keep the knot stationary over some inconspicuous mark on the table-top. E can disturb the position of the knot by pulling back or relaxing his pull on his end of the rubber band pair; S maintains the knot where he wants it by similar means. Figure 16.4 shows how this situation relates to the basic feedback diagram used near the beginning of the book.

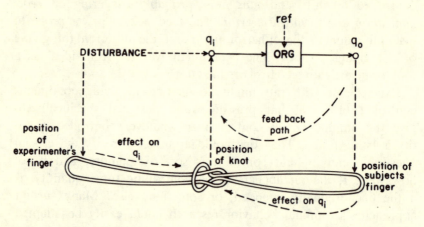

FIGURE 16.4. *Relationship of the rubber bands to the basic feedback diagram.*

The position of the knot, as seen by the subject relative to the mark on the table, is the controlled quantity, q_i. The position of the subject's finger is the output quantity q_o. One rubber band represents the environmental feedback path through which the subject's output affects his own input, the controlled quantity. The position of the experimenter's finger represents the disturbing event, and the remaining rubber band represents environmental links through which the disturbance tends to affect the same controlled quantity affected by the organism's—the subject's—output. Thus in this demonstration every aspect of the feedback control situation is visible and explicit.

If E now draws slowly back on his end of the rubber band, S will do likewise, and the knot will remain quite stationary. If E swings his end slowly from side to side, S will swing his end the opposite way and the knot will still not move. To see why it is confusing to use disturbances too rapid for the control system's appropriate time scale, E may try jerking his end around. S's control will deteriorate and transient movements of the knot will tend to mask the reference position. It will be seen that sudden and transient disturbances reveal little about organization per se.

This demonstration is a nice way to introduce feedback theory to behaviorists, though they tend to become oddly silent as it progresses. From the behavioristic point of view, E's finger-movements constitute the *stimulus,* and S's constitute the *response.* Discriminable motions of various parts of the rubber bands can also serve as stimuli. That excludes, of course, the knot, if the stimuli change slowly, for the knot moves the least or not at all! The behaviorist E would try to discover how the subject's responses depend on the stimuli. Almost inevitably, such E's will begin by applying *sudden* stimuli, for that is the traditional bias. If E can reach any conclusion, it would most likely be some statement that the subject's response is generally (statistically) opposite to the stimulus in direction. If S prevails on E to slow down, that stimulus-response law will become quite clear. But unless E happens to notice that the knot stays still, he will miss the crucial feature of the situation—the purpose of S's every movement.

This demonstration has the most impact on a behaviorist if he actually deduces the correct stimulus-response law. When he does, S can point out that the knot remains in one place, and can then show beyond doubt that the stimulus-response law is a property of the rubber bands and not a property of S. Wherever E places his finger, there is only one place where S's finger can be *if the knot is to remain stationary.* The relationship between those positions depends *only* on the relative elasticity of the two rubber bands, and could be determined in advance using no subject at all.

Adding two coins, we can illustrate "control by manipulation." Place one coin under the knot, and the other about six inches from that location, toward S. S is to keep the knot over his coin, and *E is now to place S's finger over the other coin.* S cannot control *both* his fingers and the knot: they are connected. Therefore if S wants to control the knot, E can control S's finger, as long as the result does not inconvenience S (as by running the finger into a hot soldering iron). This is an endlessly illuminating demonstration, and amusing to try.

In ordinary behavioral situations, the "rubber bands" are hidden or invisible, and the knot—the controlled quantity—is far from

obvious. All that *is* obvious is the relationship between the disturbance and the subject's output. Ponder that, and you will
understand clearly what led psychology into the fatal misinterpretation.

And be sure to carry a couple of rubber bands with you at all
times.

Exploring the Hierarchy

So far we have been dealing with behaviors involving just one obvious controlled quantity. Some readers may have noticed another
important fact: we have uniformly assumed a fixed reference
level for the controlled quantity. The Test, as outlined so far, will
not work if the reference level shifts erratically, as it might well
do as higher-order systems act to correct higher-order errors. In
order to use The Test successfully as described so far, one must
either pick quantities likely to involve fixed reference levels (avoidance of shock) or arrange to have the subject hold his higher-order
reference levels constant for a while.

The usefulness of The Test would be greatly increased if a way
could be found to make it independent of reference level. If we
could determine the *kind* of variable being controlled without having to know its momentary preferred value or state, we could perhaps learn to separate levels of control system without putting un-
natural restrictions on the subject.

In order to devise such a method we must use The Test in a way
a little closer to the way it is used in control engineering. In identifying a controlled quantity, we are basically looking for a response to a disturbance that has the opposite effect on the controlled quantity. That basic relationship will not be affected on
the average even if the reference level changes randomly. If behavior is already going on, making the controlled quantity track a
changing reference level, a disturbance will call forth added
changes in output, superimposed on those already occurring.

If we simply employ random disturbances—random in direction
and amount—there should be no observable correlation with the
system's output unless a controlled quantity is being disturbed. If
a controlled quantity is disturbed, even relative to a changing
reference level, the proper measure of output will show a definite
average relationship to the disturbance.

That "proper measure" is, of course, the predicted effect of the output on the hypothesized controlled quantity. The disturbance, too, must be expressed in terms of predicted effects on the same quantity.

Actually, it is not necessary to measure the system's output, for we are interested mainly in the controlled quantity itself. Rather than looking for a correlation between disturbance and output, we can look for *lack* of correlation between the behavior of the defined quantity and a disturbance that is known (on physical grounds) to be able to affect the quantity.

In order to eliminate the effects of a changing reference level, these correlations must be expressed in terms of *changes*. A change in the value of the disturbing variable should, on the average, produce no change in the controlled quantity (or far less change than physics would predict).

This approach must take into account the fact that control systems all have speed limits. When the amount and direction of disturbance are changed, there must be a delay before sampling the state of the controlled quantity or else confusing dynamic effects will take over. This delay should be varied to find the point at which transient effects die out.

In some situations—at the moment I can think of only a few simple tracking experiments—the method of correlating changes separated by a time delay can be done rather easily and rigorously. It is a happy fact that the *cross-correlation function* of a disturbance and a controlled quantity can be continuously monitored and will yield the desired relationship directly in usable form if the "driving function"—the disturbance—takes the form of random noise. All that is needed is some ingenuity in the monitoring equipment which must embody the definition of the controlled quantity. But that is what engineers are for, especially those who have been using techniques such as these, although not in this theoretical context, for years.

Reaction Time Experiments

In a hierarchy of control systems, lower-order systems must necessarily have a faster response than higher-order systems. That is a basic stability requirement. Since part of the slowness of behavioral control systems results from a true time delay during which neural events propagate from input to output, it must be true that lower-order systems will respond to a disturbance before higher-order systems even begin to respond.

Here is an illustration I thought of many years ago and have yet to see fail. Have someone hold his arm straight out, and place your hand on top of his, lightly. Ask him to move his arm rapidly downward when you signal by giving his hand a short, sharp downward push. The result will be a two-stage reaction. The signal push will deflect the arm downward, and it will immediately begin to return to the original reference position. I have verified that this is an active response involving a control system, and not an effect of muscle elasticity (using an electromyograph). After a delay, the reference position will be reset, and the arm will then accelerate downward for good. I have yet to find a subject who can eliminate this "hitch" in the response, no matter how long he or she practices. Direction makes no difference.

I interpret this experiment (not very daringly) as evidence of at least two levels of control. One level of control maintains the arm at a reference position; the higher level defines that reference position. The initial signal is only a disturbance to the lower-order system and is resisted, while the higher system detects the fact that the signal has occurred and finally gets around to resetting the lower-order position reference.

This simple approach may prove useful in determining relative order of control organizations. Obviously a system which reacts within the response time of another one *has* to be of lower order if the slower system acts by adjusting the reference level of the faster one. As far as I can see, the opposite ordering of speeds would have to create violent oscillatory instability. Thus a ranking of control organizations by latency or response lag might provide an important clue to the structure of the hierarchy of control.

Studies of Reorganization

The one aspect of this book that seems to create puzzlement is my concept of the organizing system. The most common objection arises from failure to grasp the difference between a change in the *actions* of a control system (which occurs when disturbances arise) and a change in the *properties* of a control system. Perhaps by discussing how I propose to investigate learning I can make this distinction clearer (and perhaps doing the experiments will prove me wrong—who cares, as long as they get done?).

Suppose we have successfully identified some controlled quantity and are sure of its nature and can continuously monitor it. What would happen if we then introduced a change in the environment such that the organism's outputs were no longer effective in controlling that quantity? Assuming that loss of control creates intrinsic error, we would predict that reorganization would commence and would continue until control were restored or that control system were dismantled altogether. By continuously monitoring the controlled quantity and the effects of disturbances on it, we would be able, in effect, to observe the transfer function of the system changing, to monitor the process of reorganization itself.

This would permit us to ask and answer some basic questions about this process. Is it random, or does it begin altering parameters immediately toward the final values? Is it variable in speed? Does its progress relate to physiological signs of stress, such as blood pressure, heart rate, respiration rate, vasoconstriction, or galvanic skin reflex? Does it lead to a logically preferable solution or simply to the first one that works? Does it improve with practice? (It shouldn't.) Does it depend on conscious attention? (It should.)

Before reorganization can be studied meaningfully, we must clearly know a lot about existing organization and develop methods to keep track of it continuously. This does not mean we have to understand the whole hierarchy before starting to investigate reorganization, but it does mean that work on existing organization must be the first order of business.

The Levels

There has been no mention in this chapter of the specific structure of levels I have proposed, because I consider those definitions to be no more than a starting point. We should not, however, totally ignore them because they do represent the outcome of a long period of informal observations of behavior, and it seems unlikely to me that they would be completely in error.

Perhaps the best way to view the definitions of the nine levels is as a source of hypotheses for test. It is not difficult to arrange an experiment in which a subject is given control of some exam-

Chapter 16

ple of intensity, sensation, configuration, motion, sequence, or relationship, the first six levels. Investigations of higher levels—program, principle, and system concept—will be difficult to instrument, but these kinds of behavioral organization are not usually investigated quantitatively anyway. At these higher levels, experiments will verge on therapy sessions and the methods of applying The Test will involve one-to-one interpersonal interactions.

There is another reason for keeping this chapter general rather than proposing specific experiments oriented around my definitions of levels. We do not have to grasp at straws. The correctness or incorrectness of the definitions is and should be a matter of indifference, for those definitions do not represent our only hope of understanding behavior. The real power of this theory comes from the basic concept of behavioral control. Defining the levels helped me to see how that basic concept could be applied to *all* behavior, so in a way the levels have already had a useful life. We are now in a position to examine them critically, knowing that the same experiments that may force change in the definitions will supply the needed improvements. If we cling too lovingly to the particular structure in this book, we may miss the chance to make major improvements in the near future. We do not want to let psychology fall into another sixty-year-long rut as a result of being defensive about some small and temporarily useful discovery.

Therefore, let us concentrate on putting a firm base under the basic concepts of this theory, if we can, and let the structure build on that however it wants to. Confidence in the basic ideas will make defenses unnecessary.

General Comments

I do not want to leave this chapter before correcting a possible impression that only rigorous and instrumented experiments are of any use. The opposite is probably closer to the truth for the time being. Getting a useful grasp of this theory means spending much time merely getting the feel of it. The everyday world is full of examples of disturbances being resisted, strong hints as to the nature of controlled quantities, and even chances to do a little nudging to test hypotheses without becoming too obnoxious. But practically every opportunity to apply the theory proves also to be a challenge to some comfortable preconception of How People Work. Psychological theories may not seem to have much to do with ordinary life, but it is amazing to see how behavioristic concepts permeate our thought and our language. Perhaps I have it backward—perhaps behaviorism arose from a far older and more deeply entrenched misconception of human nature. In any case, trying to watch people as if they were control systems will reveal some dramatic contrasts between feedback theory and other more widespread "theories."

It does not make sense to rush into formal experimentation before having given this whole system concept a chance to fill out and become solid. Some of my more painful experiences have come from listening to proposals for research based on a half digested mixture of feedback and behavioristic, or feedback and humanistic principles. I appreciate the enthusiasm but deplore what seems to be an unconscious effort to preserve the more precious of one's misconceptions. And I think at this stage, after twenty years of consideration, I can call at least some ideas misconceptions without being arrogant.

Let us approach human behavior from this new point of view as we would begin exploration of virgin territory. If we see familiar things along the way as we innocently follow our noses, so much the better, time will have been saved. I expect that much previous work in psychology and related sciences will prove salvageable and valuable, but we should, to avoid confusion and prejudice, approach the exploration of this theory as if we were ready to start psychology all over again, from a second foundation.

References

Powers, W. "A Feedback Model for Behavior: Application to a Rat Experiment." *Behavioral Science* 16 (1971): 558–63.

Verhave, T. "Technique for Differential Reinforcement of Rate of Avoidance Responding." *Science* 129 (1959): 959–60.

17

Conflict and Control

In this final chapter we will look into applications of this model of human behavioral organization. The reasons for applying this model even in its present rudimentary state are twofold. First, the results are interesting and even useful in ordinary living; it is a theorist's prerogative to think so. Second, this is the best way I know to combat the "nothing-but" syndrome. The second reason may be the most important for the future of this theory.

The "nothing-but" syndrome is the demonstrated tendency of human beings to upgrade similarities to the status of identities. Thus I have heard that the reorganizing system is "nothing but" drive-reduction theory, that the control-system unit of organization is "nothing but" reafferent stimulation, that higher-order perceptions are "nothing but" concepts. Each nothing-but-er was attempting, often with generous intent, to find a niche for this control-system model in some established scheme. It is my present conviction that all such attempts will fail, not because this theory owes nothing to its predecessors (it owes everything), but because it carries us beyond its predecessors into new territory. It makes us think about behavior in new categories. Attempts to make this model congruent with older non-control-system concepts always, in my experience so far, require a misinterpretation of the properties of control systems or a direct contradiction of a postulate in the model. I do not object to justified contradictions, but only to accidental and thus indefensible contradictions.

Such contradictions can arise from the fact that older theories are based on and in turn are used to "prove" basic assumptions about human nature that are directly denied by the control-system analysis. The kinds of distortions that typically occur are precisely those that permit older ideas of human nature to be retained, almost as if the implications of control theory had been grasped and rejected as unthinkable; the well-intentioned student distorts the theory to eliminate the unthinkable consequences, often, no doubt, with the friendly motive of refusing to believe that I could be so stupid. For example, it is amazing how long a listener can go on smiling and nodding, busily reinterpreting my words to mean something else, without really understanding that control systems control their inputs and do not "control" their own outputs.

The best approach I have found to forestall the "nothing-but" syndrome and consequent misinterpretations of this theory is to use the theory to develop specific implications concerning experience and behavior. That procedure at least defines as clearly as possible the real differences between this approach and older ones. It also gives me the well-deserved opportunity to speculate somewhat less restrainedly.

In this final chapter I will use the properties of the model to develop a theory of conflict, showing first what the term *conflict* means in the context of this model and then how conflict can be the most serious form of malfunction possible in the human hierarchy (short of physical destruction). To many readers the implications of this theory of conflict for psychotherapy will be obvious and I hope exciting. I will not, however, try to develop a therapeutic approach in this book.

Instead, I will close by applying the theory of conflict to show the impracticality of one of the most common modes of human action and interaction: self-control and mutual control of behavior. I think it can be shown that the idea of controlling behavior—one's own or that of other people—stems from an old but incorrect concept of human nature, incorrect because it fails to recognize the control-system properties of human nature. What we commonly think of as control is not control at all but *conflict*. Intrapersonal and interpersonal conflict thus result directly from our misunderstanding of the feedback control process in ourselves and in others.

Logical Conflicts

This subject is a red herring, and I discuss it here only because of the way it can throw us off the track. Logical conflicts are *paradoxes*. Paradoxes sound like conflicts, but only if one arbitrarily restricts himself to unrealistic rules at one level of perception. Logical conflicts are little more than a game one can play or not, as he chooses, and are easily transcended if one reminds himself of the full range of choices available to human beings.

Most paradoxes boil down to a simple contradiction: *A* implies not-*A*. The card that says on one side, "The sentence on the other side is true," and on the other side, "The sentence on the other side is false," is an example, as is the old story about the man who claims he always lies. A subtler example is the Prisoner's Dilemma (Rapoport and Chammah, 1965). Two prisoners accused of the same crime are held separately. Both can be convicted only if at least one confesses. If only one confesses, he alone gets a lightened sentence for implicating the other. If both confess, both receive a harsh sentence. Each prisoner is faced with the same dilemma: *not* confessing could lead to either freedom or a harsh prison term, while confessing could lead to either a mild or a harsh prison term, depending on the other prisoner's decision.

This is a pretty paradox as long as one plays the game as a seventh-order program bound by fixed rules. Going up a level, however, destroys the paradox, as is the case for all self-contradictions. Then one sees that the Prisoner's Dilemma is a dilemma only within a very restricted set of assumptions having nothing to do with real situations. If this problem were programmed into a real computer so that the stated rules were perfectly obeyed, the result would be that neither simulated prisoner would confess. Instead, the computer would cycle endlessly between the two possibilities, each looking better until chosen, and it would never finish running the program. A human prisoner who faithfully followed the same rules would also come to no decision. There *is* no decision he can reach on grounds of logic alone. If he does make a decision, he must have introduced other considerations outside the rules originally specified. He may decide to adopt a principle of truthfulness, in which case he will confess or not confess on grounds having nothing to do with the other prisoner's choice. He may base his decision on an estimate of the other prisoner's ability to see the advantage of not confessing; that estimate will then govern what decision is made, unambiguously. He may flip a coin and hope for the best. He may decide that this is his lucky day, and not confess, "knowing" that he will go free. He may confess in a way that will later prove to contradict the facts of the case, hoping to get word to the other prisoner during the confusion. Given the real range of human ingenuity, one can hardly treat the Prisoner's Dilemma seriously, *except* as a game.

When any paradox of the form A implies not-*A* is built into a real device, something specific will happen, but it will happen outside the assumed universe of discourse. A relay circuit set up as a logical contradiction simply *buzzes;* that is the basis for a simple and useful device. Logical relationships leave out time and numerous other considerations. That is why logical processes do not occupy the highest level in the human brain, and that is why making logic too important in human affairs is a mistake. Human conflicts are far more serious than logical conflicts, especially when there is no logical way out of them. If one cannot decide between letting logic run his life and letting his feelings run his life, how can he find a logical way out of *that* one?

Conflict

A person is said to be "in conflict" when he wants two incompatible goals to be realized at once. Since the time of Freud and no doubt for much longer than that, inner conflicts have been recognized as a major cause of psychological difficulties. Unresolved conflict leads to anxiety, depression, hostility, unrealistic fantasies, and even delusions and hallucinations. In fact as I have come to realize what inner conflict means in terms of this feedback model, I have become more and more convinced that conflict *itself*, not any particular kind of conflict, represents the most serious kind of malfunction of the brain short of physical damage, and the most common even among "normal" people.

The reasons for the extraordinarily bad consequences of conflict are not to be found in specific behavioral effects, although disruptions of overt behavior certainly can make life difficult. Our model, however, tells us that mere practical consequences of specific conflicts are secondary to their major consequence, which is to remove parts of the brain's organizations from action as effectively as if they had been cut out with a knife, yet without getting rid of their undesirable influences on the whole hierarchy. The worst aspect of conflict between control systems is that the higher the quality of the control systems, the more violent and disabling is the result of conflict.

On the basis of our model, we can build up a picture of how conflict works. Many variations are possible if we consider systems of different sensitivities, different limits on maximum output, different dynamical properties, and different responses to extreme overloads of signal strength. There is no need to ring all the changes, however. We can see the major principles of conflict in a simple two-way conflict involving reasonably well-designed control systems of about equal sensitivity and having about equal output capabilities. Once the basic situation is understood, variations can easily be constructed to take care of any specific variant of experience.

The basic mechanism behind conflict is *response to disturbance.* Conflict is uniquely a control-system phenomenon. A rock rolling to rest against a tree is pushed against the tree by precisely the same force that made the rock roll; the rock does not redouble its efforts when it finds its progress halted. Only a system that senses the consequences of its behavior can suffer true conflict, and that conflict arises directly from opposition to the outputs of the system.

When two people arrive simultaneously at opposite sides of a swinging door they do not simply stop as two rocks rolling against each other would stop. The efforts they employ suddenly rise to ten, twenty, fifty times the amount normally required to open the door. Muscles can be pulled loose from their attachments by such an encounter before higher-order systems can alter lower-order reference levels for the position of the door.

Conflict is an encounter between two control systems, an encounter of a specific kind. In effect, the two control systems attempt to control the same quantity, but with respect to two different reference levels. For one system to correct its error, the other system must experience error. There is no way for both systems to experience zero error at the same time. Therefore the outputs of the systems must act on the shared controlled quantity in opposite directions.

If both systems are reasonably sensitive to error, and the two reference levels are far apart, there will be a range of values of the controlled quantity (between the reference levels) throughout which each system will contain an error signal so large that the output of each system will be solidly at its maximum. These two outputs, if about equal, will cancel, leaving essentially no net output to affect the controlled quantity. Certainly the net output cannot change as the "controlled" quantity changes in this region between the reference levels, since both outputs remain at maximum.

This means that there is a range of values over which the controlled quantity cannot be protected against disturbance any more. Any moderate disturbance will change the controlled quantity, and this will change the perceptual signals in the two control systems. As long as neither reference level is closely approached, there will be no reaction to these changes on the part of the conflicted systems.

When a disturbance forces the controlled quantity close enough to either reference level, however, there *will* be a reaction. The control system experiencing lessened error will relax, unbalancing the net output in the direction of the *other* reference level. As a result, the conflicted pair of systems will act like a single system having a "virtual reference level," between the two actual ones. A large dead zone will exist around the virtual reference level, within which there is little or no control.

In terms of real behavior, this model of conflict seems to have the right properties. Consider a person who has two goals: one to be a nice guy, and the other to be a strong, self-sufficient person. If he perceives these two conditions in the "right" way (for conflict) he may find himself wanting to be deferential and pleasant, and at the same time wanting to speak up firmly for his rights. As a result, he does neither. He drifts in a state between, his attitude fluctuating with every change in external circumstances, undirected. When cajoled and coaxed enough he may find himself beginning to warm up, smile, and think of a pleasant remark, but immediately he realizes that he is being manipulated and resentfully breaks off communication or utters a cutting remark. On the other hand if circumstances lead him to begin defending himself against unfair treatment ("Joe, you can't let him get away with that!"), his first strong words fill him with remorse and he blunts his defense with an apologetic giggle. He can react only when pushed to one extreme or the other, and his reaction takes him back to the uncontrolled middle ground.

In theory and in reality, conflicted reference levels seem to have two major consequences: they define a fixed and restricted range within which behavior will keep the controlled quantity, and they destroy control *within* that range. The behaviors that do occur are always negative in their effects; they cause a strong avoidance of either reference level. Thus conflict frustrates the purpose for which either system was set up.

Conflicted pairs of control systems may exist anywhere in the hierarchy. However, conflict is highly unlikely to occur except between systems *of the same order.* Systems of different order control different classes of perceptions and are thus unlikely to share a single controlled quantity. Even within a given order of control systems, it is not likely that interactions among systems (which cause no special problems) will turn into exact opposition. Raising the forearm with the biceps tends to rotate the forearm as well; that rotation can be stopped by pronator muscles without their preventing the elbow from bending. Conflict can occur only when two control systems control the same kinds of variables, so closely related that they are essentially one variable. When a conflict occurs, then, we may assume that it occurs at a particular order in the hierarchy. The effects on higher and lower orders of organization are predictable in terms of our model.

Conflict is only possible when perceptions define mutually exclusive states of lower-order sets of perceptions. I cannot perceive myself as looking angry at the same time I am looking pleasant— if I could there would be no conflict in deciding to appear both angry and pleasant. As a result of this fact, a given lower-order system receives conflicting reference signals from conflicted systems of higher order—those *are* the "opposing outputs." In our model, however, there can be only one net reference signal for one control system; the lower-order system responds as if to a single reference signal that is the average or vector sum of the conflicting ones; that is what creates the appearance of a virtual reference level.

Systems of order lower than the conflicted systems therefore behave normally. Our man in the example may not know what attitude to take, but whatever it happens to be he is able to speak words appropriate to the attitude. All he has lost control of is the attitude itself; everything works fine at lower orders. He can answer questions, tell jokes, and offer opinions—the only strange thing about his behavior is the way he fluctuates aimlessly between bellicosity and propitiation while he does these things.

If nothing disturbs the controlled quantity of a conflicted pair, an equilibrium point will be reached somewhere between the reference levels. The result will be a fixed virtual reference level for a given lower-order system. This seems to explain the stereotypy of behavior seen in persons with severe inner conflict. The compulsive hand-washing syndrome of classical literature is a specific example. There is nothing wrong with the way a compulsive hand-washer washes his hands; the only strange thing is that he does it whether his hands are dirty or not. Something is wrong with the systems that *choose* hand-washing as a goal, not with the systems that carry it out.

Higher-order systems are affected by conflicts at lower orders in two main ways. Sending reference signals to the conflicted systems will *not* result in appearance of the corresponding present-time perceptions; something unintended will be perceived. Fixity of lower-order reference signals will create the other main effect: unwanted lower-order avoidance of certain perceptual states, or almost equivalent, lower-order behaviors that interfere with achievement of the higher-order goal. It is hard to play ping-pong if one's hand avoids grasping the paddle's handle, or if one's hands insist on washing each other.

In any case there is a likelihood that conflict will tend to create higher-order errors. If the conflicted systems are only one part of the means available for achieving higher-order goals, the result will be a switch to alternate means of control or a readjustment of other reference signals at the level of the conflict. One can always hold the ping-pong paddle in his teeth. Higher systems can *compensate* for the parasitic presence of the conflicted systems. Our brave/timid friend can go to parties where everyone has the same problem, so that nobody is overly critical or friendly, a polite crowd. Or he can stop seeing people altogether. Then his little parasite will keep quiet.

One of the important features of higher-order compensations must be avoidance of situations in which a perception drifting in the dead zone between conflicted reference levels is forced to approach either reference level. Such an event will make the presence of the conflict strongly felt, as explained above. As long as the controlled quantity remains safely in the dead zone the conflicted systems seem quiescent (in reality they are both producing maximum output, but the outputs cancel). A disturbance that brings the controlled quantity very close to one of the conflicted reference levels unbalances the conflict and meets strong resistance, a pseudo-avoidance reaction that is caused by relaxation of the output that was aiding the disturbance.

If that "disturbance" is nothing more than a result of one's normal behavior, that behavior will be disrupted by an automatic resistance to some aspect of it. This resistance is felt as a reluctance to carry out the behavior leading to some goal, even a total inability to perform the required actions. Our man in the example may want a job, but finds that when he gets to the office for the interview he cannot make himself open the door. His own need to be aggressive arouses the conflict, for he thinks he is going to have to be extra nice to get the job.

Severe conflict involves abnormally large error signals, and I think there is reason to consider that condition, occurring anywhere in the hierarchy, as an intrinsic error condition. The state of chronic large error is felt as anxiety, a state which seems universally unwanted. Thus a likely result of chronic conflict is *re-organization*. If that reorganization alters perceptions or choice of goals so as to eliminate the conflict, all is well, but unfortunately nature does not guarantee that a reorganization will have good long-term effects. In many situations the chronic error can be largely corrected by means that leave the conflict in full effect: avoiding situations requiring the use of the conflicted systems, substituting imagined information for the uncontrollable perceptual signals from the conflicted systems, or even altering one's rules of logic in ways that are temporarily useful but in the long run will create even worse intrinsic errors. All these temporary but eventually dangerous methods are well known to the therapists; they are called *defenses*. What the system defends itself against is not anything external, but the threat of experiencing the error due to conflict.

My objective here is only to show how conflict can be analyzed in control-system terms, not to carry the analysis to the point of discussing psychopathology and therapy. That is a separate task, and a large one. I hope it is established that conflict among the control systems in the human hierarchy leads directly to serious psychological problems, perhaps even being the primary source of such problems. Understanding how the effects of conflict arise from the properties of control systems should suggest new approaches for helping people resolve conflicts and, I hope, new and more effective methods of therapy.

Arbitrary Control of Behavior

The purpose is rather to show that attempts to control behavior arbitrarily—one's own or that of other people—accomplishes nothing in the long run but to produce conflict and consequent pathology. What do I mean by *arbitrary* control? I mean attempts to make behavior conform to one set of goals without regard to other goals (and control systems) that may already be controlling that behavior—that *must* already exist, since behavior exists.

Inside one person this kind of control appears as a resolve to alter one's behavior (or its consequences) by simply *overcoming* the unwanted behavior. Sometimes this is the only solution in an emergency situation, but it is not used only in emergencies. It requires no modification of the offending higher-order motives, no understanding of one's own properties. All it requires is deliberately setting up a conflict to remove an unwanted system from action, and substituting a "better" system. The payment for a lifetime of "overcoming" one's weaknesses, base desires, and forbidden habits is to spend one's last years in a snarl of conflicts, one's behavior restricted to that tiny part of the environment that leaves all conflicts quiescent, if any such place still remains. The rigidity of many elderly people is, I believe, the rigidity of almost total conflict, in which every move is made against massive inner resistance. The contrast of such people with others who have reorganized their conflicts away instead of overpowering their own unwanted behaviors is one of the more striking anomalies of old age. Equally striking is what happens to old people as their brains lose their functions, due to strokes or simple deterioration: the conflicted person finds one side of a conflict removed, and begins suddenly to show some extreme or bizarre behavior. The unconflicted person simply declines gracefully and without distress, at peace with himself.

When one acts without conflict there is no sense of trying to act. One does not have to persuade or bully oneself into action. One does not have to stand aside and tell himself what he ought to do, what his duty is, what terrible things will happen if he doesn't act, or what lovely things will happen if he does. One feels like himself, he feels free, he feels effortless. He does not have to *control* himself, in the sense of forcing himself against his own wishes to behave in a particular way. The late Abraham Maslow described the unconflicted person far better than I can (1971). I wish he could read this chapter.

That state of being, which so few of us experience more than fleetingly, is destroyed by attempting to overcome unwanted behaviors through force of will. The very act of destruction, however, feels good: higher-order errors may well be corrected, or even intrinsic error. Indeed, self-control is commonly taught as part of raising children, and it is taught by reward and punishment, by inducing and then relieving intrinsic error. Thus, creating inner conflict actually has the temporary result of decreasing intrinsic error or even erasing it, since children seldom experience intrinsic errors as severe as those induced by punishment when left to themselves. Through social custom and the use of reward and punishment, therefore, we have perpetuated the teaching of self-control and have thus all but guaranteed that essentially everyone will reach adulthood suffering severe inner conflict. Self-control is a mistake because it pits one control system against another, to the detriment of both. Exactly the same reasoning applies if the two control systems are in separate human beings. Arbitrary control of the behavior of one person to suit the goals of another person ignores the goals that are already governing the behavior of the other person, and inevitably creates conflict.

Interpersonal Control

The history of civilization is a history of people attempting to control people; the implication of our model is that this approach of controlling people is probably the main cause of the problems that control is supposed to cure. In what follows here, I will speak about control as essentially a symmetrical situation, as if one person's attempts to control another result from his personal preference. This alone will be enough to enrage some readers. People who want to control other people seldom admit that they *want* to, that controlling people gives them any personal satisfaction, or that they in any way are to blame for their own behavior. Rather they prefer to objectify the situation, saying that morality requires control, or logic requires it, or self-preservation requires it, or scientific experiment proves its necessity, or the good of society demands it (and who am I to go against society?). This attitude is a direct result of having been brought up in a society that believes in control and that encourages us to pretend to be controlled. Thus my argument here will not be against morality, or logic, or self-preservation, or science: to speak of justifications at all is to miss the point. The point I want to make can be seen simply by examining the probable consequences of attempts at interpersonal control, using and extrapolating from the properties of our model of human nature.

First let us consider two modes of control that are often employed under the impression that they are innocuous. In fact they can be innocuous, but are not likely to be if one person not only wants to satisfy his own goals for his own perceptions, but specifically wants control—arbitrary control—of another person's behavior as well.

If A knows what B is controlling, he can select a disturbance that can be countered by B only through one behavior. If producing that behavior creates no inner conflicts, B will produce it, and A will have "made" B behave as A wanted. This method of control satisfies A without dissatisfying B, and creates no problems when it works.

Controlling a person's behavior by disturbing his controlled quantities, however, requires great care and knowledge if done surreptitiously. One must first be sure he has correctly defined the controlled quantity. That can be difficult at times, but not as difficult as the other major requirement: one must know *all* the other person's controlled quantities at *all* levels in his hierarchy as well as all his intrinsic reference levels. Without such full knowledge, there is the strong possibility that the behavior A wants to perceive B carrying out will come into conflict with B's other goals. B, for example, may be quite capable of detecting A's strategy and may object to being manipulated.

Even if A does succeed in mastering B's structure of goals, A must restrict his disturbances to amounts that B can counter without being inconvenienced. In other words, A must not succeed in disturbing anything that matters to B, not to any significant degree. A can cause B to pick up a telephone receiver by dialing B's number, making B's phone ring. But he must not do this too often or at the wrong hours lest B become inconvenienced and change his telephone number or answer the call in a way that thwarts A's reasons for wanting B to pick up the phone.

The greatest inconvenience A can cause for B is to maneuver B into a situation that creates intrinsic error in B. While acting to counter A's disturbances, B may injure himself, or become overly fatigued, or have to skip lunch, or lose his wife. Such results can cause reorganization of B's control hierarchy, which in turn invalidates A's map of B's organization. A then has to start all over, and may now find that he has to protect himself against a hostile and suspicious B.

A's difficulties in using the method of control by disturbance arise largely from A's desire to control B arbitrarily, without arousing B to resistance. If A really wants to control B, he does not want to satisfy B's goals, but A's, to make B do anything A wants. That, of course, is not possible to do by this method; attempting that will end in direct violent conflict.

The best A can hope for is to get B to behave in ways that satisfy A's goals without preventing B from satisfying his own. This situation is most readily achieved by telling B what is going on and trying to get B's cooperation. In return, of course, A will have to agree to modify his goals and behave as B wants, provided that A can still achieve his higher-level goals.

In fact, this kind of interaction seems to me the only practical way for hierarchies of negative feedback control systems to coexist: each system controls its *own* perceptions, avoiding those behaviors that disturb what matters to other such systems, helping other systems correct their errors in return for similar favors.

Another approach A might try is to alter B's perceptions, to create preselected errors that B has to correct with the behavior that A wants. One cannot literally alter another's perceptual organization, but it is possible to use words to manipulate imagination, and to take advantage of ambiguities and of limitations in the number of perceptions that can be handled simultaneously. This is really another version of the method just discussed, except that there is no direct interference with controlled quantities in the external world. Thus Johnny can tell Linda, "Your mother says go home right now," and thus get the swing Linda was occupying. A more grown-up version of the same approach is, "Girls, use our toothpaste and all the boys will want to kiss you."

Words are not the only medium for manipulating perceptions. One can show rapt attention to another's opinions as a way of preventing him from looking around and seeing his car being stolen; a gambler can let a sucker win enough to become confident, and then clean up; a robber can hold a pencil in his pocket and make his victim pass over the money in order to avoid being shot by the pencil, perceived as a gun. Such deceptions can control behavior, but fail as a general principle for controlling behavior. They are sooner or later found out, and become ineffective. Since misrepresentations of the external world are involved, deceptions create a basically undesirable situation: they destroy the normal connection between controlled perceptions and effects on intrinsic state. The girl who relies on toothpaste as her only means of getting male companionship will starve for sex, since using toothpaste is definitely not enough to do the job. She will reorganize and perhaps quit perceiving toothpaste as an effective error reducer.

The basic disadvantage of deception, however, is not in indirect effects but in the way deception is *used*—to cause B to behave according to A's goals, without regard for B's goals. Even if deception does not bring B into conflict with A, it will probably bring B into conflict with himself when he tries to do something that creates error in his own hierarchy (or intrinsic error). Deception must lead to conflict if the behavior it affects seriously disturbs anything that matters to the victim. The attempt at arbitrary control is itself the basic flaw in this mode of human interaction.

In most societies that consider themselves civilized, there is an ideal of achieving control of individual behavior by nonviolent means. Children are taught respect for religious principles, secular laws, and duly constituted authority; they are taught to adopt principles and system concepts that are intended to create a smoothly running social system. If these principles and system concepts were self-consistent and consistent with human nature, if all persons adopted them as their personal reference levels, and if the teaching of these concepts did not itself create intrinsic error, everyone would behave in such a way that violence would never be necessary.

The failure of every large-scale system to achieve this goal has produced two different reactions: to try harder to make the system work, or to revolt and introduce a new system. Behind either reaction is the implied idea that the methods used for control need revision, partial or total. Such revisions have occurred over and over during human history, yet somehow crime, distrust, prejudice, hatred, and active hostility are still with us, as strongly as ever. It is not unreasonable to conclude that we have missed something vital in all our violent struggles to achieve peace on earth.

I think we have missed something vital, and for a good reason: the rigorous theory of control systems had its first feeble beginnings in the 1930s, only forty years ago. Ninety-nine percent of civilized history went by with no clear understanding of the laws governing control systems, which is to say the basic properties of human nature. The model I propose here is not necessarily the one that will solve our problems, but I am convinced that what we need is to be found in this general area.

As I will now attempt to demonstrate, control theory shows clearly how our methods of teaching principles and system concepts (not to mention the principles and system concepts we teach, themselves) are themselves the roots of violence. Our difficulties do not arise from the fact that this set of principles is inconsistent or that system concept is ineffective in controlling social behavior, but from the fact that our principles and system concepts are incompatible with human nature. We have tried to deal with behaving systems as we deal with inanimate objects, because until the advent of feedback theory the precise difference between animate and inanimate objects could not be correctly understood.

The behavior of an animate object—an organism—is governed by internal reference signals. The ultimate determinant of the organism's choice of reference signals is its set of intrinsic reference levels, which are not only internal to the organism but are inaccessible to external influences. The behavior of an organism can be influenced—that is, its observable actions and their environmental consequences can be influenced—by the actions of another organism or by other natural events, but the behavior of organisms is not organized around the control of overt actions or any randomly noticed effects they produce. It is organized around control of perceptions. That is why the two methods of control we have just discussed seem to work if not carried too far. They do not in fact control perceptions, but only actions. Organisms do not care how they *act* as long as the actions do not disturb the *perceptions* they *do* care about.

Human beings (I cannot speak here for other organisms) are so organized that they do not have to know each variable affecting their intrinsic states: they can *feel* intrinsic error. It is not necessary to understand why behaving in a certain way corrects intrinsic error, nor without specifically constructing theories can we say we *ever* know what it is about what we do that corrects intrinsic error. All that nature has given us is a single simple signal: feeling good or feeling bad. If we feel bad we reorganize our behavior until we feel good again. Feeling good overrides all other considerations; the correction of intrinsic error takes precedence over any other error-correcting activity (at least when our organizations are not hopelessly conflicted). I speak of course of our real intrinsic errors, not just those we consider important for learned reasons. An "ascetic" living on a spare diet of water and whole grain may come closer to satisfying his real intrinsic reference levels for nutrition than a person we would consider to be "eating well." Maybe.

What I am getting at is this: anything we do to each other that involves the creation of intrinsic error *will* result in reorganization. What we want to happen or think ought to happen is quite beside the point. If we have a high moral principle that proves to cause intrinsic error as we obey it, the principle will eventually be reorganized so it means something else or disappears altogether. We may cling frantically to the principle, try to force ourselves to keep behaving the same way, but such struggles will accomplish nothing. If the struggles are getting in the way of correcting intrinsic error, they, too, will be reorganized away.

It sounds as if I am saying that everything will turn out peachy if we only leave the situation alone. But we *are* the situation. What I am doing right now is the result of reorganizations that occurred in my early years because of the bad feelings developing from other people trying to control me (and from my efforts to resist). What you are reading right now *is* part of the process of reorganization that results from our treating each other like inanimate objects. One has to appreciate the time scale on which the organization of our highest levels changes; generations may be involved. Information is passed along not only in the genes but in books and institutions and customs. One generation forces the next to adopt its principles and system concepts, so that individuals do not develop "naturally" so as to experience zero intrinsic error. What each person ends up with as his highest-order organizations represents a copy of what his parents adopted, modified only slightly by the reorganizational processes resulting from flaws in those system concepts. That is why change is so slow, and why a new concept could have the potential of effecting enormous changes in our well-being.

Obviously if we were to discover and eliminate something that causes intrinsic error, something that is common to all the principles and system concepts that we pass on from generation to generation, a step change in the human condition could result. If I seem reluctant to get to my final point, it is because I cannot really believe that the answer is so simple, nor can I see any reason why I should be the one to point it out. There is quite literally nothing special about me; indeed I know less about human beings than most of the human beings I meet, which is not a great number. I can invoke no authority of my own, no long string of past accomplishments to lend credence to this thesis. I must rely on each reader's confronting these theoretical notions directly, out of sheer curiosity or good will, making an effort to understand that I cannot force or even influence. I, too, was raised in a society in which control of behavior is accepted as natural and necessary. I cannot help feeling anxious about the thought of leaving so important a concept, having such enormous potential importance, open to each individual's private decision to consider or not consider, to believe or not believe. But my own theory tells me that I can do nothing else!

Freedom and Dignity

The only way in which one person can arbitrarily control the behavior of another person, without regard to the other person's goals, is through reward and punishment. That is, only by having the power to create and then alleviate intrinsic error in another person can one truly cause that other person to reorganize and behave in any way desired. That is why in *every* major society, whether before or after a revolutionary change of principles and system concepts, reward and punishment have been retained as the principal methods of social control. That is why B. F. Skinner's methods have received so much attention; they promise to perfect this technique of behavioral control, the one people have always believed was right. And Skinner proposes to control people through the use of rewards alone, which sounds much nicer than using punishments.

But there is a fatal flaw even in the idea of using rewards. This flaw is not in the idea that people will eagerly alter their behavior in order to get rewards—that will always be true. The built-in contradiction arises from the *contingencies* that must be established before one can begin using a schedule of rewarding reinforcements to control behavior.

When an experimenter decides that a rat will have to press a lever in order to get food, he simply carries out the decision. Relative to the rat, the experimenter is a combination of God and Superman; whatever rules the experimenter chooses to set up will be the rules that the rat has to learn. Not only is the experimenter immensely stronger than the rat, so he can put the rat in the cage despite its every attempt to escape, but the experimenter possesses an order of magnitude greater intellect. The conditions that are set up cannot be understood by the rat's minicomputer brain in the same terms in which the experimenter perceives them. The rat cannot perceive that it is being forced ignominiously to bend to the will of the experimenter; I suppose that the rat might even be joyful that such an easy way to feed itself has appeared, if the lever produces enough food to satisfy hunger.

That is not at all the situation when human beings are involved. One human being can create a contingency because he is capable of perceiving and controlling seventh-order perceptions. But another human being can see that the contingency has been set up, and can see who did it. He can challenge the other person's right to create the contingency in the first place: "What gives you the right to say that I may not have food until *my* behavior suits *your* goals? Why can't *I* set up a contingency such that *you* have to do what *I* want in order to eat?"

Therefore human beings will not allow one another to set up the contingencies that make rewards work, not without strenuous and often violent objections. A putative controller who wants to use the disbursement of food as a reward must first gain control of the food supply; if those he wishes to control can get their own food whenever they want it, food cannot be used to control their behavior. Food rewards *will* cause modification of behavior, but how do you set up the conditions that give you sole control of the food supply? That is the step which Skinner and those who admire his methods have completely overlooked. That is the step that leads directly to violence.

It has been said that one does not have to cause deprivation deliberately in order to use rewards to control behavior. There are naturally occurring needs already unsatisfied that can be taken advantage of. But those who say this overlook one fact: if the controller wants to use something people already need as a reward, he cannot simply give it to them as soon as it is available. He must let the people know the reward is available (they will find out anyway the first time it is given) and then he must withhold it until his victims change their behavior to suit him. He cannot hide the act of withholding. What he can do is piously claim that he has no choice: social order or moral commandments force him to act as he does so he cannot be held personally responsible. That will hold some people off for a while, but not all of them, and none of them indefinitely. Some people will see immediately, and others eventually, that this is a deception. The controller is in fact using his control of the rewarding thing in order to shape behavior according to his private beliefs; his disclaimers of personal responsibility are a sham.

It is true that people can be persuaded to go along with a system of rewards based on withholding. Those who want to control behavior may present a very convincing case, disbelieving which would create severe inner conflict. People can be persuaded to adopt the principle of control through withholding rewards, to give it their strong support, and to teach it to their children. But—and this is the fatal flaw—they cannot live up to that principle. They never have been able to and they never will be able to. *It causes intrinsic error*.

If what is withheld is truly needed to correct intrinsic error, then throughout the period of withholding, reorganization will be occurring. The only thing that will stop reorganization is for the person suffering the error to correct or at least minimize the intrinsic error. He will reorganize until he is able to circumvent the withholding—get control of what he needs so that he can prevent intrinsic error before it can trigger off reorganization. In short, he will learn to cheat the system. He cannot help it. He will automatically reorganize anything, including his most precious beliefs, if what he is doing is resulting in uncorrected intrinsic error. However he must rationalize, however guilty he feels, however he must distort his perceptions, however he must become unconscious of his own motives or split himself into independent subsystems, he will cheat and get the reward for himself while everyone else (he supposes) is working to get it in the approved way.

Therefore *any* system based on the control of behavior through the use of rewards (or, of course, punishments) contains the seeds of its own destruction. There may be a temporary period, lasting even for many generations, during which some exciting new system concept so appeals to people that they will struggle to live within its principles, but if those principles include incentives, which is to say arbitrary deprivation or withholding at the whim of human beings, inexorable reorganization will destroy the system from within: nature intervenes with the message, "No! That feels bad. *Change!"*

The only way in which one person or any group of persons can control behavior successfully (behavior other than their own) is to comprehend completely the effects of what they do on each person's intrinsic state, including reflexive effects on their own. To be able to do this without creating violent interpersonal conflict, one must devise a system such that any possible deviation of any individual from playing his part in that system would increase that person's intrinsic error, resulting in his reorganizing back to a state in which he is once again a full participant. That is what has probably happened to ants and bees.

But one person cannot feel another's intrinsic errors. We do not even know our requirements for reaching the state of zero intrinsic error. We have no list of our intrinsic reference levels, and we may never have such a list. It might be incomprehensible to a mere brain. However well-intentioned he may be, no person is wise enough to be able to control the behavior of other people without creating intrinsic error. The only intrinsic error a person can be relied upon to correct successfully is *his own.* He cannot design a utopia in which everyone's intrinsic errors will be corrected; his very attempt to make others adopt his system will assure its failure.

There is only one way I can see for fallible, ignorant human beings to live in accord with their own real natures and that is to discard forever the principle of controlling each other's behavior, dropping even the *desire* to control other people, and seeing at every level the fallacy in the logic that leads to such a desire. Whatever system concept we adopt in the effort to reach the conflict-free society, it must contain one primary fact about human beings: they cannot be arbitrarily controlled *by any means* without creating suffering, violence, and revolution. The major premise of civilization has, I submit, been proven wrong.

Let me clarify this. In our American society there is a widespread belief in the rule of law (enforced by physical punishment) and in the use of incentives tied directly to our ability to stay warm, well fed, and otherwise happy. There is a stubborn insistence that our worsening social problems can *only* be solved by strengthening the punishing force behind the law and by sternly withholding necessities from those who will not behave properly. Even further, there is a strong belief that these methods are all that are preventing total collapse of our system, and that increasing social tension is traceable to insufficiently vigorous and consistent use of reward and punishment. If we are to trust the theory in this book, however, we must conclude the exact opposite. The more faithfully we adhere to the system of incentives and the rule of law, the closer must the country approach a state of open revolt. What our leaders (and we ourselves) are doing in an effort to save the country from dissenters, revolutionaries, and malcontents is the direct cause of the increase in numbers of such persons.

We simply have to take an honest look at the realities of our society, the way things really work, not the way we are trying to get them to work. Management insists that the incentive method is the only rational way to control the productivity of workers. Labor responds not by working harder but, as soon as management makes it known that incentives are available in the form of more money, by going out on strike and demanding the reward *now*. Parents try to train their children to "know the value of a dollar" by setting arbitrary tasks for them to perform to earn their allowances, and the children dress themselves in rags and say, "I don't *need* your fucking dollars." The best jobs are reserved for college graduates with the highest grades, so the college students have their work done by hired professionals. Profits are held up as the highest reward for honesty and quality and hard competition, and businessmen substitute advertising claims for reality, cheat each other short of provable crime, and collaborate to eliminate competition.

Incentives and laws *ought* to control behavior, but they don't. Everyone who does not *voluntarily* live within the system cheats, or sees himself as a special case, or finds exceptions to the rules, or takes advantage of technicalities, or finds someone else to blame for his actions, or finds *some* way to get beyond the restrictive rules of The System as it is formally understood. Why do people, some people, work so hard to amass great amounts of money? Not just for power—that is understood to be an aberration when sought as its own reward. Money ultimately means freedom, the freedom to organize oneself so as to correct his own intrinsic errors when they hurt and not when someone else gives him permission. The goal of working one's way up through this "free society" is to escape its painful grasp.

Our whole society is a maze of contradictions that can be traced directly to attempts to run it by means of arbitrary control; no matter what else is good about our society, that one factor will destroy it. As long as each person feels a powerful need to control other people (even just *some* other people) in order to avoid being controlled himself, conflict is inevitable, and conflict between control systems is the worst thing that can happen to them short of physical destruction. Obviously, physical destruction is a highly likely outcome.

Control of behavior is not wrong or sinful or irrational or evil. It is simply inconsistent with the facts of human nature. If we become trapped into talking about control in terms of right and wrong, we will miss the essential point completely. We will start arguing over who will control the controllers, and so on, tacitly assuming that control is really possible in the first place. It is not possible. People cannot get inside each other's brains to operate the control systems there, and those control systems are what cause behavior. People can *disturb* each others' behavior, but unless they could actually feel the other person's intrinsic errors they could not be sure whether that person would cooperate or turn violent.

I can see many ways in which the theory in this book could be wrong. The nine levels I have proposed will probably not survive ten years' experimentation; they are only a starting-point. The hierarchy may exist in the form of stored information, not wired-in circuits; the hierarchical organization may extend up only a few levels, changing to a network or a general-purpose computer after that. None of these possible changes concerns me particularly; I would rather know how we really work than persuade everyone to accept a wrong model.

I would, however, be exceedingly surprised if the basic idea behind this theory failed to hold up to test: the concept of behavior as a feedback process organized around the control of perception, and *re*organized as a way of maintaining ourselves in a peculiarly human condition defined by intrinsic reference levels. That much is all we need in order to see the fallacy of interpersonal control; the rest is dispensible detail. In order to avoid self-destruction, I think that all we need do is consider openly and very carefully the implications of this basic concept of human nature. That one concept, so antithetical in its implications to the ways in which people have always thought about each other and themselves, gives us a place to stand from which we can move the world.

References

Rapoport, A., and Chammah, A. *Prisoner's Dilemma, A Study in Conflict and Cooperation.* Ann Arbor: University of Michigan Press, 1965.
Maslow, Abraham H. *The Farther Reaches of Human Nature.* New York: Viking Press, 1971.

Appendix: Control System Operation and Stability

This discussion is intended to acquaint the reader only with the most elementary aspects of control system theory—just enough to aid in appreciation of the basic rules of thumb about stable control systems. For more advanced information see any text listed under "Servomechanisms" or "Control Systems."

Linear Analysis of a Control System

Figure A.1 is the standard control-system diagram used elsewhere in the book. Here, however, each relationship is considered quantitatively.

The k-constants shown represent a linear approximation to the actual input-output relationships of the various functions involved. Thus for the input function, the constant k_i relates the perceptual signal p to the input quantity $q_i : p = k_i q_i$.

The error signal ϵ is taken to be equal to the difference between the reference signal r and the "perceptual" signal p. In actuality this is more likely to be a *weighted* difference, but the weighting factors are most conveniently absorbed into k_i and k_o. Thus $\epsilon = r - p$. The sign is chosen so that feedback will be negative.

The output quantity q_o depends on the error signal ϵ according to $q_o = k_o \epsilon$.

The output quantity q_o and the input quantity q_i are physical quantities and are expressed in physical units, whereas the signals

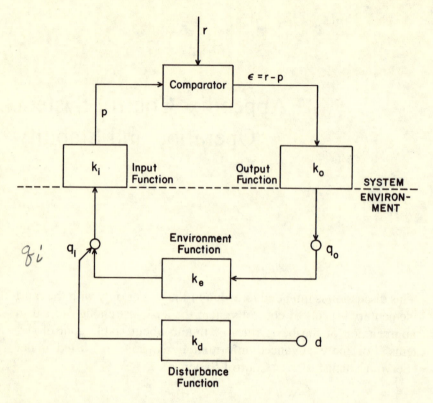

FIGURE A.1. *Control system and environment, with annotations for linear analysis.*

p, r, and ϵ are neural events and must be expressed in signal-units (impulses per second). Thus k_o has units of *physical units per impulse per second,* and k_i has units of *impulse per second per (other) physical units.* The environmental function k_e and the disturbance function k_d have units of input per output unit and input units per disturbance unit respectively. We assume q_o and d to be linearly additive in their effects on the input quantity q_i, so that $q_i = k_c q_o + k_d d$.

We now have a list of system-environment equations:

1. $p = k_i q_i$
2. $\epsilon = r - p$
3. $q_o = k_o \epsilon$
4. $q_i = k_e q_o + k_d d$

These equations represent the steady-state conditions of the variables under the assumptions that only one such condition exists at a time, and that transient effects die out rapidly to zero. Solving the equations first for p and then for q_o, we can investigate the meanings and effects of the various constants.

$$p = k_i k_e [k_o (r - p)] + k_d d$$
$$p = k_i k_e k_o r - k_i k_e k_o p + k_i k_d d$$

$$5. \quad p = \frac{k_i k_e k_o r + k_i k_d d}{1 + k_i k_e k_o}$$

To see most clearly what equation 5 means we need to do some normalizing—to select some reference scale of magnitudes to anchor our judgments of what is a "large" or a "small" signal. The most fruitful place to begin is with the perceptual signal p.

Let the maximum value of the perceptual signal p be arbitrarily called *one signal-unit*. The three signals inside the system can then all be expressed in those units.

Also, let the value of the input quantity q_i that corresponds to the maximum perceptual signal be called *one environment-unit*. Both q_o and d can then be expressed in environment-units. However, their values are not limited; they may be such as to drive the control system out of its range of normal operation. The relationship between signal-units and environment-units is expressed by the dimensions of k_i, the input function; the magnitude of k_i is 1, which is the basic normalization we were seeking.

When we normalize in this way, we make all perceptual scales equal in "sensitivity"; the magnitude of any perceptual signal is judged in terms of its maximum attainable magnitude. This is a far more useful measure than threshold of detection. It gives a standard for comparing two stimuli of different kinds that are well above threshold.

With this normalization the sensitivity of the control system has only one meaning: *output per unit error*, which is simply k_o. We judge the sensitivity of a control system in terms of the amount of error required to produce a given amount of output. It is convenient to make that "given amount" the *maximum possible output*, for that immediately reveals the maximum error that can exist when the system is operating normally.

Equation 5 can now be given with $k_i = 1$:

$$6. \quad p = \frac{k_e k_o r + k_d d}{1 + k_e k_o}.$$

The product $k_i k_e k_o$ represents all of the multiplication factors that are encountered in one trip around the control loop, say from p back to p. It is called the "loop amplification factor" or "loop gain." In order for good feedback control to exist, this loop gain must be high. Suppose it has a value of 10 (the product $k_i k_e k_o$ is dimensionless). In that case,

$$7. \quad p = \frac{10}{11} r + \frac{k_d d}{11}.$$

If the loop gain has a value of 100,

$$8. \quad p = \frac{100}{101} r + \frac{k_d d}{101}.$$

Clearly, an increase in $k_e k_o$ has two effects: it reduces the effect of the disturbance on q_i (given by $k_d d$) and hence on p, and it brings p closer in magnitude to r, the reference signal. For an infinitely sensitive system, $p \cong r$. Thus the first rule of thumb for a sensitive control system: it keeps its perceptual signal equal to the reference signal.

Let us see how the output and the disturbance are related. First, consider the form of equation 6 with $d = 0$ (before the disturbance appears). An asterisk indicates the zero-disturbance value.

$$9. \quad p^* = \frac{k_e k_o r}{1 + k_e k_o}$$

The *error* is $\epsilon^* = r - p^*$, or

$$\epsilon^* = \frac{k_e k_o r}{1 + k_e k_o}$$

$$\epsilon^* = \frac{r + k_e k_o r - k_e k_o r}{1 + k_e k_o}$$

$$10. \quad \epsilon^* = \frac{r}{1 + k_e k_o}$$

The output q_o^* is equal to $k_o \epsilon^*$:

$$11. \quad q_o^* = k_o \epsilon = \frac{k_o r}{1 + k_e k_o}.$$

Going through the same derivation with the disturbance acting $(d \neq 0)$, we have

$$12. \quad q_o = \frac{k_o r}{1 + k_e k_o} - \frac{k_o k_d d}{1 + k_e k_o}.$$

The first term on the right is simply q_o^*. Thus

$$13. \quad q_o = q_o^* - \frac{k_o k_d d}{1 + k_e k_o}.$$

If the loop gain is large, so that $1 + k_e k_o \approx k_e k_o$, an approximate form of equation 13 can be written:

$$q_o \cong q_o^* - \frac{k_o k_d d}{k_e k_o}.$$

$$14. \quad q_o \cong q_o^* - \frac{k_d d}{k_e}.$$

Finally, rearranging terms, we have

$$15. \quad k_e(q_o - q_o^*) \cong -k_d d.$$

The left-hand member expresses the effect of a change in output on the input quantity; the right-hand member expresses the effect of a disturbance on the input quantity. Thus we have the second major rule of thumb concerning how the control system operates: when a disturbance occurs, its effects on the input quantity are approximately cancelled by an equal and opposite change in the effects of the output on the input quantity.

If we call d the "stimulus" and $(q_o - q_o^*)$ the "response," the stimulus-response law is simply the ratio k_d/k_e. From figure A.1 it can be seen that k_d and k_e are properties of the environment.

Range of Control

Most control systems are limited mainly by the amount of output they can produce. Hence the normal range of operation is usually definable in terms of maximum possible output.

Assuming maximum q_o, the effect on q_i is computable from knowledge of the environment function k_e, which is observable. This immediately predicts the range of disturbances which the system can counter: the effect of any disturbance on q_i must not exceed the maximum effect which the system's output can have on q_i.

Obviously the system can act as a control system only if its output is not required to exceed the maximum possible output.

Measurement of Loop Gain

Because of normalization, q_i is numerically equal to p; hence we may substitute q_i for p in any equation with appropriate change of units. Also, we can determine the value of q_i at which $p = r$, for at that value $\epsilon = 0$ and $q_o = 0$. Manipulating a disturbance d so as to reduce q_o to zero, we can measure q_i^* and say that it is numerically equal to the setting of the reference signal r. Thus q_i^* is the *reference level of the input quantity,* and can be substituted in equations in place of r, with appropriate change of units. This permits transforming equation 6 to

$$16. \quad q_i = \frac{k_e k_o q_i^* + k_d d}{1 + k_e k_o},$$

which can then be solved for $k_e k_o$, the loop gain:

$$17. \quad k_e k_o = \frac{k_d d - q_i}{q_i - q_i^*}.$$

In equation 17, the only unobservable is k_o, so it is possible to determine its value experimentally.

Nonlinearities

If the output function is nonlinear, the rules of thumb will still hold provided that the loop gain never drops below some minimum value. Equations 7 and 8 show that for a linear system, any value of $k_e k_o$ greater than 10 will keep the perceptual signal within 91 percent of the reference signal (with no disturbance). Whether this is close enough to allow one to accept the rule $p \cong r$ depends on the precision one requires in predicting the system's behavior.

If the nonlinearities of an output function never result in a loop gain less than the acceptable minimum, the rule of thumb will hold. Conversely, the system will obey the approximate rule at least as well as a system with a constant k_o such that the actual function $q_o = f(\epsilon)$ always lies above the line $q_o = k_o \epsilon$. This assumes, of course, that the system remains dynamically stable.

*An asterisk indicates the zero-disturbance value.

A nonlinear input function involves exactly the same consideration. However, the input quantity q_i is no longer numerically equal
to the perceptual signal p except at maximum (the normalizing
point). In general, if the perceptual signal p depends on the input
quantity q_i according to $p = g \ (q_i)$, then $q_i = g^{-1}(p)$ and $q_i^* = g^{-1}(r)$. If the loop gain remains high enough, the condition $p \cong r$
implies $q_i \approx q_i^*$ as before, and q_i will vary nearly as the inverse input
function of the reference signal. The form of the input function
determines the relationship between the reference signal (often
called the "command" signal in neurology) and the external quantity q_i affected by the system's output. The form of the output function is almost immaterial as long as the loop gain remains high
enough.

Local Minima

Some analyses of complex behavioral feedback systems attribute
abrupt changes in behavior to systems so nonlinear that the loop
gain varies several times from positive to negative and back again
over the range of operation. A large enough disturbance could
cause the system's output to fall, permitting the controlled quantity
to change and the error to grow. At some larger amount of error the
output would rise again, preventing further change.

When the output falls for increasing error, feedback becomes
positive rather than negative. If the system does not burst into wild
oscillations at that point, it will drive itself immediately to the
next state (if any) where the feedback is once again negative. The
effect will be a jump in the magnitude of the error signal when the
disturbance becomes just large enough to cause the beginning of a
decrease in the opposing output, and then the output will again be
large, opposing the disturbance.

If the system is sensitive, the largest possible output will occur
when the error is a small fraction of the reference signal. Whatever
jumps in error magnitude occur, therefore, must occur within this
"small fraction." Hence local minima in the form of the output
function will not alter the basic operation of the control system,
provided only that oscillation does not occur and the loop gain
remains high enough in the negative feedback regions.

Local minima in the form of the environment function (k_e) will
have much the same effect, but the observed output q_o will jump

from one value to another as the positive-feedback region is traversed. This will have little influence on the rules of thumb since the environment function is observable.

Local minima in the input function will result in a jump in the value of q_i^* at certain levels of disturbance and certain settings of the reference signal. The perceptual signal will still obey the rule $p \approx r$, if the loop gain is high enough in the negative feedback regions.

I have not yet seen behaviors in which a model having local minima is called for. Perhaps some examples will be found when very complex situations are analyzed, which I have not yet ventured to do.

Stability

Perhaps the hardest task facing a servomechanism engineer is that of stabilizing a control system while obtaining maximum possible speed of response. A stable control system responds to a disturbance of its controlled quantity with one fast adjustment of output. Contrary to some common notions, good servomechanisms do not "hunt" back and forth about the final steady state. Only poorly designed or on-off ("bang-bang") control systems show permanent oscillations after a disturbance. A good control system properly designed for the disturbances it is most likely to encounter produces outputs which at all times cancel out the effects of varying disturbances, doing this so well that special instruments are needed in order to detect any variation at all in the controlled quantity.

While we do not have to design the behavioral control systems we are attempting to understand, we have to consider stability in order to see why certain approaches to understanding feedback control itself are wrong.

The most common beginner's error in analyzing how a control system works is to trace the effects of an abrupt disturbance step by step around the closed loop. Such analyses are almost always qualitative, and therefore do not reveal the quantitative difficulty created by that approach.

Suppose we have a very insensitive control system, having a loop gain of only 2. Such a system would show very poor control behavior, being able to cancel only ⅔ of the effect of a disturbance on the input quantity. Let us try a step-by-step analysis.

Let the beginning value of the input quantity be zero, and assume we have already found that q_i^* is 5 (in some appropriate units). The initial error, $q_i^* - q_i$, is thus 5. Since the loop gain is 2, the next value of input quantity will be 2×5 or 10. The error, $q_i^* - q_i$, is now $5 - 10$ or -5. The next value of q_i is thus -10, and succeeding values will be $+30$, -50, $+110$, -230, and so forth. Even though we set the system up for negative feedback, it is producing not control but wilder and wilder oscillations.

If we had applied this analysis to a better control system—say, with a loop gain of 10 or 20—the oscillations would have been even more extreme. We have clearly left something out, since a real control system does no such thing.

In fact, if any control system were designed so that events took place sequentially as in our analysis, exactly that kind of extreme oscillation would inevitably occur, even if the time between events were microseconds. The problem is not the time scale, but the fact that time itself is left out of a sequential-state analysis. By leaving out time, we have in effect asserted that it makes no difference—that we can perform the sequence of calculations at any speed we wish and still get the right answer. That assertion is wrong.

There are time delays in every real control system. The output cannot actually cancel the effect of a disturbance on a controlled quantity at the instant the disturbance occurs. But in every successful control system, there is a physical limitation built into the system which in effect slows the action of the system dynamically. This limitation prevents some variable in the system—usually its output—from jumping abruptly from one value to another. If a sudden error occurs implying that the output should suddenly change from 1 unit to 10 units, the output does not suddenly become 10 units. Rather, it *begins to change* toward the new value.

The speed of this change is the critical factor. For a system with a given sensitivity and a given inherent time delay, the speed must be such that oscillations do not build up. Where in the system the rate-of-change limitation occurs is unimportant, but such a limitation must exist.

Suppose in the initial example the natural time delay around the closed loop had been one second. The initial error of 5 units would then lead to an output sufficient to create $+10$ units of input quantity *one second later*. Attempting to stabilize this system, we might limit the speed of actually making this change so that, for example, only half the ultimate change could occur in one second. On each round of computation, we would calculate the error, compute the new value of q_i, and then allow only half the computed change to take place before making a new computation one second later. The resulting series of values of q_i would then be 0, 5, 2.5, 5, 2.5 . . . .

Now the extreme buildup of oscillation is gone, but the system is not approaching a steady state. Let us therefore decrease the speed still more to allow only 0.4 of the calculated change to take place on each round. This yields the series, 0, 2, 3.6, 3.28, 3.3444, . . . 3.333.

Now the system is stable; it approaches the final steady state with $q_i = \frac{2}{3} r$. For any slow-down factor less than $\frac{1}{2}$, in fact, the steady state will eventually be reached, the optimum slow-down being a factor of $\frac{1}{3}$. Further slowing will simply delay the final steady state more than necessary.

The more sensitive the control system, the smaller fraction of the calculated correction must be permitted on each round of calculation and the more slowly must the system change its output if stability is to be maintained. This is how time can be taken into account in a sequential-state analysis of a control system. When time is properly taken into account, the sequential analysis gives the same steady-state result as the continuous-variable (algebraic) analysis. Otherwise it yields only nonsense.

There are far more sophisticated methods for analyzing system stability, and I do not pretend to be expert enough to present them here out of my own knowledge. But the analysis just given communicates the important facts about the relationship between time delay and speed of response permitted for a system having a given loop gain. When one is trying to understand the organization of a control system that is already known to be dynamically stable, knowing about this relationship is essential to seeing the overall situation correctly.

If a control system is known to be dynamically stable, the rules of thumb presented earlier can be applied without taking time into account, provided only that one adopts a time scale on which the outputs of the control-system appear to change instantly in response to a disturbance. On that time scale, delays within the system are negligible.

Glossary

Many of the terms used in the following definitions are themselves defined in the glossary.

ADDRESS: Information sent into a memory device to specify which recordings are to be retrieved.

ADJUST: To affect in such a way as to achieve a preselected perceptual result. See CONTROL.

ANALOGUE: A variable the state of which is a measure of the state of some other physically distinct variable, or which is some regular function of some set of other variables.

AWARENESS: A subjective phenomenon associated with reception of perceptual signals by the reorganizing system.

COMPARATOR: The portion of a control system that computes the magnitude and direction of mismatch between perceptual and reference signals.

CONSCIOUS PERCEPTION: The combination of awareness with one or more perceptual signals.

CONTROL: Achievement and maintenance of a preselected perceptual state in the controlling system, through actions on the environment that also cancel the effects of disturbances.

CONTROL SYSTEM: An organization that acts on its environment so as to keep its inner perceptual signal matching an inner reference signal or reference condition.

CONTROLLED QUANTITY: An environmental variable corresponding to the perceptual signal in a control system; a physical quantity (or a function of several physical quantities) that is affected and controlled by the outputs from a control system's output function.

DETECT: *A* is said to be detected when a device creates a signal *B* such that *B* is an analogue of *A*.

DISTURBANCE: Any variable in the environment of a control system that (a) contributes to changes in the controlled quantity, and (b) is not controlled by the same control system.

ENVIRONMENT (of a control system):   All that directly affects the input function of a system and is affected by the output function of the system. See REALITY.

ERROR: The discrepancy between a perceptual signal and a reference signal, which drives a control system's output function. The discrepancy between a controlled quantity and its present reference level, which causes observable behavior.

ERROR SIGNAL: A signal indicating the magnitude and direction of error.

FEEDBACK (-LOOP):   A closed unidirectional causal chain (loop), relating a system and its environment. See NEGATIVE FEEDBACK, POSITIVE FEEDBACK.

FUNCTION: A rule making the state of one variable dependent on the states of one or more other variables. A physical entity embodying processes described by the function rule.

HIERARCHY OF CONTROL SYSTEMS: A layering of control systems into orders of control, a system of order *n* receiving reference signals from systems of order $n+1$, and controlling its own perceptual signals by adjusting reference signals sent to systems of order *n*-1. The acquired organization of the brain.

IMAGINING: Replay of stored perceptual signals as present-time perceptual signals, in combinations that did not ever occur before. See MEMORY.

INFORMATION: A characteristic of a signal that remains the same as the signal travels from one point to another, and that the receiving device is designed to detect.

INPUT FUNCTION: The portion of a system that receives signals or stimuli from outside the system, and generates a perceptual signal that is some function of the received signals or stimuli.

INSTABILITY: [Dynamic]: Existence of large self-sustained oscillations of all variables in a feedback loop, in the absence of changing disturbances.

[Static or Absolute]: A "flip-flop" condition in which a feedback loop is dynamically stable only at the limits of its operating range.

Instability results from positive feedback.

INTRINSIC ERROR: A discrepancy between any intrinsic quantity and its intrinsic reference level. The driving force for reorganization.

INTRINSIC REFERENCE LEVEL: The state of an intrinsic quantity at which there is no contribution to an increase in the rate of reorganization.

INTRINSIC REFERENCE SIGNALS: Information against which intrinsic quantities are compared. Part of genetic message; some may vary with physiological state.

INTRINSIC STATE: The physiological state of an organism that causes reorganization to cease or reach a minimum rate. The state defined by the set of all intrinsic reference signals.

INTRINSIC QUANTITY: A physiological variable or a variable that is a function of several such variables, that belongs to the set monitored by the reorganizing system. Ashby's "essential variables," approximately.

LEARNING: A loose term covering memory, programmed problem solving, and reorganization.

MEMORY: The storage and retrieval of the information carried by perceptual signals. See REMEMBERING, IMAGINING. The physical apparatus of storage and retrieval. See ADDRESS.

MODEL: A mental representation of external reality, describing an external state of affairs which economically accounts for the regularities in directly perceived reality. See ORDERS OF PERCEPTION.

NEGATIVE FEEDBACK (dynamically stable): A feedback situation in which a disturbance acting on any variable in the feedback loop gives rise to an effect at the point of disturbance which opposes the effect of the disturbance.

NEURAL CURRENT: The number of impulses per second passing through any cross-section of a nerve fiber, or bundle of fibers carrying the same information.

ORDER: Relative position in a hierarchy. The question of why a given perception is controlled as it is leads to higher orders of control; the question of how leads to lower orders.

ORDERS OF PERCEPTION: Each is a function of lower-order perceptions.

    I. INTENSITY: Magnitude of stimulation of sensory receptor; energy flow.

    II. SENSATION: quality of intensity; vector.

    III. CONFIGURATION:.   An object, pattern, arrangement, or invariant of the present moment.

    IV. TRANSITION: Time and space changes; partial derivatives.

    V. SEQUENCE OR EVENT: A fixed succession of lower-order elements; ordering.

    VI. RELATIONSHIP: A regularity in the simultaneous space-time behavior of two or more independent lower-order elements.

    VII. PROGRAM: A network of choice-points characterized by tests at the nodes.

    VIII. PRINCIPLES: Generalizations drawn from many different examples of lower-order perceptions; facts, heuristics, laws, beliefs.

    IX. SYSTEM CONCEPTS: Organized entities; models; beings.

OUTPUT FUNCTION: The portion of a system which converts the magnitude or state of a signal inside the system into a corresponding set of effects on the immediate environment of the system.

PERCEPTION: A perceptual signal (inside a system) that is a continuous analogue of a state of affairs outside the system. See PHYSICAL QUANTITY.

PERCEPTUAL SIGNAL: The signal emitted by the input function of a system; an internal analogue of some aspect of the environment.

PHYSICAL QUANTITY, PHENOMENON: A perception identified as part of a physical model of external reality.

POSITIVE FEEDBACK: A feedback situation in which a disturbance acting on any variable in a feedback loop gives rise to an effect at the point of disturbance that aids the effect of the disturbance. See INSTABILITY.

REALITY: [Directly perceived]: The world as subjectively experienced, including mental activities, feelings, and concepts, as well as the subjective impression of a three-dimensional outside universe.

[External]: A directly-perceived set of hypotheses, beliefs, deductions, and organized models purporting to explain directly perceived reality in terms of underlying phenomena and laws. See PHYSICAL QUANTITY.

REFERENCE CONDITION: The state of a controlled quantity at which a control-system's output ceases to tend to alter the controlled quantity. The state toward which a control system's output tends to alter the controlled quantity.

REFERENCE LEVEL: A reference condition considered as a quantitative point on a scale of magnitudes. The term "level" is used as in "water level" or "level of effort."

REFERENCE SIGNAL: A signal inside a control system which specifies the state of zero error, and thus determines the reference level of the controlled quantity.

REINFORCEMENT: [Positive]: Anything that reduces intrinsic error. [Negative or aversive]: Anything that causes or increases intrinsic error.

REMEMBERING: Replay of stored perceptual signals as present-time perceptual signals, in combinations that actually occurred at some time in the past. See MEMORY.

REORGANIZATION: The process of changing the forms of functions in the hierarchy of control systems. See INTRINSIC ERROR.

REORGANIZING SYSTEM: The inherited aspect of the brain's organization responsible for modifications of or additions to the hierarchy of control systems. See INTRINSIC-.

SIGNAL: A physical variable inside a system that gives processes at one location a quantitative unidirectional effect on processes at another location. A train of neural impulses having a magnitude measured in units of neural current, or impulses per second, See INFORMATION.

STABILITY (in feedback): Existence of a steady-state condition to which a system will return after a disturbance has been applied and removed. See INSTABILITY.

STEADY STATE (of control system): A state in which all variables in a feedback loop remain essentially constant during any time-interval of the order of the total time-delay encountered in one trip around the feedback loop. A condition in which transient terms in the describing differential equation are negligible.

STIMULUS: A loose term indicating an effect on sensory nerves, but not specifying whether the source is part of the feedback loop or not.

VARIABLE: An entity identified by characteristics of the location at which it is measured, and having a number or a continuum of detectably different states. A meter-reading associated with a physical phenomenon.

VOLITION: Injection of arbitrary signals (probably reference signals) into the hierarchy of control systems by the reorganizing system.

Index

Behavior: The Control of Perception
by William T. Powers

PUBLISHER / ALEXANDER J. MORIN
MANAGING EDITOR / CURT JOHNSON
MANUSCRIPT EDITOR / JOANNE JOHNSON
PRODUCTION EDITOR / JANET E. BRAEUNIG
PRODUCTION MANAGER / MITZI CAROLE TROUT

DESIGNED BY ALDINE STAFF
COMPOSED BY SSPA TYPESETTING, INC., CARMEL, INDIANA
PRINTED BY PRINTING HEADQUARTERS, INC.,
ARLINGTON HEIGHTS, ILLINOIS
BOUND BY BROCK AND RANKIN, CHICAGO